Wailua Falls

MAUI TRAILBLAZER
Where to Hike, Snorkel, Surf, Drive
Maui, Molokai, Lanai
sixth edition
written by Jerry Sprout
photographs, art direction, production by Janine Sprout

For Thomas Mobius and Sara Emmaline Sagues, Carmen Frances and Lucia Jane Sagues, Lea Alexandra Butler, and Kylan Solei, Bodin, and Iyla Sprout

ISBN: 978-0-9913690-2-7
ISBN E-book: 978-0-9913690-4-1
ISBN Amazon print-on-demand: 9781976810145
Library of Congress Catalog Card Number: 2001127203

Diamond Valley Company, Publishers
89 Lower Manzanita Drive, Markleeville, CA 96120
www.trailblazertravelbooks.com, www.trailblazerhawaii.com
trailblazertravelbooks@gmail.com

Copyright ©2002, 2003, 2004, 2005, 2006, 2007, 2008, 2009, 2010, 2012, 2014, 2015, 2016, 2018
by Jerry and Janine Sprout

All rights reserved. No part of this book may be reproduced or copied in any form by any mechanical or electronic means or stored in a data retrieval system without written permission from the publisher.

Mahalo Nui to our Trailblazer ohana:

The Hyde family, Mark, Vicki, Blair and Spencer; Paula Pennington and Jimmy Dunn; John and Patty Brissenden; John and Suzanne Barr; Gail and Brian Butler; Deanne Hawkins; Brian and Sue Kanegai; Georgia Sagues; Michael and Cynthia Sagues; Jack and Sandy Lewin; Carol Mallory and Jim Rowley; Rich and Kate Harvey; Greg Hayes and Joan Wright; John Manzolati and Linda Kearney; Ellen Scott and Joe Stroud; Rob, Moser, Lynn Braitman; Judy Farnsworth, Barbara and Gary Howard. Marsha Wienert, Maui Visitors Bureau; Lucienne de Naie, Maui Tomorrow; The Aina family at Huialoha Church, Alan Bradbury, Garden of Eden; Larry Rodrigues and friends, Baldwin Beach; Mana at Kumu Farms, Pi'ilani Kikaha Lewis at Pi'ilanihale Heiau, Gary Kaufman, Pacific Whale Foundation; Tom Vrbensky, Yarrow Flower at Kapalua; Kaleo Amadeo; Christopher and Caroline from Germany; Marian Feenstra, Department of Parks and Recreation; Joe Norwood; Steve Knight, Island Marine; Bob Chambers, Dave Castles, and Captain Rae, Maui Dive Shop; Stacey, Wailuku Main Street Assn.; Mike Townsend, Haleakala National Park; Lahaina Restoration Foundation; Maui Historical Society; Robert at Hotel Lanai; Dexter Tom, Carol Sh'e, Hattie, and Chris, Department of Land and Natural Resources; Becky and others at Haleakala National Park; Sarah from Kai Pali Place; Melissa Kirkendall, State Historic Preservation Division; Rosalyn Baker, Leanne, Office of Economic Development; Russell Sparks, Division of Aquatic Resources; Brittney Dinson, Anuhea Rodrigues Auld, Debi and Dan Strick; Kate Zolezzi, Liz Smith, Maui Ocean Center; June Friewald, Pacific Whale Foundation; Polly Rhodes, Maui Eco-Adventures; Kaau Abraham and Patty Miller, Humpback Marine Sanctuary; Meiling Rossi, Hana Cultural Center; Jason Coloma, Kim Gaines, Swinging Bridges; the late Alii Chang, Maui Kula Lavender; Paula Heggle and Tara, Tedeschi Vineyard; Sandy and Tammy Hueu from Keanae; Ben, and J.D. Wyatt, Hawaii Nature Center; Linda Domen and Kahena at Kaupo Store; Roslyn Lightfoot, Maui Historical Society; Toni and Margo, Maui Natural History Association; Kamaui from Kahanu Gardens; Malia Carvalho from Keanae, surfer Dan Moore, and photographer Frank Quirarte.

Proofreader: Greg Hayes
Cover photo: Baldwin Beach Park

MAUI TRAILBLAZER is an offering to these islands, to all their plants and animals and living things in the sea, and to all persons who dedicate their lives to fulfilling the promise of Aloha.

Iao Needle

MAUI
Trailblazer

Where To
Hike, Snorkel, Surf, Drive
Maui, Molokai, Lanai

Jerry and Janine Sprout

Diamond Valley Company
Markleeville, California . Kilauea, Hawaii
Publishers

©2018

TABLE OF CONTENTS

INTRODUCING MAUI   8

MASTER MAP   12
Getting to and Around on Maui

HOW TO USE THIS BOOK   14
    Calculating Hike Times
    Key to Reading Trailhead Descriptions

BEST OF   17
    What do you want to do today? An index that lets you choose a place and activity to suit your mood and the day.

        Hikes, Beach Walks   17
        Whale Watching, Snorkeling, Swimming   18
        Surfing, Windsurfing, Kayaking, Picnics   20

TRAILHEAD DIRECTORY   22
    A list of activity trailheads for each region, showing recreational options and page numbers.

TRAILHEADS, DRIVING TOURS, MAPS,
AND ACTIVITY DESCRIPTIONS

        Sunny South, Trailheads 1-9   24
        Valley Isle, Trailheads 10-20   48
        Windward Coast, Trailheads 21-34   80
        Hana Highway, Trailheads 35-44   110
        Haleakala, Trailheads 45-52   142
        Molokai, Lanai, Molokini Trailheads 53-55   174

FREE ADVICE & OPINION, DISCLAIMER
    Safety tips, regulations, and nonsense   199

Calabash

Timeline	206
Maui: World's Vacation Hot Spot	208
Haleakala Miscellany, Maui Man	213
Whales, Sharks, Turtles and Other Creatures	214
Climate, What to Do in Bad Weather	217
Packlist, Farmer's Markets, Hula Shows, Luaus	220
Surfin' da Net	222

Trailblazer Kids   223

Resource Links

Public Agencies, Transportation	230
Visitor Info, Supplemental Maps, Reference Books, Newspapers	232
Museums, Attractions, Gardens	233
Preservation, Cultural Groups, Outfitters	234
Where to Stay, Camping	238
Where to Eat	243
Stores, Gifts, Art, Crafts	246

Hawaiian Glossary	247
Index	249
About Diamond Valley Company	256
How to order books	

Maps

Master Map – shows all trailhead sections	13
Map 1: Sunny South	28
Map 2: Valley Isle	54
Map 3: Windward Coast	84
Map 4: Hana Highway	118
Map 5: Haleakala	152
Lanai	180
Molokai	188

INTRODUCING MAUI

Aficionados of Hawaii debate which is the favorite among the islands, a discussion akin to picking the most charming rock star in a universally beloved band. People on this island have an expression meant to cut the friendly rivalry short—*Maui No Ka Oi,* Maui Is The Best.

With eighty-plus beaches, more than any other island, Maui will make converts of those whose primary quest is for sand, sun, and surf. The entire west coast—from Kapalua, Ka'anapali and Lahaina in the north to Kihei, Wailea and Makena in the south—is a run of beaches and coves, all with usually safe swimming. As an added bonus, offshore are enticing views of the sister islands that make up Maui County—Molokai, Lanai, Molokini, and Kahoolawe.

West Maui beaches (the island is hour-glass shaped, connected by an isthmus) will tweak most people's image of a Hawaii vacation: a run of resorts and condos dotted with coco palms that shade white sand beaches. Inland loom dark green valleys and ridges 5,000-feet high. This side of Maui is about two-million years old, twice the age of East Maui, giving nature time to add shape and nuance.

The beaches of Kihei and Wailea, sometimes called the Gold Coast, lie at the foot of Haleakala, a 10,000-foot high active volcano that rises into another dimension on East Maui. In the lee of the volcano, this coast is more arid and sunnier, although gardens and parks add greenery to the coastline. South of the resorts, Makena State Park and the Ahihi-Kinau Reserve are natural areas, with beaches and lava peninsulas that serve up near-pristine snorkeling and out-there coastal hiking.

Having explored these areas, beachcombers will just be beginning. Maui's windward east coast has rain forests, an arid wilderness coast, and more coco palms and white sand beaches—along with red, black, and yellow sand beaches. Add in as well, remote boulder bays, pastoral bluffs, and lava reefs fringed by forests.

Along this windward side is Paia, the world capital of windsurfing, and just south of that is Jaws, where freakishly huge waves lure surfers from all over the world. And if surf's not up here, try Honolua Bay just north of Kapalua, another five-star wave ride. For tamer water sports like snorkeling and scuba, Maui offers dozens of coral reefs, including several Marine Life Conservation Districts. Molokini Island, just offshore, is considered one of the best dive spots in the world.

For all these reasons—the mind reels at the scope—beach lovers may well agree that *Maui No Ka Oi*. But beaches are only part of the the story. Hikers will be drawn to West Maui's tropical mountains and streams, like Iao Valley and Waiheʻe Ridge. The north coast is an undeveloped series of bluffs and bays, made for whale-and-wave watching, or hiking grasslands toward the jungly interior.

Kapalua

The road to Hana zigzags over fifty-plus one-lane bridges, penetrating rain forest that is one of the wettest spots on earth. The highway is a world-class attraction, and driving it sets heads gimbaling and eyes popping. The coast is wild, where waves meet cliffs. A new waterfall appears at every turn, punctuated by tropical flora literally too copious to comprehend. Visitors can pause at several arboretum and garden hikes, and take side trips to villages where Old Hawaii lives on.

It's a tall order not to be an anticlimax after such a highway, but Hana has the quiet charm to pull it off. History and pastoral scenery overlay the town, set beside a pleasantly diverse coast that ranges from sculpted lava bluffs, to red-cinder coves, to a white-sand beach at Hamoa.

The pilgrimage to Hana ends down the road, at the Pools of Oheo, which are the lower section of Haleakala National Park. Nature's bathtubs await in a stream, while a trail inland ascends to towering waterfalls in a subtropical forest and bamboo grove—one of the very best waterfall hikes in Hawaii.

The upper part of Haleakala National Park bears no resemblance to the lower—or really to anywhere else. The crater at the summit (technically an eroded valley) is some 20 square miles, into which millions of visitors roam each year. This is Maui's main event in an all-star array of attractions. Bike down it, hike within it on miles of trails past cinder cones and mysterious lava caves, or stroll from roadside turnouts to sky-high overlooks. The drive to the top is the steepest in the world, and along Haleakala's slopes are eight biological zones, designated as an International Biosphere Reserve.

All these charms have made readers of national travel magazines tout Maui as the "World's Best Island" for several years running. Visitors can choose from a range of accommodations—rustic beach cottages, wilderness camping, country bed-and-

Ritz Carlton

Hana

breakfast cottages, beachside condos, and the destination resort strips at Kaʻanapali and Wailea. Maui's fine restaurants and art galleries are numerous.

Even considering all these glitzy superlatives, the most surprising aspect of the island is its wealth of cultural sites and archeological ruins. Some are well preserved, like the Halekiʻi-Pihana Heiaus State Historical Monument in Kahului and the Piʻilanihale Heiau near Hana. Others are overgrown and uncharted, like many along the Kaupo coast, Kipahulu, and the interior valleys of West Maui. Here are reminders of the Hawaiian culture and geographical wonders. For many visitors, these intrigues will overshadow the island's allure as a vacation wonderland.

GETTING TO AND AROUND ON MAUI

AIRLINES
Most flights to Kahului Airport in Maui include a stopover and change of terminals in Honolulu. Most international airlines service Honolulu. Some airlines have non-stop flights to Maui: From Los Angeles, check with American, Delta, and United. From San Francisco try United, and from Seattle, give Hawaiian a call. Hawaiian has fewer length-of-stay restrictions and the most flights.

Hawaiian and Mokulele airlines are the major inter-island carriers. Several small airlines travel to Lanai and Molokai, as do passenger ferries. See *Resource Links* for all telephone numbers.

CAR RENTAL
All the major companies, plus a few local companies, service Maui. Book early and phone around to get the best deals. Some companies, such as Avis, offer mini-leases, if you're planning to stay longer. Numbers are in *Resource Links*.

Most highways and streets have bike lanes, and it's possible to navigate by bicycle as a means of transportation. But most roadways also have traffic, and dedicated bike paths and quiet rural thoroughfares are uncommon. Traffic jams appear around Lahaina, Kahului, Paia, and Kihei (that's just about everywhere). A public bus services Kihei and the Lahaina-Kaʻanapali Coast. Tour companies and shuttle taxis are widely available. For independent travelers, a car is essential.

WHEN TO COME
High season is when school's out during the summer, and also briefly around Christmas and New Year's. Maui visitation doesn't drop off much during any month. But if you'd like a slack time, early autumn and mid-to-late winter are the best bets. Room occupancy rates vary from 60 to 80 percent.

See *Driving Tours* at the start of each trailhead section for specific road descriptions. Also see *Free Advice & Opinion* for driving conditions and tips.

KAHULUI AIRPORT TO:
Hana 55 mi., 2.5 hr.
Wailuku, 5 mi., 10 min.
Maʻalaea 14 mi., 30 min.
Lahaina 28 mi., 40 min.
Kaʻanapali 32 mi., 50 min.
Kapalua 39 mi., 1 hr.
Kihei, 10 mi., 20 min.
Wailea, 15 mi., 30 min.
Makena, 20 mi., 45 min.

KAʻANAPALI TO:
Lahaina 4 mi., 10 min.
Kihei 25 mi., 50 min.
Haleakala summit 65 mi., 2.5 hr.
Hana 83 mi., 3.5 hr.

KIHEI TO:
Haleakala summit 45 mi., 2 hr.
Hana 62 mi., 3 hr.
Lahaina 25 mi., 50 min.

MAUI
SECTION MAP

VALLEY ISLE
TRAILHEADS 10-20
PAGE 54

WINDWARD COAST
TRAILHEADS 21-34
PAGE 84

HANA HIGHWAY
TRAILHEADS 35-44
PAGE 118

SUNNY SOUTH
TRAILHEADS 1-9
PAGE 28

HALEAKALA
TRAILHEADS 45-52
PAGE 152

HOW TO USE THIS BOOK

Use the INDEX to locate a trail or place that you've already heard about. Use the TABLE OF CONTENTS and MASTER MAP to find a part of the island you'd like to explore. Then use the TRAILHEAD MAP for each region to focus on a particular spot, and go to the descriptions to pick out a hike or other activity that looks good to you. Each trailhead contains hikes of varying lengths, and most have water sports. Use the Activities Banner in the TRAILHEAD DIRECTORY to see which recreational opportunities are available and where. Go to the BEST OF section to locate a hike or other activity that suits your interests, mood, and the day.

Use RESOURCE LINKS to find listings and phone numbers for public agencies and organizations, museums and attractions, tours and outfitters, accommodations and restaurants, and all other visitor information. For advice on obtaining SUPPLEMENTAL MAPS, see page 232 in Resource Links.

CALCULATING HIKE TIMES

Hikers in average condition will cover about 2 mph, including stops. Groups and slower-movers will make about 1.5 mph, or less. Well-conditioned hikers can cover 3-to-3.5 mph. Everyone should add about 30 minutes for each 800 feet of elevation gain. Also add 60 minutes to daylong hikes, for a margin of error, and just because this is Maui—trails are not generally easy, and people tend to look around more.

To check your rate of speed: 65 average-length steps per minute, equals about 2 mph; 80 steps per minute, about 2.5 mph; 95 average steps per minute, about 3 mph.

KEY TO READING TRAILHEAD DESCRIPTIONS

| 23. TRAILHEAD NAME | ACTIVITIES BANNER |

WHAT'S BEST:
PARKING:

HIKE: *Hike Destination (distance, elevation)*   *(SAMPLE)*

Hike descriptions.
Talk Story:
Be Aware:
More Stuff:

SNORKEL: SURF:
Snorkeling, Surfing descriptions

"23." TRAILHEAD NUMBER: These correspond to the numbers shown on the five Trailhead Maps, plus the three outer islands. Numbers begin with Map 1, Sunny South, continue to Map 5, Haleakala, and conclude with the three outer islands. In most cases, trailhead numbers that are close together numerically will be close geographically. There are 55 trailheads, listed sequentially in the text of the book. When looking for a particular trailhead, "TH23" for example, you may find it easier to flip through the text rather than look up the page number in the Trailhead Directory.

TRAILHEAD NAME: Each trailhead offers one or more of the activities—hiking, snorkeling, and surfing. Some trailheads have one parking place and a single activity. Other trailheads have several parking places, all close together, and several recreational activities. Some trailheads take a whole day, or more, to explore, while others can be combined with other nearby trailheads to fill out a day of adventuring.

ACTIVITIES BANNER: This shows which of the three recreational activities are available at this trailhead. Activities are always listed in the same order.

> **HIKE:** Hikes, ranging from long treks to easy strolls.
> **SNORKEL:** Snorkeling and swimming, including freshwater pools.
> **SURF:** Surfing, with boards, boogie boards, and bodies. Also includes windsurfing and kiteboarding.

WHAT'S BEST: A brief description of what to expect when visiting this trailhead.

PARKING: Gives specific directions from the nearest highway to the parking spot for the trailhead's primary hike destination, which will be listed first in the descriptions that follow. Secondary *Driving* directions are also given, sometimes in the activities paragraph. Additional parking directions are always *noted*, in italics. Directions reference mile markers (mm), the highway signs that mark each mile, or half-mile in some cases. It will help if you use your car's trip odometer to measure mile fractions.

HIKE: The first paragraph after the **HIKE:** symbol lists each **Hike Destination** available at the trailhead, followed by the (distance, and elevation gain) for each hike, in parentheses. Distances are given to the nearest .25-mile. Only elevation gains of 100 feet or greater are noted. All hiking distances in parentheses are ROUND TRIP.

The second paragraph after the **HIKE:** symbol often gives background and history for the trailhead (*Talk Story*). Following paragraphs give trail descriptions. The first reference to a **Hike Destination** is boldfaced. Trail descriptions include junctions with other trails, the type of terrain and walking surface, as well as elevation changes and landmarks along the way. **Second Destinations** follow in subsequent paragraphs, boldfaced and described in the order they are listed in the first **HIKE:** paragraph.

Talk Story: Gives historical or other background information. Rooted in the islands' oral traditions, 'talk story' is the term locals use for reminiscing about the old days.

Be Aware: Notes special precautions and difficulties associated with a hike or other activity. Also read *Free Advice & Opinion* for listings of rules and hazards.

More Stuff: Gives other hikes and activities available at this trailhead that are not among the primary listings. Normally these are out-of-the-way spots, sometimes with difficult access and terrain. Fewer visitors will be at these places.

SNORKEL: SURF: Descriptions for snorkeling and surfing follow, in order, after the hike paragraphs. Descriptions include where to go for these water sports, as well as notations for precautions. Parking directions for these activities will be included in the descriptions—unless they have already been listed in the parking directions or hike descriptions above. For example, parking directions for a snorkel or surf spot will most often be among those already given for a beach walk. **Snorkel** and **Surf** locations are boldfaced. One trailhead may have several locations for each activity.

Kahului, Windward Coast

The Best of Maui

WHAT NOT TO MISS ON MAUI

Everything in this book is recommended, but these places are among Hawaii's best. Lists are in ascending order of trailhead numbers.
TH = trailhead

HIKES

RAIN FOREST, STREAM VALLEYS, WATERFALLS
Olowalu Valley, TH12, page 58
Iao Valley, TH25, page 92
Twin Falls, TH35, page 119
Falls at Makahiku, TH44, page 137

GARDENS, ARBORETUMS
Kumu Farms, TH26, page 95
Keanae Arboretum, TH37, page 124
Kahanu Gardens, TH 39, page 128
Kula Botanical Gardens TH47, page 162

TRAILS WITH A VIEW
Waihe'e Ridge, TH22, page 86
Iao Valley Tablelands, TH25, page 92
Halemalu'u Trail, TH46, page 157
Sliding Sands Trail, TH46, page 159
Skyline Trail, TH47, page 162

SHORT WALKS TO EXQUISITE PLACES
Olowalu Landing, TH12, page 60
Kukuipuka Heiau, TH22, page 87
White Hill Summit, TH46, page 158
Pu'u Maneoneo, TH51, page 170

BEACH WALKS, WHERE THE TOURIST ACTION IS
Wailea Coast Walk, TH6, page 38
Kamaole Beach Walk, TH7, page 41
Ka'anapali, TH14, page 66

BEACH WALKS, NATURAL SETTING
Big Beach, TH3, page 34
Spreckelsville, TH30, page 101
Baldwin Beach Park, TH31, page 102

SEASCAPES WITH CRASHING WAVES
Hawea Point, TH15, page 69
Dragon's Teeth, TH15, page 69
Nakalele Blowhole, TH17, page 74
Wainapanapa, TH37, page 130
Nu'u Landing, TH51, page 170

ARCHEOLOGICAL SIGNIFICANCE
King's Trail, TH1, page 29
Halei'i-Pihana Heiaus, TH24, page 91
Halehaku Heiau, TH34, page 109
Pi'ilanihale Heiau, TH39, page 129

FAMILY OUTINGS
Humpback Sanctuary, TH8, page 44
Maui Ocean Center, TH9, page 47
Lahaina Town, TH13, page 62
Kepaniwai Gardens, TH25, page 92
Maui Tropical Plantatin, TH26, page 95
Haleakala Crater, TH46, page 156

TOWN STROLLS
    Lahaina, TH13, page 62
    Maui Swap Meet, TH28, page 96
    Paia, TH32, page 104
    Makawao, TH45, page 153

BIRDWATCHERS-WATERFOWL
    Wetlands Boardwalk, TH9, page 45
    Kanaha Pond, TH29, page 99
    Waihou Springs, TH45, page 154
    Hosmer Grove, TH46, page 157

WHALE WATCHING

    McGregor Lighthouse, TH11, page 56
    Olowalu Landing, TH12, page 60
    Lipoa Point, TH16, page 72
    Kahakuloa Head, TH20, page 78

SNORKELING

EASY ENTRY COVES, ROCKY
    Dumps-Ahihi Cove, TH2, page 32
    Makena Landing, TH4, page 36
    Olowalu Landing, TH12, page 60
    Honolua, TH16, page 73

SANDY BEACH
    Polo and Wailea beaches, TH6, page 40
    Ulua Beach, TH6, page 40
    Kamaole II and III, TH7, page 42
    Olowalu Beach, TH12, page 61
    Black Rock, TH14, page 67
    Kapalua & Napili bays, TH15, page 70

WHERE THE TOUR BOATS GO
    Black Sand Beach, TH3, page 34
    Turtle Town, TH4, page 36
    Coral Gardens, TH11, page 57
    Olowalu, TH12, page 61

KEIKI (KID'S) BEACHES
    Kalepolepo Beach Park, TH8, page 44
    Puʻunoa & Lahaina TH13, page 65
    Baby Baldwin, TH30, page 102
    Spreckelsville, TH32, page 106

FRESHWATER POOLS
    Twin Falls, TH35, page 119
    Keanae (Sapphire) Pools, TH37, page 125
    Pools of Oheo, TH44, page 137

HIKE-TO COVES
    Kakaeloa Aquarium, TH2, page 32
    Lipoa Point, TH16, page 73
    Bellstone Pools, TH19, page 75
    Nuʻu Landing, TH51, page 170

LOCALS BEACHES
    Maluaka Beach, TH4, page 35
    Palauea, Poʻolenalena, TH5, page 36
    Keawakapu Beach, TH6, page 40
    Puʻunoa Beach, TH13, page 65
    Baldwin Beach Park, TH31, page 102

A CLASS OF ITS OWN
    Molokini, TH53, page 177

Pools of Oheo

SURFING

LEARNER'S BEACHES
Cove Park, TH8, page 45
Puamana Beach Park, TH13, page 66
Hanakoʻo Beach Park, TH14, page 68

OFFSHORE BREAKS
Lahaina Seawall, TH13, page 66
Hana Wharf, TH41, page 134

WHERE THE BIG BOYS GO
Maʻalaea Bay, TH9, page 47
Slaughterhouse, TH16, page 74
Honolua Bay, TH16, page 74
Hoʻokipa, TH32, page 107
Jaws, TH33, page 108

TIERS, LEFT AND RIGHT
Ironwoods, TH15, page 71
Windmills, TH16, page 74
Honomanu Bay, TH37, page 126

PLACES TO WATCH SURFERS AND WINDSURFERS
Maʻalaea Breakwater, TH9, page 47
Lahaina Seawall, TH13, page 66
Honolua Bay, TH16, page 74
Kanaha Beach Park, TH29, page 100
Hoʻokipa Lookout, TH32, page 107
Jaws, TH33, page 108

WINDSURFING-KITEBOARDING

Mai Poina ʻOe Iau Beach, TH8, page 45
Kanaha Beach Park, TH29, page 100
Waiehu Beach Park, TH24, page 91
Hoʻokipa, TH32, page 107

KAYAKING

La Perouse Bay, TH1, page 91
Makena Landing, TH4, page 36
Puʻunoa Beach, TH13, page 66
Kahekili Beach Park, TH14, page 68
Hoaloha Park, TH28, page 98
Maliko Bay, TH33, page 109
Keanae Landing, TH37, page 126
Hana Bay, TH41, page 134

PICNIC SPOTS

HIDDEN BEACH PARKS
Waipuilani, TH8, page 44
Haycraft, TH9, page 47
Waiheʻe Beach Park, TH24, page 90
Koki, TH42, page 135
Kipahulu Point (bluff), TH44, page 140

PRIME LOCATIONS
Kamaole I and II, TH7, page 41
Kahekili Beach Park, TH14, page 67
Kepaniwai Heritage Gardens, TH25, page 92
Kanaha Beach Park, TH29, page 99
Hana Beach Park, TH41, page 132
Rice Park, Kula Driving Tour, page 150

Kanaha

TRAILHEAD DIRECTORY

HIKE: Hiking, Strolling
SNORKEL: Snorkeling, swimming
SURF: Surfing, bodyboarding, wind sports

SUNNY SOUTH – Trailheads 1 through 9

1. La Perouse Bay .... HIKE, SNORKEL 29
2. Ahihi-Kinau Natural Area Reserve .... HIKE, SNORKEL 31
3. Makena State Park .... HIKE, SNORKEL, SURF 33
4. Makena Landing .... HIKE, SNORKEL, SURF 35
5. Po'olenalena Beaches .... HIKE, SNORKEL, SURF 37
6. Wailea Resorts Coast .... HIKE, SNORKEL, SURF 38
7. Kamaole Beach Parks .... HIKE, SNORKEL, SURF 41
8. North Kihei .... HIKE. SNORKEL, SURF 43
9. Ma'alaea Bay .... HIKE, SNORKEL, SURF 44

VALLEY ISLE - Trailheads 10 through 20

10. Lahaina Pali East .... HIKE 55
11. Lahaina Pali West .... HIKE, SNORKEL 56
12. Olowalu-Launiupoko Valleys .... HIKE, SNORKEL, SURF 58
13. Lahaina .... HIKE, SNORKEL, SURF 61
14. Ka'anapali Coast .... HIKE, SNORKEL, SURF 66
15. Kapalua Bays .... HIKE, SNORKEL, SURF 68
16. Honolua Marine Preserve .... HIKE, SNORKEL, SURF 72
17. Nakalele Blowhole .... HIKE 74
18. Eke Crater & Ohai Loop Trails .... HIKE 75
19. Waikalai Plateau & Bellstone Pools ..... HIKE, SNORKEL 76
20. Kahakuloa Village .... HIKE 78

Twin Falls

WINDWARD COAST - Trailheads 21 through 34

21.	Seabird Bluffs	HIKE	85
22.	Waiheʻe Ridge	HIKE	86
23.	Swinging Bridges	HIKE	89
24.	Waiheʻe Beaches	HIKE, SNORKEL, SURF	89
25.	Iao Valley	HIKE	91
26.	Kapilau Ridge-Tropical Plantation	HIKE	94
27.	Wailuku Town	HIKE	95
28.	Kahului Harbor	HIKE, SURF	96
29.	Kanaha Beach Park	HIKE, SNORKEL, SURF	97
30.	Spreckelsville	HIKE, SNORKEL, SURF	100
31.	Baldwin Beach Park	HIKE, SNORKEL, SURF	102
32.	Paia-Hoʻokipa	HIKE, SNORKEL, SURF	104
33.	Jaws	HIKE, SURF	107
34.	Halehaku Heiau	HIKE	109

HANA HIGHWAY - Trailheads 35 through 44

35.	Twin Falls	HIKE, SNORKEL	119
36.	Koʻolau Forest Reserve	HIKE	121
37.	Keanae	HIKE, SNORKEL, SURF	124
38.	Nahiku	HIKE	127
39.	Piʻilanihale Heiau-Kahanu Garden	HIKE, SNORKEL	128
40.	Waianapanapa State Park	HIKE, SNORKEL	131
41.	Hana	HIKE, SNORKEL, SURF	133
42.	Hamoa Beaches	HIKE, SNORKEL, SURF	136
43.	Venus Pool	HIKE, SNORKEL	137
44.	Pools Of Oheo	HIKE, SNORKEL	138

HALEAKALA - Trailheads 45 through 52

45.	Olinda Upcountry-Makawao	HIKE	153
46.	Haleakala National Park	HIKE	156
47.	Kula Forest-Polipoli Park	HIKE	160
48.	Great Tahiti	HIKE	164
49.	Manawainui Gulch	HIKE	166
50.	Huakini Bay	HIKE	167
51.	Nuʻu Bay	HIKE, SNORKEL	169
52.	Kaupo	HIKE, SNORKEL	171

OUTER ISLANDS - Trailheads 53 through 55

53.	Molokini	SNORKEL	177
54.	Lanai	HIKE, SNORKEL, DRIVE	180
55.	Molokai	HIKE, SNORKEL, DRIVE	188

Sunny South

Big Beach, Makena State Park

SUNNY SOUTH

You'll need fingers and toes to count all the beaches along the twenty-plus mile coast from La Perouse Bay to Ma'alaea. Take a survey on this snorkeling safari. Although sun, sand, and surf remain near-constants, the settings range from the rugged lava wilderness of the King's Trail, to swank destination resorts with poolside gardens, to neighborhood beach parks with lawns and coco palms, and finally to a harbor where the tour boats return and nearby cliffs are perches to watch whales.

DRIVING TOUR
PICKING THE RIGHT DAY

This is called the Sunny South—and also Maui's Gold Coast—for a reason: In the lee of the trade winds and the rain-shadow of Haleakala, the southwest coast has reliable beach-going weather—320 days a year of sunshine. Volcanic smog (vog) can sometimes drift up from the Big Island. The isthmus, a land bridge between West and East Maui, moderates ocean currents. You may want to save this tour for a day when weather is inclement elsewhere. Beach parks and local's beaches, in the middle section of the tour, will see more action on the weekends. For a quieter time, pick a weekday.

THE ROADS

From Makena State Park to La Perouse, the road is narrow and bumpy in places, but easily navigated. From Makena north, the roads are all good, but traffic can be a problem. By starting in the south in the morning, you will avoid the slow going on Highway 31 that occurs in the afternoons. South Kihei Road, fronted by condos and small malls, has pedestrians and cross traffic. But a slow pace is compatible with sightseeing—you could miss things even going the speed limit.

THE COURSE

Follow along on the Sunny South map, page 28. Refer to trailhead descriptions beginning on page 29 for more details.

EARLY MORNING. BEGIN LA PEROUSE BAY. Snorkelers hit the water early at **La Perouse Bay**, which is also the best time to venture on the sun-baked lava fields for a look back to ancient times on the **King's Trail**. Then return to the present with a refreshing dip in the bay, or move up the road a short distance and get in the water at **Ahihi Cove**. The drive takes you across the flow of Maui's most recent eruption, several hundred years ago, and the likely spot for Haleakala's next blow, which will occur ... sometime in the future.

Wailea Resorts

MID-MORNING. Move north to the main parking area for **Makena State Park**. A short beach walk leads to the point separating **Big Beach** from **Little Beach**. You can also take the scamper up Pu'u Olai for a great view, beginning here, or from the trail at **Black Sand Beach**. Then get back in the car, and, past the Maui Prince Hotel, head to Makena Landing. Meander the shade and gardens of **Keawalai Church**, and then take the road north, hugging the coast past Chang's Point, as well as **Po'olenalena** and **Palauea beaches**. Locals will be here as soon as it warms up on the weekends.

NOON. North of Palauea Beach, you'll come to the parking for **Polo Beach Park**. Here is the south end of the **Wailea Coast Walk**, a promenade past several beaches and opulent resorts. You can opt for an out-and-back on part of this paved path—or a driver can drop off walkers and then drive north around the resorts to pick up the walkers at **Keawakapu Beach**. For lunch, choose a plate lunch or deli sandwich from among the many choices in **Kihei**, and hang around the **Kamaole Beach Parks**. If you want beverages and snacks for sunset, pick them up here also.

Kamaole III, Kings Trail, Wailea

AFTERNOON. Continue north on Kihei Road. On weekends you might find some big doings at **Kalama Park**, or a race finale at the Kihei Canoe Club. You'll want to stop in at the **Humpback Whale National Marine Sanctuary**, where you can also visit the ancient fishpond. Birdwatchers can stop off at the **Kealia Pond National Wildlife Sanctuary** and stroll the boardwalk on the north end near the beach. Save the late afternoon for a visit to the **Maui Ocean Center** in **Ma'alaea Bay**.

SUNSET. Head out to the wharf at Ma'alaea Bay and watch the tour boats and fishermen returning from a day at the ocean. Or head to **McGregor Point**, on the west end of the bay, or Papawai Point, and watch the sun take a dive (an maybe spot a whale) from a higher elevation.

Map 1
Trailheads 1-9
SUNNY SOUTH

SUNNY SOUTH
TRAILHEADS 1-9

- **TH:** TRAILHEAD
- **HIKE:** ALL WALKING, FROM SHORT STROLLS TO FULL-FLEDGED DAY HIKES
- **SNORKEL:** BOTH FISH-VIEWING WITH MASK AND FINS, AND PLACES TO SWIM
- **SURF:** BOARD, BODYSURF, BODYBOARD, WINDSURFING, KITEBOARDING
- **MM:** MILE MARKER, CORRESPONDS TO HIGHWAY SIGNS

All hiking distances in parentheses are ROUND TRIP.
Elevation gains of 100 feet or more are noted.

1. LA PEROUSE BAY   HIKE, SNORKEL

WHAT'S BEST: The ancient King's Trail runs through historic ruins and jumbled lava fields to a remote bay. Return to snorkel in one of Maui's pristine locales.

PARKING: Take Hwy. 31 (the Pi'ilani Hwy.) south to Wailea. Continue south on Wailea Alanui for 8 mi., as the route becomes Makena Alanui and then So. Makena Rd. Road narrows and ends. Park on left at La Perouse Monument, about 2 mi. after entering the Ahihi-Kinau Natural Area. *Be Aware:* No parking or hiking access on the road through the natural area. The area was closed in 2008 for study; may re-open partially in 2015.

HIKE: King's Trail to: **Oasis Beach (4 mi., 150 ft.)** or **(Kanaio Beach (5.5 mi., 200 ft.); Cape Hanamanioa (3.25 mi.)**

Talk Story: The parking area is within **Keoneoio Village**, a 65-acre historic district. Some of the lava-rock ruins date back about 500 years. The bay is named for French Admiral Compte de la Perouse, who thought this a "dismal coast" when he laid anchor in 1786, the first documented landing by Europeans on Maui. Historians long believed that four years after La Perouse's departure a wave of lava three-miles wide swept down from above—the most recent flow of Maui's million years of volcanic activity. New charcoal dating by volcanologists suggest this eruption may have occurred 400 years earlier—and La Perouse simply had not included the flow on his map. Captain George Vancouver mapped the Cape Kinau flow in 1793, spawning the notion that the eruption had taken place between the two visits. *Be Aware:* Take care not to disturb any ruins. Bring plenty of water and sun protection.

For the **King's Trail to Oasis (Kaunahana) Beach and Kanaio Beach**, walk the coastal trail through the village site, to the left as you face the ocean. (You can also walk the gated road that skirts the village inland.) You'll come to a grove of large kiawe trees

Ahihi-Kinau Natural Area Reserve

and then reach an open area with a small sandy shore, called **Beau Chien (Pretty Dog) Beach**. Just past the trees, about .5-mile from the parking, go left, departing the shore road and pass through an opening in a wire fence. Turn right on the wide, lava-stone trail, and you'll soon come to a large sign noting the **Hoapili Trail**—named for Maui's governor in the early 1800s who improved the roads built by King Pi'ilani in the early 1500s. The King's Trail is also called the alaloa, literally the "long road" that encircled Maui—metaphorically, the path of life that we all travel from birth to death.

The 8-foot-wide stone trail ascends gradually for a mile from the trailhead sign, reaching a rise. **For Oasis Beach**, look for coastal greenery as you descend from the rise. Leave the main trail and stay left of a rock enclosure at the beginning. The going is rough and the trail sketchy as you circle left of kiawe trees and then drop right to the (somewhat) sandy beach, which lies at the base of Cape Hanamanioa. **To continue to Kanaio Beach**, the former site of Kamanamana village, stay on the main trail as it descends for a mile from the rise and reaches the welcome shade of kiawe trees at the shore. White sand and coral among the black rocks will interest beachcombers, as will ancient rock enclosures located at the southern end of the little bay. *Note:* For more on this area, contact Project Kaeo; see *Resource Links*, page 234. *More Stuff:* The King's (Hoapili) Trail continues for another 10 miles across no-man's-land, although the footing is rougher and the trail is less defined and more overgrown after Kanaio Beach. See Manwainui, TH49, page 166 for access from other side.

To reach **Cape Hanamanioa**, the light beacon at the southern end of La Perouse Bay, follow the trail at water's edge to Beau Chien Beach. Keep right on the road closest to the water—passing two short connector trails that lead to the King's Trail. Follow the rough road to your right as it climbs briefly onto the cape. You'll get views of the bay and also inland toward the lava flow. The beacon is at the tip of the cape.

SNORKEL: The **north side of La Perouse Bay** is one of Maui's four marine preserves. From the parking area, head to your right, passing the haggard, barbed-wire fence. Land access is prohibited but it's okay to enter the water. You'll find a few smooth spots to sit down, but this rocky area is tough for tenderfoots. Booties will help. Swim across the sandy-bottomed bay, and then out the lava fingers of Cape Kinau, which forms the northern border of the bay. More adventurous snorkelers can try the **Beau Chien Beach**. To get there, see directions for the King's Trail. Look for a sandy channel just as you reach the greenery of the beach. *Be Aware:* Feeding fish is not allowed.

2. AHIHI-KINAU NATURAL AREA RESERVE   HIKE, SNORKEL

WHAT'S BEST: Rugged trails lead across jagged lava to sacred fishponds, a hidden beach, and a rugged coast (though much of the preserve my be closed for environmental study). The reserve offers some of the best the snorkeling on Maui.

PARKING: Take Hwy. 31 (the Pi'ilani Hwy.) south to Wailea. Continue south on Wailea Alanui for about 4 mi., as route becomes Makena Alanui and then So. Makena Rd. The Ahihi-Kinau boundary sign is about 1 mi. past last entry to Makena State Park, after the road narrows. *For Dumps Coast:* About .3-mile from the reserve boundary, just beyond where the road comes close the shore of Ahihi Cove, you'll see a large trailhead parking on your right. *Kalaeloa Cove (Aquarium)-Halua Pond:* Drive across the barren lava of Cape Kinau—about 2 miles from the reserve boundary—to road's end at the La Perouse Monument (same parking as previous trailhead). *Be Aware:* No parking or hiking access on the road between Dumps and La Perouse. Most of the reserve was closed for study in 2008. Access to the hiking and snorkeling below may be limited. Heed signs.

HIKE: Dumps Coast (1.25 mi.); Kalaeloa Cove (Aquarium)-Halua Pond (2 mi.)

For the Dumps Coast hike, which follows the northern end of the natural area and reaches a small pond, take the well-trod path from the parking area to the coast. You continue left around the southern lip of **Ahihi Bay** and reach a sign noting "end of trail" at a small kiawe grove. Cut left inland at the sign on a trail marked by coral chunks and smoother rocks. You'll reach the shore again and find passage along black boulders that skirt the edge of the rougher a'a lava heaps. The shore transitions to coral chunks, a beach of sorts, with scrub kiawe at the backshore. After that is the pond, roughly 100 by 30 feet, with a squiggly shore. Fresh water and sea water surface and mingle near shore to form these ponds. *Note:* Hiking access may be limited beyond Dumps.

For Kalaeloa Cove (Aquarium)-Halua Pond, walk the road back about one-tenth mile from the La Perouse Monument parking. The trailhead is just after a walled and gated driveway, marked by a round mirror. The trailhead sign may not be present,

Aihi-Kinau Natural Area Reserve

but step over a low pile of rocks and take the sandy trail along the fence line, under the shade of kiawe trees. After a couple hundred feet you break into the open. **For Halua Pond**, keep right at an obscure junction, following the direction of the fence, avoiding options that lead left toward La Perouse Bay (and Kalaeloa Cove). The trail meanders over broken tabletops of lava. You'll come to the first pond, **Kauhioaiakini**, with greenery at its banks. Go right—avoiding another left-bearing option—keeping the pond on your left. You'll reach a black-cinder trail above the pond that continues due west toward the ocean. **Halua Pond** will be visible from the low ridge. Sitting close to the sea, this is one of several brackish ponds in the lava fields where ancient Hawaiians raised large mullet. Stay to the left of the pond and make your way down to the small bay that lies just beyond. This bay is marked by a good-sized kiawe tree, casting precious shade upon a rare patch of sand, a perfect spot to plant the fanny. *Be Aware:* This route is hard to follow and *may be closed*.

For Kalaeloa Cove (Aquarium), stay left on the trail as you leave the fence line, heading toward La Perouse Bay. On lava gravel, you'll head seaward along the bayshore and reach a little pond. Continue along water's edge. You'll reach a second pond, with orange-tinted shores. Keep this pond to your right. Climb a low bluff and negotiate a rocky chute—the route's roughest section—and then reach a more defined route that ends at the cove. The lava shore of the cove is tricky to walk. Stay left for the easier going. *Be Aware:* Double back to a known spot if lost. *This area may be closed.*

SNORKEL: Dumps is the best snorkeling in the reserve, and some of the best on Maui. You'll find a good entry spot at the far end of the lava shore, backed by shade trees. Waters are pristine and current normally calm. **Ahihi Cove** also offers very good snorkeling with easy access, located just .1-mile from the boundary sign. Parking at the inlet has been restricted, so you may want to park at the new Dumps lot and walk back to the cove. The best entry is on the north side of the cove, via a smooth submerged rock. Access to the cove and to Dumps was not changed by the environmental closure.

Kalaeloa Cove, also known as the **Aquarium**, offers excellent snorkeling, although considering the rough trail to get there, its over-popularity, and the difficult entry, you might conclude that it is overrated. See the hiking description above. Low surf and clean lava make for great visibility, and the fish are bountiful. *Be Aware:* Don't feed fish in this natural area. This area is subject to closure, due to environmental impacts.

3. MAKENA STATE PARK — HIKE, SNORKEL, SURF

WHAT'S BEST: People watching, wave-play, sunning, scenery, and snorkeling: Makena (Big Beach) is one of Hawaii's superstar natural beaches. You can also take a short hike to a Maui landmark with a view of geographical significance.

PARKING: Take Hwy. 31 (the Pi'ilani Hwy.) south to Wailea. Continue south on Wailea Alanui, which becomes Makena Alanui. Pass the entrance to Makena Resort Maui and then pass Keonoio Rd. Four access points: *For Oneuli (Black Sand) Beach*, go .2-mi. past Keonoio Rd. and turn right dirt road. Continue .25.-mi. to an unimproved lot. *Big Beach has three access points and two parking lots;* the first lot is .4-mi. past the Keonoio Rd. and is usually more crowded since it is closest to Little Beach; the second lot is less than .2-mi. beyond the first. After the second lot are roadside turnouts where you can can easily access the less-crowed, far end of Big Beach. *Note:* A parking fee of around $5 may be charged at some of the state park lots.

Makena State Park

HIKE: Puʻu Olai (1 mi., 350 ft.); Big and Little Beach (up to 1.5 mi.)

Known variously as Hill of Earthquakes, Round Mountain, and Red Hill, **Puʻu Olai** is the volcanic hillock that is prominent from many viewpoints on the west side of Maui. To reach the summit from the lot, backtrack a short distance from the beach and traverse up through the trees, near a multi-signpost. After a short, steep burst, you'll reach a trail that heads directly to the top of the north side of the puʻu. The top is a crater, overgrown with greenery. Head to your left along the rim. Once at the south side of the crater, the trail circumnavigates the rim, and you'll wind up making a loop. *Be Aware:* Heed warning signs. Though short in distance, this is a rugged walk.

Talk Story: According to local lore, Puʻu Olai was near the epicenter of an earthquake in the last century. A fishing shrine, or heiau, once adorned its summit. On a clear day you'll see Mauna Loa and Mauna Kea on the Big Island.

For the **Big and Little Beach** stroll, turn in at the first Big Beach access. A short path leads through trees from the lot to the northern end of the beach. *Note:* This parking lot fills up first; if arriving later on a weekend, try the second lot or use roadside parking where the road narrows. From the first lot access, the wide sand beach extends about .5-mile to the left, or south. Big Beach is officially called Oneloa Beach, and is also known as Makena Beach.

To walk to **Little Beach** head to your right along a path that skirts the sand, toward the point that marks the north end of Big Beach. You'll reach a short sand-and-rock connector trail (hands required) that takes you up and over to Little Beach. You'll also want to walk out through trees to the point, a lava terrace with sunset views and tide pools. *Be Aware:* Although nudity is unlawful in Hawaii, Little Beach has become a popular clothing-optional beach. It's normally way more crowded than Big Beach.

SNORKEL: The south end of **Oneuli Beach**, or **Black Sand Beach**—see first access parking—attracts snorkeling and scuba tours. Swim out along the base of Puʻu Olai. Lack of freshwater runoff creates clear waters here when the surf is low. The reef has good snorkeling, with occasional turtle sightings. At **Big Beach**, go the the far north end and snorkel the calmer waters below the point, where the trail leads up to Little Beach.

Snorkelers couples will also like pretty **Kanahena Cove**. *Driving:* Shoreline Public Access is .3-mile south of the second Makena parking lot. You can park at a turnout marked by a "speed bump" sign or along a lava wall that extends from the turnout. The access is just past address 6900. A sand channel leads out to the right of the small sand beach. Although wave action can make entry difficult, fish viewing is good.

SURF: Bodysurfers are drawn to **Little Beach**, although the shore break can be hazardous. Keep a lookout for spinner dolphin, who like to play offshore of Puʻu

Little Beach

Olai. Surfers and boogie boarders like the south end of **Big Beach**, particularly in the summer when the Kona surf is up. Pass all park entrances, and park along the road for the easiest board access. In the winter, skim-boarders ride the down-sloping wet sands of Big Beach and ride up the shorebreak—an entertaining sight.

4. MAKENA LANDING   HIKE, SNORKEL, SURF

> **WHAT'S BEST:** Snorkeling, beachcombing, and historical sites combine for a full day of fun at this less visited coastline.
>
> **PARKING:** Take Hwy. 31 (the Pi'ilani Hwy.) south to Wailea. Continue south on Wailea Alanui, about 2 mi. The road becomes Makena Alanui past Kaukahi St. Pass first Makena Rd. (and Makena Surf) and turn right on second Makena Rd. *For Chang's Point,* continue for less than .25-mi. to a Shoreline Public Access, located between high-end homes before ascending a hill. *For Maluaka Beach Loop,* continue over the hill, pass Makena Landing Co. Park and Honoiki St. Park at the lot across from Keawalai Church.

HIKE: Chang's Point (.25-mi); Maluaka Beach loop (up to 1.25 mi.)

For the **Chang's Point** stroll, walk out a low lava wall and look for graves to your left—remnants from the 1800s when Chinese emigrants had a settlement on this

Keawalai Church

coast below their larger villages in Kula. (We'll see what Chang's spirits have to say about the impolite encroachment of the new homes.) Continue out to water's edge and make your way a short distance to the end—its formal name is Nahuna Point.

The **Maluaka Beach loop** is a stroll along one of Maui's underrated beaches. It is below the Makena Resort Maui, which is scheduled to be torn down and replaced by mega-condos. Start the stroll by exploring the pleasant gardens and Hawaiiana around the **Keawalai Church**, built in 1832 using coral rocks (memorable services are held Sunday mornings at 7:30 and 10). Then continue walking a short distance down the road to where a parking turnout provides access to the beach. Walk the tree-fringed swath of sand, which is sometimes confusingly called Makena Beach Park.

At the end of the beach, you can skirt the golf course and new large homes to **Maluaka Point**, with its view of Pu'u Olai. Then backtrack, cutting inland at the south end of the beach toward the Makena Resort Maui. A flagstone path runs through rolling lawn and gardens, between the hotel and the beach. *More Stuff:* You can also access Maluaka Beach, and the south end of the paved path, by driving past the resort entrance on Makena Alanui and, about .6-mile later, making a hairpin right on Keonoio Road. This short spur of the old road leads to a big parking lot, less frequented by beachgoers, but also the locale of a large beach villa development.

SNORKEL: Five Graves, also known as **Turtle Town** and **Five Caves**, is destination for snorkeling tour boats, which anchor a couple hundred feet offshore. You can swim here, using a narrow entry to the left of the point. An easier entry, but longer swim, is at **Makena Landing County Park**, just over the hill from Chang's Point. Swim from the sandy landing entry to your right, a few hundred yards, out to the point. After the swim, you'll find a small sunning beach just around the shore from the county park. The lawn areas at the park are perfect for kicking back.

Makena Landing County Park

The five caves, accessible only by experienced scuba divers, are underwater off the north side of the point. *Talk Story:* From 1850 to the early 1900s, Makena was Maui's busiest port, used to ship sugar and also to send cattle to a large ranch on Kahoolawe.

The second access to explore Turtle Town/Five Caves is from **Chang's Point**, as per the hike description above. Look for a small black-rock cove set in from the point. You'll have to do less swimming from this entry. Sea turtles commonly swim just off the point. *Be Aware:* Surf and rocks can make entry at Chang's Point tricky. Also, if swimming a distance off the point, watch out for boat traffic.

SURF: **Maluaka Beach** has a good bodysurfing break during summer swells.

5. PO'OLENALENA BEACHES HIKE, SNORKEL, SURF

WHAT'S BEST: In spite of new development, you'll find space on weekdays at these local's beaches, made for strolling, surfing, snorkeling, or just hanging out.

PARKING: Take Hwy. 31 (the Pi'ilani Hwy.) south to Wailea. Continue south on Wailea Alanui. After 1 mi., turn right on Kaukahi St., just past the Fairmont Kea Lani Hotel. At the bottom of the hill, turn left on Makena Rd. Three access points: *For Palauea Beach,* continue .25-mi. to unimproved parking amid shade trees across from new homes. *For Po'olenalena Beach,* continue on Makena Rd. another .5-mi. until it loops back out to Makena Alanui. Turn right and then turn right immediately on short access road to a signed, gated parking lot. *For Chang's Cove,* stay on Wailea Alanui, which becomes Makena Alanui past Kaukahi St. Pass the first Makena Rd. jct. Just before second Makena Rd. jct., turn right at a Shoreline Access (just past a fire hydrant) to Makena Surf condos into improved lot with a half-dozen spaces.

HIKE: Palauea to Poʻolenalena Beach walk (up to 2.25 mi.)

Talk Story: Off the main road between the Wailea and the Makena beaches, this mile-long run of sandy beaches interrupted by lava points is a longtime local's favorite. You'll find shade trees, swaths of sand, safe swimming, with views of Molokini and Kahoolawe. *More Stuff:* Ancient ruins are scattered about in nearby kiawe grove and wiliwili trees. Some 670 acres have been set aside for conservation; contact the local Sierra Club (see page 235) to join in hikes on these private lands, and elsewhere on Maui. Fees are nominal and tourists are welcomed.

To walk from **Palauea Beach to Poʻolenalena Beach**, make your way to the beach through the shaded backshore and head left, or south. You'll soon run out of sand climb up and over low-lying **Haloa Point**. Look for a fishing shrine, or heiau, on the point. You drop down from Haloa Point and reach the north end, called **Little Poʻolenalena Beach**. After crossing the first stretch of sand, you top a small point and reachn **Poʻolenalena Beach**, which runs for nearly .5-mile before hitting the rugged point on which the Makena Surf condos are situated. *More Stuff:* For a shorter walk that avoids rock hopping, follow the directions in *Parking* above to Poʻolenalena. The beach runs mainly to the south from this access but—hot tip—you can also go right, or north, over a low point (or take a trail to the right at a yellow gate through kiawe trees along a rock wall) to reach the hidden, less crowded **Little Poʻolenalena Beach**. Sweet.

SNORKEL: Haloa Point, which is at the south end of **Palauea Beach**, has a reef offshore, but it's known more as a scuba zone. Although condo dwellers sun here, **Chang's Cove** is a secret among tourists and can be an ideal little snorkeling stop. From the lot described in parking directions above, walk the brick path down through buildings to the small, sort-of-sandy cove. Surf can be an issue here, but on calm days you'll have plenty of fish habitat in which to float. A marker for Hale Waʻa, an ancient canoe site, sits above the cove; to the left is a pathway to Chang's Point. **Poʻolenalena** and **Palauea beaches** both offer good swimming for a day at the beach.

SURF: Poʻolenalena and **Palauea** draw wave riders in the summer. Board and bodysurfers gather, along with the occasional windsurfer.

6. WAILEA RESORTS COAST   HIKE, SNORKEL, SURF

WHAT'S BEST: A paved path runs beside five beaches and the gardens of luxury resorts and beach villas. People-watch, take a swim, and treat yourself to a luxury lunch.

PARKING: Take Hwy. 31 (the Piʻilani Hwy.) south to Wailea. Continue to the end, turn right on Wailea Ike Dr. *To Polo Beach (south access, primary hike description):* At the stop light, turn left on Wailea Alanui. After about 1 mi., turn right on Kaukahi St., just past the Fairmont Kea Lani, and follow signs to Polo Beach Shoreline Access. *To Keawakapu*

Wailea Resorts Coast

Beach (north access): Turn right at the stop light on Wailea Alanui. Turn left on Okolani Dr., go downhill, and make a hairpin left at a "Wailea" sign on an extension of So. Kihei Rd. Follow .25-mi. to beach access parking. *Note:* Direct access to the middle beaches is given below in *Snorkel*.

HIKE: Wailea Coast Walk (up to 4.25 mi.)

Talk Story: The five beaches of the Wailea are all curves of golden sand (which is sometimes depleted by storm surf) ranging from less than .25-mile to almost .5-mile in length, separated by low lava fingers, and flanked inland by the lawns, gardens, and poolside paraphernalia of destination resorts. Offshore, Kahoolawe is the island view, although West Maui to the north appears to be the separate island it once was. Picking your favorite among the beaches tough. Why bother?

Begin the **Wailea Coast Walk** on the lawn and picnic area of **Polo Beach Park** and head to your right on the paved path. Above Polo Beach are the gleaming turrets **Fairmont Kea Lani Resort**. After Polo, the path rounds **Wailea Point**, a lava shelf with a viewing area amid a lush Hawaiian plants garden. After 15 minutes, you'll cross a bridge and come to **Wailea Beach**, which is shared by the tastefully appointed **Four Seasons** and **Grand Wailea Resort**. The resort's sprawling pool is complete with caverns, waterfalls and rapids: well worth a saunter. Inside, check fourth-story plaza that dwarfs huge Botero bronze statues and a lake-sized fountain surrounding a bar. Outside are the serene lawns of the chapel, with more statuary, a fountain, and royal palms. Off the front portico is another garden hosting a large Kamehameha Statue.

After Wailea Beach, the path crosses the lawns above the lava at the **Marriott** and then drops alongside sweet **Ulua Beach**. The path peters out as you reach the next beach north, **Mokapu Beach**, which fronts the newer **Andaz Maui at Wailea**. Mokapu Beach blends with **Keawakapu Beach**, which is the longest run of sand on the walk. *More Stuff:* For hoity-toity shopping (Gucci, Vuitton, Fendi, etc.) local art, and dining, try the **Shops at Wailea**—off Wailea Alanui Drive, near the light at Wailea Ike Dr.

SNORKEL: For all the Wailea beaches, snorkeling can be very good, although wave action can create turbidity and erode sand. **Polo Beach** has two entry points: At the left, or south, end of the beach near the beach club, which is a shorter swim; and to the right, or north, at Wailea Point, where you need to swim out a little farther but are rewarded with more colorful coral. At **Wailea Beach**, you want to go to the left, or south, to Wailea Point and flipper out around the lava. Some of the best coral on this coast awaits. *Driving:* Head south (left) on Wailea Alanui from Wailea Ike Drive. Pass the entrances to the Grand Wailea Resort and look for a black-marble **Wailea Beach** sign; drive down a short distance to a large, shoreline access lot 106.

Another prime snorkeling spot is the lava point at north end of **Ulua Beach**, which is also the south end of **Mokapu Beach**. *Driving:* Turn north, or right, on Wailea Alanui from Wailea Ike Drive. Look for an access sign and road on your left, across from Hale Ali'i Place; the access is just south of the Andaz Maui resort. Ulua Beach will be just left from the beach facilities, and Mokapu is just to the right. The point is a good spot for novice snorkelers. **Keawakapu Beach** offers a long run of resort-free sand, gentle surf, and offshore views. It's the locals' choice for hanging out. *Driving:* Try the public access at the end of South Kihei Road; additional access to Keawakapu is via a big lot at Kilohana Drive, toward Kihei on the north end of Wailea.

SURF: Bodysurfers and bodyboarders head to **Polo Beach** and **Ulua Beach** to catch the shore break. Afternoons are the best bet, and surf is usually bigger in the summer. During the summer, **Wailea Beach** is the site for the windsurfer race to Molokai, a spectacle you'll want to behold.

7. KAMAOLE BEACH PARKS   HIKE, SNORKEL, SURF

WHAT'S BEST: Four beach parks offer excellent swimming, spacious lawns, a coastal trail, and shaded picnic spots—combining to make Maui's best family beach scene.

PARKING: *North access:* Take Hwy. 31 (the Pi'ilani Hwy.) south toward Kihei and Wailea. About 2.25 mi. south of jct. with Hwy 311, turn right on Lipoa St. Continue to South Kihei Rd. Turn left, continue for 1 mi.(passing Kalama Beach Park) and veer right on Ili'ili Rd., at Cove Park. Go to the end and park at the corner of Ili'ili and Kaiau Pl. (location of Charley Young Beach Park). Or turn left on Kaiau for one block and park at a large lot. *South access:* Take Hwy. 31 about 4 mi. south of the jct. with Hwy 311. Turn right on Keonekai Rd. Continue and turn left at South Kihei Rd. Park at a lot for Kamaole III Beach Park. *Notes:* Hiking description starts at north access. On busy days, use the big lot at the Kihei Boat Ramp, which is just south of Kamaole III.

HIKE: **Kamaole Beach walk to Eddie Pu Trail (up to 2.5 mi.)**

Talk Story: These pleasant beach parks are across a busy street from oodles of mid-range hotel and condo resorts, local-style eateries, souvenir and sundries stores, kayak rentals, and dive shops. Kihei is abuzz with the sandy-footed and sunburned, playing hard and living the good life on their Maui vacation. On weekends, local families join the fray. Each beach has lifeguards on duty until late afternoon. At sunset, bring a picnic dinner and thank yourself for having the good sense to be in Hawaii.

The **Kamaole Beach walk** begins at tiny **Charley Young Beach Park**, set on a palmy terrace that affords a postcard look south toward **Kamaole I**. Head down to the sand and walk to your left. After less than .5-mile, you'll run out of beach and need to cross the broad grassy bench in front of a large hotel. Then descend again to the sands of **Kamaole II**. Stroll the palm-fringed shores before ascending once again, to the point that is the north boundary of **Kamaole III**, and home to the lifeguard office. Walk the grassy bluff or the beach at the south end of Kam III, where you pick up the wood-

Kamaole Beach walk

chip pathway that is the **Eddie Pu Trail**. Benches and interpretive signs line the trail, which continues through the **Kihei Boat Ramp** and then through shade trees and along the outer lawn of the **Kihei Surfside Resort**. From here you can continue to **Keawakapu Beach** and along the Wailea Resorts path. *Talk Story:* Local consevationist Eddie Pu used his time off every year for 25 years to walk the entire shoreline of Maui.

SNORKEL: Usually, the best snorkeling is off the rocky point that separates **Kamaole II** from **Kamaole III**. Park at Kam III. Begin either at the north end of the sand at

Vancouver monument

Kam III and snorkel toward the point, or start at the south end of Kam II and stroke out the same point. At Kamaole III, you can also snorkel closer to the shore on the south end of the beach—heading toward the bluff at the Kihei Boat Ramp. At **Kamaole I**, dip your mask on the south end of the sand, out and around the lava rocks in front of the Royal Mauian Hotel; or try the north end, off the steps at **Charley Young Park**. Unless the surf is up, which is rare, the waters along the beach parks are safe for beginning snorkelers.

SURF: Body surfers and boogie borders ride the shore break, mostly during summer, at all three **Kamaole beaches**, but this shore is not known for wave sports.

8. NORTH KIHEI   HIKE, SNORKEL, SURF

WHAT'S BEST: Beach parks and historic sites are often missed by visitors to this section of the sunny coast. For whale watchers, this trailhead is a must.

PARKING: Drive to the junction of Hwy. 31 (the Pi'ilani Hwy.) and Hwy. 311 (Mokulele Hwy.). At traffic signal where these highways join, go south on South Kihei Rd. *Note:* Further directions follow, starting from this north point and proceeding south.

HIKE: Vancouver Monument to Sugar Beach (2 mi.); Hawaiian Islands Humpback Whale Sanctuary (.25-mi.); Waipuilani Park (.75-mi.); Cove Park to Kalama Park (.75-mi.)

Talk Story: The 4-mile coastline of north Kihei, featuring narrow sand strips, shallow waters, and rocky embankments, was in ancient times home to saltwater fishponds. Today, this coast is mostly a State Beach Reserve, buffeted by mid-range resorts, condos, and quiet neighborhoods. A stop-and-go, driving lollygag is the best way to visit.

Vancouver Monument to Sugar Beach is a relaxing stroll. *Driving:* Park at **Mai Poina 'Oe Iau Beach Park**, just south of the junction with Highway 311. The modest monument is less than .5-mile down the beach (at mile marker 1, across from the Maui Lu). Walk to your left as you face the water and look for a patch of coco palms. A totem pole erected was in 1968 to commemorate Captain George Vancouver, the British explorer who visited in 1793 and is credited with fostering peace among the warring Hawaiians. From the monument, double back northward, to walk the fine sands of **Sugar Beach**. Less than .5-mile north of the beach park, are the remnants of **Kihei Wharf**, where Henry Baldwin's men shipped sugar in the late 1800s, and today paddlers of the Kihei Canoe Club put in. North of here is the long sweep of Ma'alaea Bay.

The **Hawaiian Islands Humpback Whale National Marine Sanctuary** is probably Maui's most underrated attraction. *Driving:* It's at 726 South Kihei Road, about .25-mile south of the Vancouver Monument. The center is a living classroom, where interpretive displays and knowledgeable docents teach the history and ecology of the seagoing mammals. Free programs are normally offered Tuesdays and Thursdays at 11. On the water is the visitors center, set in a historic building with a whale-watching deck (with complimentary binoculars). To the left of the center is **Kalepolepo Beach Park**, home to the ancient **Koieie Loko Ia Fishpond**. The he nonprofit Association of Fishponds in Maui has restored large semicircle of lava stone at the shore, which, centuries ago, were handed down in a human chain of workers from the uplands miles away. To the right of the center, look for a sandy trail that leads to another section of the **Kalepolepo Beach Park** that is a favorite among moms with kids.

Sweet **Waipuilani Park**, for some reason, is absent from most maps. *Driving:* Turn right on Waipuilani Road at mile marker 2, less than a mile south of Kalepolepo Beach Park. Continue to road's end. The park offers a palm-dotted expanse of lawn, with a view of West Maui, looking like another island. This strip of sand is a prime sunset stroll. Ancient fishpond ruins are offshore.

The stroll from **Cove Park to Kalama Park** is most interesting on weekends. *Driving:* Continue on South Kihei Road and turn right into Kalama Park, just past Waimahaihai Street, before mile marker 4. On weekends, the grassy expanses of the park are often the site of community festivities. Not to be missed is **Pacific Whale Foundation's Whale Day**, usually held in mid-February and often featuring Grammy-winning entertainment, local-style food, booths by nonprofit organizations, and artwork. Continue southward from Kalama to a roadway bridge, across which is cozy Cove Park.

SNORKEL: Kalepolepo Beach Park's **Koieie Loko Ia Fishpond** is a safe place for the keikis to take a dip. Good-sized fish breach the rock walls at high tide. But the better bet for families is to walk the short dune trail to the right of the center to a sandy kids' beach at **Kalepolepo Beach Park**. For a close-in getaway, drive to **Cove Park**. Then walk fifty feet up Iliʻili to a **Shoreline Public Access**; a little beach awaits!

SURF: Cove Park, with a modest break at the mouth of the cove, is Maui's best place for beginning board surfers. Just north, at **Kalama Park**, boarders ride the 4- to 9-foot summer swells, breaking both left and right. Body and board surfing is fairly good at **Mai Poina ʻOe Iau Beach Park**, but the real action here is for windsurfers.

9. MAʻALAEA BAY   HIKE, SNORKEL, SURF

WHAT'S BEST: Birdwatchers, exercise walkers, and joggers can roam free at Maui's longest beach and largest wildlife ponds. Then stop in at the harbor for seagoing shops and a visit to the Maui Ocean Center.

PARKING: *For Maʻalea Bay-Kealia Coastal Boardwalk:* Take Hwy. 31, which is North Kihei Rd., north from Kihei; or take Hwy. 31 south from its jct. with Hwy. 30 (Honoapiʻilani Hwy.) Park at the boardwalk's gated parking lot, west of Kealia Pond and

Maalaea Bay

near mm2, or at unimproved shoulder farther down the road. *For Kealia Pond:* Take Hwy. 311 (Mokulele Hwy.) north from north Kihei. At mm6—be alert—make a left across the divided highway toward the the signed refuge gate. *For Ma'alea Harbor-Maui Ocean Center:* Take Hwy. 30 west (toward Lahaina) from its jct. with Hwy. 31. The harbor is with on the left within a mile.

HIKE: Ma'alaea Beach (up to 5.5 mi.) or Kealia Coastal Boardwalk (1.25 mi.); Kealia Pond Refuge (.75-mi); Ma'alaea Harbor-Maui Ocean Center (.75-mi.)

After crossing the dunes to the left of a pavilion at the parking area, you will be about in the middle of **Ma'alaea Beach**. To your left is a 1.5-mile run of sand, near the highway, that leads to **Sugar Beach**. Headed to your right, you can look forward to 1.75 miles of open sand, with coastal wetlands and a large cane field as an inland buffer. The beach ends at **Haycraft Park**, near Ma'alaea Harbor. *Talk Story:* At night, from July through December, beachgoers include hawksbill turtles, who come ashore to lay eggs at the high-tide line; watch out for the egg pits in the sand of these endangered reptiles. In the late 1700s, King Kalaniopu'u of the Big Island used these shores to invade Maui, and 800 of his elite warriors were annihilated in the Battle of the Sand Hills. In 1944 the U.S. Marines came ashore here in preparation for the taking of Iwo Jima.

The 2,200-foot **Kealia Coastal Boardwalk** opened in 2005. Head to the right from the parking area. An eight-foot wide, railed deck manders along coastal mudflats and good-sized **Kealia Pond**, which is a gathering places for both shorebirds and waterfowl.

Wetlands Boardwalk, Humpback Whale Marine Sanctuary, stingray at Maui Ocean Center, North Kihei windsurfer, Kihei Canoe Club

Among the dozens of species to be seen here are Hawaiian ducks and stilts. Golden plovers, ruddy turnstones, and wandering tattlers—migrating here from more than 2,000 miles away in Alaska and Canada—will be among the shorebirds.

Birders may like **Kealia Pond National Wildlife Refuge**. The U.S. Fish and Wildlife offices and **new visitors center** are about .5-mile in from the highway. Levees between rectangular fishponds provide raised trails around the water. In the 1600s, villagers dug a channel through the dunes, creating a pond for shore-dwelling fish. Kealia Pond was also the island's salt source. *Note:* Normal hours are weekdays, 7:30 to 4:30, but they close on lots of holidays.

At **Ma'alaea Harbor**, your first stop might be the **Maui Ocean Center**, featuring the largest tropical aquarium in America. Whale life, ocean ecology, and Hawaiian culture exhibits are evocative as well as educational. The aquarium's sea tunnel makes you feel like you're snorkeling without getting wet, and the shark tank makes you glad you're not. Plenty of staff are on hand to personalize your visit, and local art vendors sometimes set up inside. Sea turtles and a living reef highlight outdoor exhibits, along with a new home for hammerhead and tiger sharks. *Note:* Admission is pricey, pushing thirty bucks for adults and twenty for kids. Weekly passes and coupons save money.

Highlighting the shopping center next door to the center is the **Pacific Whale Foundation**, offering non-touristy ocean tours and a wealth of nature-related gift ideas. Below the complex is the **Ma'alaea Harbor Village**, and behind that is the Ma'alaea **Small Boat Harbor**. Take a saunter out the wharf to view the comings and goings of whale-watching vessels and fishing boats.

SNORKEL: Hidden **Haycraft Beach Park** is a find for visitors seeking quietude. *Driving:* Head inland .5-mile from the harbor village on Hauoli Street. Pass all the condos to the end, at the **Ma'alaea Community Garden**. Haycraft, a less-used starting point for beach walkers, has a shower, tables, and a pretty beach with a winning view toward Haleakala, Molokini, and Kahoolawe. The fish are few, but swimming is good.

SURF: During the summer, **Ma'alaea Bay** brings the board heads running. There are three spots: **Mud Flats**, offshore in the middle of the bay, is a right-breaking 3- to 10-foot swell; watch out for the reef at low tide. **Breakwater**, accessible from the harbor, features a larger right break with long rides. The breakwater is a good place to view surfers under the right conditions. Big waves sometimes wash the parking lot.

The third spot, **Kapoli Beach Park**, is tough to find: Head toward Lahaina from Ma'alaea Harbor, pass Ma'alaea Bay Place, and look for an unsigned left turn, leading down a rugged road. Sometimes called Little Cape St. Francis, this spot offers long right-breaking tubes in the summer. Windsurfers, usually in the summer, can be seen offshore of **Haycraft Beach Park**. You'll also see windsurfers taking off from the middle of Ma'alaea Beach.

Valley Isle

Ukumehame Valley

VALLEY ISLE

West Maui is almost two million years old, twice the age of Haleakala, but the years have been kind. Nature—rain, wind, waves, erosion—has cleaved 3,000-foot deep valleys into the old volcano and adorned them with tropical greenery. From the west side, you view these classic green chasms opening inland from a coast that is almost continuous beach. As you go north, the coast becomes a series of bays and bluffs, and the tropical forests encroach the road. Finally, on the north, the coast is mainly steep cliffs, more arid here, with grassy upslopes that give way to forested ridgelines.

Resort beaches and coves are plentiful, and Lahaina is Maui's best strolling town for history buffs and window-shoppers. Take your pick from several wave-watcher's walks along sea-sculpted bluffs, hike into the forest, and turnouts with panoramic views. You can afford to be fickle in the Valley Isle trailhead section, since the distance between being a beach potato or hardcore eco-adventurist is not far, in terms of miles.

DRIVING TOUR
PICKING THE RIGHT DAY

Get an early start to the north shore, and you'll feel like you're discovering the place. But don't go during or just after big rains: You'll get a discomforting look at erosion in progress, as mud and rocks wash into the roadway. In the winter, weather hits from Kapalua north. As you go south, sun is more likely. From Kaʻanapali down to Olowalu will often be in the sunny lee of minor storms, giving a view of the weather in the West Maui Mountains while you bask in the sun.

THE ROADS

From McGregor Point to Lahaina, traffic often flows in a steady stream from midmorning to nightfall. You move along fine, but merging and getting across the highway can be exasperating—although a new road is planned (or at least talked about a lot) to bypass the coast, which would ease the congestion. This driving tour has you going south during that period to minimize the hassle. Traffic bogs down in Lahaina, and Kaʻanapali, especially since several beach parks front the road. But then it's normally smooth sailing on Highway 30 going north, since this newer road bypasses the condo coast at Kahana.

North of Kapalua, the scenery shifts dramatically. The highway becomes a nicely swerving view road for the next dozen miles along the north shore—until the abyss at Kahakuloa. Here, the road takes a several-mile dive through the valley, and you might grip the steering wheel like the reins on a wayward steed. Traction and clearance are no problem—four-wheel drive is not needed—but a two-foot wide car would be helpful. Cars tend to wait for others oncoming, and then drive through in small caravans. After Kahakuloa, where the route becomes Highway 340, you encounter more one-lane spots, but they are shorter in length. This tour takes you down to Kahakuloa and back again, without circumnavigating West Maui.

THE COURSE

Follow along on the Valley Isle map, page 54. Refer to trailhead descriptions beginning on page 55 for more details.

BEGIN EARLY MORNING. TAKE HIGHWAY 30 NORTH TO KAHAKULOA VILLAGE. Get a cup of java to go and breakfast in a bag, and drive in the morning light. This tour plans for stops on the way back. Make your first stop **Kahakuloa Head**, the "Tall Lord" of a mountain that anchors the north side of the bay. Then double back and stroll the town—probably joined by roosters and barnyard beasts. Being here early will lessen concerns about navigating the narrow roads. When you drive back out—the way you entered—you may want to hike the first ten minutes of the **Waikalai Road**, which affords a view of the bay, or take the short jaunt down to **Bellstone Pools**.

Lipoa Point, Waikalai Road

Lipoa Point

MIDMORNING. DRIVE THE NORTH SHORE. Some of the best whale-watching bluffs are along the highway over the next several miles heading back toward Kapalua. You'll find the half-mile **Ohai Loop Trail** and other unmarked trails that skirt the cliffs and descend to seaside decks. Also keep an eye inland for segments of the alaloa, the King's Trail, that is identifiable because the ancient road builders didn't contour gullies, but instead went straight across, dipping and rising. You have an option of taking the short walk to Maui's sea geyser, the **Nakalele Blowhole**. Sometimes on this drive you will follow a whale family as it swims around the island.

Then continue on Highway 30, dropping through rough-sculpted Honokahau Bay. Farther down the road, stop in and catch the surf scene at **Lipoa Point**, where world-renowned waves roll in. From the overlook, you can also check out **Honolua Bay** to decide if this is a good morning to swim with the fishes in the marine preserve. Just as the road gets wider, you may want to swing in to check out **D.T. Fleming Beach Park**, a good place to let kids play.

Noon. Continue back on Highway 30 and then turn right on Office Road toward the Ritz Carlton and Kapalua. A tasty place to stop is the **Honolua Store**, where you can pick up treats to suit any yen. If you'd like to laze in luxury for a spell, check out the **Ritz Carlton**, one of Maui's best. Office Road connects with Lower Honoapi'ilani Road—turn left—and take your culinary prize to **Ironwood Beach**, to relax on the sand.

Continue south on Lower Honoapi'ilani. This is the Condo Coast that the highway bypasses. On the north end you'll pass **Kapalua** and **Napili bays**, which are snorkeling and strolling havens. Then continue south on the coast road, a drive-by-sight-see.

Afternoon. If you feel like an unfettered beach walk, pull into **Kahekili Beach Park**. Or, to gawk at the resort scene, try Dig Me Beach on the coast path at **Ka'anapali**. But save most of the afternoon for **Lahaina**. Visit the north end of town by veering right on Front Street, to see the **Mala Pier** and **Jodo Mission**. Then drive straight through the hoopla on Front to park at the south end of town at Shaw Street. Just follow your senses around **Lahaina Harbor**. If you wander around for a couple of hours, you'll see everything. The Thomas Edison vintage film at the **Wo Hing Museum** is … you gotta see it.

Breaching Humpback, Kahakuloa Head, Hanakoo Beach Park

Lahaina Harbor

SUNSET. Many will want to finish the shift in **Lahaina**, letting afternoon slide into evening, perhaps enjoying a cool beverage while watching the various vessels returning to harbor, or holding down a bench at **Banyan Tree Square** as the craft's fair winds down. Thoughts of moving to Maui might enter your mind.

Others can savor the waning hours with a drive south on Highway 30. Over the next few miles you'll pass several beach parks, beginning with **Puamana** where the local canoe club may be putting in for a late-day paddle. Each beach park offers a quiet spot under coco palms to view Lanai, and Haleakala to the south, which looks like an island from this coast. Inland are the green crags that gave Maui its nickname as the Valley Isle. The hot ticket for this experience is **Olowalu Landing**. If you want to look for the green flash of sunset from a higher elevation, continue on Highway 30 through the Lahaina Tunnel, and use the unimproved turnouts on the right, before reaching the logjam of sightseers at well-marked **Papawai Point**.

54 | VALLEY ISLE MAP

VALLEY ISLE
TRAILHEADS
10 - 20

TH:	TRAILHEAD
HIKE:	ALL WALKING, FROM SHORT STROLLS TO FULL-FLEDGED DAY HIKES
SNORKEL:	BOTH FISH-VIEWING WITH MASK AND FINS, AND PLACES TO SWIM
SURF:	BOARD, BODYSURF, BODYBOARD, WINDSURFING, KITEBOARDING
MM:	MILE MARKER, CORRESPONDS TO HIGHWAY SIGNS

All hiking distances in parentheses are ROUND TRIP.
Elevation gains of 100 feet or more are noted.

10. LAHAINA PALI EAST   HIKE

WHAT'S BEST: This panoramic ridge trail was the easiest land route from Wailuku to Lahaina until about 1900. Traffic makes the trailhead approach tricky, meaning you'll encounter fewer fellow hikers. Start early or late to avoid scorching sun.

PARKING: The approach is difficult. You need to being going south, toward Lahaina, on Hwy. 30 (the Ho'onapi'ilani Hwy.). The trailhead road is on the right at mm5.6, just south of the traffic light that is the jct. of Hwy. 30 and Hwy. 310 (which is south of the jct. of Hwys. 30 and Hwy. 380). From an unlocked gate, drive in .5-mi. on the dirt road (being careful not to dent the oil pan on high rocks) to a signed parking area.

HIKE: Lahaina Pali East (6.5 mi., 1,500 ft.)

Talk Story: The **Lahaina Pali Trail**—pali means cliffs—was constructed in 1825 over Kealaloloa Ridge as a way for missionary school children to get from Wailuku to the Mauna Olu Seminary in Lahaina. Think about that when you're slogging up its famed zigzags in the noonday sun. One of the teachers called it "the crookedist, the rockiest road ever traveled by mortals." Prior to this trail, most people going this direction traveled via canoe. In the early 1900s, a crude road was built nearer the coast, and the trail was abandoned. In 1993, the trail was restored and made part of the state Na Ala Hele hiking system. Huge electricity-generating windmills, comprising the Ukuhame Wind Farm, were added to Kealaloloa Ridge in 2006, and placed along the rough road from McGregor Point Lighthouse to Pu'u Anu, at an elevation of almost 3,000 feet.

From the trailhead parking spot, a low-walled rock enclosure, the trail leaves the shade of kiawe trees and follows a rock-lined path. The shade will soon be a distant memory as you begin open switchbacks with big views unfolding at your back. The trail levels out after several miles (distances are marked on Na Ala Hele trails) and you'll contour a short distance on the rough road that comes up from **McGregor Point**. Then, following signs, take the trail leading from the road to your right to the turnaround and viewpoint at marker number 10. *Be Aware:* Bring plenty of water, sturdy shoes, and a hiking pole.

More Stuff: This trail connects with the following trailhead, creating the option of a car-shuttle hike. For a tamer stroll try the **King Kamehameha Golf Club**. *Driving:* Go north (toward Kahalui) on Highway 30 to just past mm4 and turn left at Kamehameha sign. At the top of the hill you will find a clubhouse designed by Frank Lloyd Wright. Its domes echo the surrounding countours as well as the far off view of Haleakala. Also check out the **Kahili Golf Course**, whose grounds preserve heiau ruins.

11. LAHAINA PALI WEST   HIKE, SNORKEL

WHAT'S BEST: Get sweaty on one of the west side's best view hikes, and later cool off with a snorkel at a colorful cove that is frequented by tour boats, but reachable from shore. Then whale watch at sunset from several cliff lookouts.

PARKING: Take Hwy. 30 (the Honoapi'ilani Hwy.) west from Ma'alaea toward Lahaina. Pass through the tunnel after mm10, continue for .5-mi., and look for a signed, dirt turnout on the right at the bottom of the hill, amid trees. *Note:* As the highway rounds the cliffs before the tunnel, you will see several turnouts on your left. Due to traffic, these vantage points are best visited while heading the other way, toward Ma'alaea.

HIKE: Lahaina Pali West (5.75 mi., 1,600 ft.)

From the **Lahaina Pali West** trailhead parking lot, you hop up to a portion of the old highway that was constructed by prisoners in the early 1900s. This old highway, in turn, covered up parts of the ancient **King's Highway**, or alaloa—the long road. The Lahaina Pali Trail leaves the old road, to your left, after about 100 feet, beginning its steady climb up red dirt and boulders to a high point on **Kealaloloa Ridge**. During the climb you'll cross several gulches, all signed since this is a Na Ala Hele state hiking trail. On the way, watch for pioneer petroglyphs—rock etchings made by missionary school children and paniolos, or cowboys, who trod this path in the 1800s. Most are before and after the number 9 signpost.

You cross the canyonlike **Manawainui Gulch** almost 2 miles from the trailhead, and then walk an open grassy area. The high point comes near signpost number 10, serving up views toward Haleakala, Molokini, and Kahoolawe. But for a slightly more enticing view, continue just 10 minutes more, as the trail joins the **McGregor Point road** and contours **Malalowaiaole Gulch**—at signpost 11 you'll be able to see down toward the Lahaina Pali East trailhead, and also get a look at the ruins of a trailside shelter. *Be Aware:* Wear hiking shoes and bring water.

More Stuff: To access several whale-watching turnouts, and **McGregor Point Light**, head back toward Ma'alaea on Highway 30 from the trailhead parking. After leaving the tunnel, within the first .5-mile, look for two dirt turnouts that were part of the old highway. Inspiring viewpoints await. Farther along, after mm9, is the well-marked and popular turnout at **Papawai Point**. For more solitude with your view, continue a bit farther—past mm8 and just before mm7—and take a right on the dirt spur road that leads a short distance to the beacon light at McGregor Point. Safe, but steep, trails lead down to weirdly shaped formations.

SNORKEL: Coral Gardens is a small cove featuring acres of coral heads and waters that are calm on days when trade winds make other snorkeling spots choppy. To get there from the Lahaina Pali West trailhead, walk the back along the highway toward the tunnel a short distance to where the guardrail ends. Make your way down the rugged trail to a rock-and-sand beach. You can walk rocks toward the point or start swimming in that direction. Tour boats moor on both sides of the point, depending on wind and wave conditions. *Be Aware:* Due to currents and (rarely) sharks, this cove is for advanced snorkelers.

For easier access, go to **Papalaua Beach Wayside**, which is across the highway from this trailhead; walk down the beach to your left and swim out toward the rocks. Or, if more challenging entry is what you seek,

Coral Gardens bound, Lahaina Pali West

advanced snorkelers can try **Wash Rock**, which is below McGregor Point; walk down from the historical maker near the light and curl around to your right on the rocks.

12. OLOWALU & LAUNIUPOKO VALLEYS   HIKE, SNORKEL, SURF

WHAT'S BEST: Get off the tourist track and into the wild: two classic tropical valleys, lots of snorkeling coral, rideable surf, and historical curiosities that span centuries.

PARKING: Take Hwy. 30 (the Honoapi'ilani Hwy.) toward Lahaina. *For Olowalu Valley-Petroglyphs:* At mm15, turn right into the lot for Olowalu General Store. Drive to the left of the left of the store, pass gate, and then turn right. Veer left at .3-mi. toward Olowalu Cultural Preserve and park at .5-mi. from the gate, at the petroglyph site. *For Olowalu Landing:* Turn left from the highway directly across from the store at mm15. Go immediately left for .25-mi. to an unimproved parking area at a gate. *For Launiupoko Valley:* Continue on Hwy. 30 to the traffic light at mm18. Turn right (opposite the beach park) on Kai Hele Kua and go left at the roundabout on So. Lauhoe Pl. (opposite Haniu Pl.). Then go right on Punakea Loop So. for .6-mi. and park at yellow fire hydrant #P-17.

HIKE: Olowalu to: Petroglyph hill (up to 1 mi., 200 ft.), or Olowalu Valley (2.25 mi., 325 ft.); Olowalu Landing (.5-mi.); Launiupoko Valley (4.75 mi., 400 ft.)

On the north side of **Petroglyph hill's** vertical face are the rock etchings made centuries ago. The exact origins of the pictures are the subject of Hawaiian legend and anthropological consternation. To the **top of the Petroglyph Hill** (Kilea cinder cone), walk the road past the petroglyphs and rock barrier, and curl right and up. Global warming tip: Sea shell fossils indicate that during geological yesteryear, when the earth had smaller polar ice caps, sea level reached within 15 feet of the top of this cone, making it a tiny island. *Be Aware:* Heed signs that say to stay back from the petroglyphs.

To **continue to Olowalu Valley**, go left from the petroglyphs, across the stream bridge. Then take the first right (the far right in the taro fields), through an OCP gate. The road ends at a water tank almost .5-mile from the petroglyphs (you can drive this first section if OCP gates are open). The area has been improved through the efforts of the **Olowalu Cultural Preserve** (see *Resource Links* page 235 to volunteer or get more info). There is no maintained trail all the way up the valley. But if you cross the irrigation ditch at the tank, and go left near picnic tables, you'll see a feeder trail that heads toward the stream bank. The forest is dense, but you can find adequate passage. *Talk Story:* The fascination with this trail is that it was the escape route in 1790 for Chief Kalanikupule when his troops were slaughtered across the island in the Iao Valley by the forces of Kamehameha the Great. *Be Aware:* Finding the same route back can be difficult if you wander off trail.

It takes time to fully soak in the beauty from the wharf at **Olowalu Landing**. The grounds (a short walk from the parking to the right) are adorned with coco palms, Norfolk pines, and several large native Hawaiian trees. For the supreme vistas, head out to the bench on the rock-and-dirt wharf. Sea turtles often pass, as do whales, just off the point. Inland is a museum quality view of Olowalu Valley, a jagged "V" above the treetops. *Talk Story:* In 1864 this was the site of one of Maui's earliest sugar mills and its most active pier. This tranquil place was also the setting of the Olowalu Massacre, in 1790, when American merchant Captain Simon Metcalf slaughtered about 100 villagers in a dispute over a stolen boat. Later, one of Metcalf's men, John Young, was kidnapped from another ship and forced to become a military advisor to King Kamehameha I. Years later, Young's granddaughter became beloved Queen Emma, wife of Kamehameha IV.

Ukumehame and Launiupoko Valleys, Olowalu petroglyphs

Olowalu Landing

Few tourists know about the **Launiupoko Valley** hike, which gives up spectacular seaward views of West Maui and takes you along the stream into the lush crease. The first part of the trail is unappealing. Head up a horsey trail until reaching a road that contours below a line of tall power poles and above the roof tops of a rural subdivision. Go right. This equestrian route has great views. After .5-mile, you'll reach signs for the **Launiupoko Ahupua'a Archaeological Park** (a village site whose remnants are obscured by brush). After another 10 minutes, keep left at a junction. You continue along a rock-lined dam and reach a **reservoir**. There you will find an inviting covered picnic table with a view.

Continue from the reservoir on grassy track that follows an irrigation ditch up the valley. The track becomes a trail, the valley closes in, and soon you will find yourself walking the tops of lava rocks that form the ditch. You lose the valley view for good when you enter trees, as century plants, guava trees, and wild coffee trees encroach on the path. Birds are abundant. About a mile from the reservoir, you cross the stream on a short, falling-down bridge supporting a water pipe. You have to enter the ditch in places over the next two hundred yards, until reaching its end, where the stream spews uncontained out of the dark shade of the jungle. Trailblazers can proceed with caution on a pig path that continues up the valley; falling rocks are among the dangers.

SNORKEL: For some of the best and most readily accessible snorkeling on Maui, try **Kaili'ili Beach**, commonly called, **Olowalu Beach**. Use roadside parking on either side of mm14. Coral shelves spread close to shore, as well as several hundred feet offshore, where tour boats anchor. *Be Aware:* Olowalu has a reputation for being a shark hangout; but only a few attacks (including one fatality) have been reported over a 15-year period. **Olowalu Landing** is also a good snorkeling area, far less frequented. Look for the sandy ramp to the left of the long wharf, and in between a smaller boat landing. A coral bench is to your left within the reef, or, on calm days, swim out next to the wharf through a reef opening to explore deeper waters. You may spot a turtle. A small lawn under coco palms is the place to log towel time between swims.

Launiupoko Beach Park, at mm18, has a nice keiki pool, formed by a curve of rocks in the center of the park. Low tide can leave this pool high and dry. To the left is a sandy beach backed by lawn and tables. Offshore the park are good snorkeling reefs, but shallow waters and breaking waves can make this an iffy proposition. Launiupoko is a choice spot for a picnic, among palms and banyan trees, though traffic noise out-duels the surf as a soundtrack. For swimming with a sandy bottom, try **Awalua Beach**, which borders the highway south of the beach park, between mm16 and mm17.

SURF: During the summer, either side of **Olowalu Landing** is surfed, but a shallow reef break can be a problem. Just north of the wharf, a left-break surf spot also pops up during the summer. More reliable surfing in this area is to be had at **Launiupoko Beach Park** and **Awalua Beach**, directions to which are in the snorkeling descriptions. Launiupoko is a good beginners' break. In between these two is called **Kulanaokalai Beach**, but it's all the same run of sand. Small offshore reef breaks are reliable in the winter, and high surf will roll in during summer.

13. LAHAINA   HIKE, SNORKEL, SURF

WHAT'S BEST: Lahaina has always been where the action is—as the beachside enclave of kings and queens, as the bustling whaling town that was the capital of Hawaii, and, today, as night-life city and the point of departure of vessels of all sizes. Lahaina is one of Hawaii's best walk-around beach towns.

PARKING: Take Hwy. 30 (the Honoapi'ilani Hwy.) to Lahaina. On the south end of town, turn toward the ocean on Shaw St. *Choices*: Park in the lot at the corner of Shaw and Front streets, use on-street parking, or continue down Front St. two blocks to a lot at Prison St. Parking spots are at a premium from noon onward.

HIKE: **Lahaina Town stroll (up to 3.25 mi.) and Lahaina Seawall (.5-mi.)**

Talk Story: In 1802, his immense eminence, Kamehameha the Great, fresh from battles that made him the first ruler of all the southern islands, kicked back along the Lahaina shores with his entourage of several hundred family members and hangers-on, while his craftsmen fashioned some 1,000 war canoes, the peleleu fleet, in preparation for the invasion of Kauai, far to the north. A treaty was signed in lieu of an invasion.

By the early 1820s, Liholiho, or Kamehameha II, was king. Lahaina saw the arrival of both the whaling ships and missionaries—two disparate forces if there ever were. The whalers—by the 1840s, some 400 ships called each year—believed "there is no

God beyond Cape Horn." Alcohol fueled violence and rowdy behavior. In defense, Liholiho, along with his mother Queen Kaʻahumanu and Chief Hoapili, embraced the missionary influence. They built a stone prison to quell unruly whalers, and set into motion a series of social reforms that abolished the patriarchal system born of the previous decades of war. They developed an educational system that was more advanced than all but a few schools in America. After 34 years, in 1854, the kingdom's capital was moved to Honolulu, whaling subsided, and Lahaina became a sleepy cane town. Recent decades have seen its resurgence as a tourist destination.

From Shaw Street, begin the **Lahaina Town stroll** down **Front Street**. At the corner of the parking lot by the ball field, you'll find a plaque commemorating **Mokuʻula Island**, the most sacred spot on Maui, where kings and queens had palaces and were interred. Common folk were prohibited. Then continue down Front Street, on the ocean side. The lawn area open to the beach is **Hale Piula**, and the foundation remnants are those for the never-completed palace of Kamehameha III—the king preferred sleeping in his grass hut nearby. Behind the hale is **Lahaina Beach**. Continuing on Front Street, after Kamehameha III school, you reach Canal Street.

Veer left at **Canal Street**, diagonally across the **Banyan Tree Square**. The sprawling tree was planted in 1873 by the sheriff on the town's fiftieth anniversary. Its canopy of limbs is now an aviary for chattering birds and an umbrella for scores of local artisans. Near the shore behind the tree are the **old courthouse-visitors center**, and the ruins of the first **coral-block prison**, which housed unruly whalers. First-class Hawaiian music and dance enliven the square on weekends.

The **Lahaina Harbor** is in front of the old courthouse, a visitors center with knowledgeable and free walking maps. For the **Lahaina Seawall**—a must-do side-trip—walk over to the prominent **Lahaina Lighthouse**, a 30-foot high beacon that dates from 1866 and was the first in Hawaii. Then walk down the paved road along the water, past an array of tour and fishing vessels, and take a right onto the seawall. You'll be walking on big flat boulders. The seawall, completed in 1938, is a spot to view surfers, the outer islands, and boating activity. But the real reason for being here is the romantic look you get back toward Lahaina: The opening shot for a South Seas adventure flick, with jagged green peaks as a backdrop to the palmy shore.

To **continue the town stroll**, return to the lighthouse and head over to the grassy area just north to see the remains of Kamehameha the Great's brick house, built in 1800, and the **Hauola Stone**, used by ancient Hawaiians as part of a birthing ceremony to portend healthy futures for their children. The ancient taro patch was also here, where the kingdom's first monarch labored to demonstrate the dignity of work. From here, cut back up to Front Street. There you'll find the **Baldwin House Museum**, the former home of Dwight D. Baldwin, one of the earliest missionaries, whose progeny became owners of vast tracts of land. Admissions is a couple of bucks.

Lahaina

Then, continue north on **Front Street**—and you're on your own. For several blocks, until things settle down again at Papalaua Street, you'll be in the heart of town, libation only steps away, galleries and shops plentiful, with brokers hawking adventure activities and tunes blaring from open windows. For the full effect, jog up **Lahainaluna Street**, the main drag that comes in from the highway. Follow your nose, but history buffs will want to stop in at the **Wo Hing Museum**. Built in 1912 as a gathering place for Maui's society of Chinese workers, the structure was restored as a museum in 1984. Behind the museum is the rustic cookhouse, in which is shown the Thomas Edison black-and-white footage of Hawaii. Shot in 1898 and 1906, these silent flicks impart volumes in a few memorable minutes. A minimal admission is charged.

More Stuff in town: Kids—and most everyone else—will want to see the Lahaina Prison, **Hale Pa'ahao**, or "stuck-in-irons house." It's two long blocks up **Prison Street**, which is between Shaw Street and Banyan Square. You'll see the high prison walls, built from the coral stones of the old fort at the banyan tree, on your left at the corner of Waine'e Street. During the 1850s, the prison housed sailors guilty of awa (kava) drinking, furious riding, and violating fishing taboos, along with your more run-of-the-mill adulterous fornication and assault. Making noise of any kind was prohibited.

Turn right on **Waine'e Street** and walk to the **Waiola Church** and **Waine'e Graveyard**. Buried here are Hawaiian royalty, including Queen Keopuolani, Kamehameha the Great's wife, and Governor Hoapili, as well as missionaries from the 1850s, such as William Richards. Commoners, sailors, elders, and children also rest here, persons of many races reflecting the multifaceted times when the world discovered Hawaii.

More Stuff close by: You'll also want to see the huge bronze buddha at the **Jodo Mission**. *Driving:* Go a few blocks north on Front Street and turn left on Ala Moana. Then, if you're looking for an inexpensive, local-style plate lunch, try the **Lahaina Cannery Mall**, located at the far north end of town, off Front at Keawe Street. Yes, it is a mall, but locals hang out here and it's also the venue for excellent free hula performances, normally held weekends at noon and Tuesday and Thursday evenings at 7.

More Stuff up the mountain: Check out the view from museum that housed Hawaii's first newspaper. *Driving:* Go several miles inland on Lahainaluna Street, in the middle of town. You'll reach **Lahainaluna High School**, begun in 1831 and the oldest school west of the Great Divide. At the original schoolhouse—veer left at the top of the hill—is a historic landmark, **Hale Pai**, where Hawaii's first newspaper was printed in the 1830s. The view from campus makes you wonder how the kids get any studying done.

Talk Story: Some 1,400-feet up the hill from the museum is David Malo's grave, a short distance above the huge "L," which is maintained by students. David Malo, among Lahainaluna's first graduates, went on to be the kingdom's leading educator. But later in life he requested to be buried high on this hill, away from Western influence he felt would destroy the essence of Hawaiian culture.

Banyan Tree Square

SNORKEL: Lahaina Beach, at the south end of town, is a .75-mile sand strip bordered by shade trees and a quiet neighborhood. A sheltering reef offshore makes for safe swimming and decent snorkeling. This was the beach of choice for Kamehameha I, a man who could do whatever he pleased. *Driving:* From the Shaw Street lot, access the beach behind **Hale Piula** to your right; or better yet, go to the more private end of the beach, by heading south to a Shoreline Access sign near 409 Front Street.

The action is at **Puʻunoa Beach**, also called **Baby Beach**, at the north end of town. *Driving:* From the highway, turn toward the ocean on Kenui to Front Street, and then go right. *Two access points: For the south end* of the .5-mile long beach, turn left on Kai Pali Place, and look for the Shoreline Access sign. This end of the beach features the popular baby, or keiki, beach. *For the north-end access,* and easier parking, continue on Front, turn left on Ala Moana, and park just past the **Jodo Mission**. A huge bronzed Buddha rests within the manicured mission grounds, a striking sight with the jungle ridge as its background. Before hitting the beach, you may also wish to walk north through the **Puʻupiha Cemetery**, to **Mala Wharf**, a monument to folly, since it was condemned just after completion in 1922 because offshore currents rendered it unusable. A reef just offshore Puʻunoa Beach provides a wave-free snorkeling zone, which can be shallow in spots at low tide. A ten-minute walk gets you to Baby Beach's south end.

Wahikuli Beach Park, alongside the highway just north of Lahaina, offers good snorkeling and numerous picnic huts set on the grass margin above the coast. The place can be busy on weekends. Use the second parking lot to the north. This spot has rocks at the shoreline, but you can walk both left and right to find sandy entrances to the water. Traffic can make getting into and out of these lots a hassle.

SURF: **Puamana Beach Park**, at mm19 just south of Lahaina, attracts low-key locals, both winter and summer. So does the **Lahaina Seawall**, both the north tip and off the elbow at its base. Access is via Lahaina Beach, behind Hale Piula, just north of Shaw Street. **Mala Wharf** also offers a long left-break, best during the summer.

14. KAʻANAPALI COAST   HIKE, SNORKEL, SURF

WHAT'S BEST: Take your pick between a glitzy, touristy resort path and a hike along an open beach backed by time shares. You'll find all manner of surf-and-sand sports.

PARKING: Take Hwy. 30 (the Honoapiʻilani Hwy.) north of Lahaina. *For Kaʻanapali Beach Resorts:* Turn left before mm24, into Hanakoʻo Beach Park. Go to the right in the lot and park near the cemetery. *Note:* Alternate Kaʻanapali parking spots are noted in snorkel and hike descriptions. *For Kahekili Beach:* Pass Kaʻanapali exit and mm25 and turn left at a light on Kai Ala Place. Pass Westin parking and proceed to beach parking.

HIKE: **Kaʻanapali Beach Resorts walk (2.25 mi.); Kahekili Beach walk (2 mi.)**

Kaʻanapali is comprised of two long beaches, which are north and south of **Black Rock**, or Kekaʻa Point, which is at the Sheraton. The resorts walk takes in south of Black Rock, and **Hanakoʻo Park** is at the south end of this segment. For the **Kaʻanapali Beach Resorts** coastal path, cross over the little bridge at the north end of the beach parking lot (to the right as you face the water). You'll join the paved path that begins at **Hyatt Regency**. *Other Parking:* To park at the Hyatt (which will begin the hike at the essentially same place) continue north past the beach park and turn left at Kaʻanapali Parkway. Then go left on Nohea Kai Drive, pass Shoreline Accesses 209 and 210, and continue past the back side of the Hyatt to Shoreline Access 208. You could also park at 209 or 210, lots near the Maui Ocean Club, which will shorten the hike.

The gardens and man-made lagoon of the **Hyatt** highlight the first, quieter section of the walk. Joggers, pool boys, and people wearing name tags may share the flagstone walkway. You then pass the **Maui Ocean Club**, with poolside gardens and chaise lounges supporting acres of glistening flesh. Here you may wonder why this path is called the **Kaʻanapali Historical Trail**. Then comes **Whaler's Village**, a rather drab, open-air mall, which opens to the path, presenting an opportunity to Hawaiianize your wardrobe or eat battered shrimp. Not far after the mall, about 1.25 miles into the walk, is the deep run of sand that stretches in front of the old-timey **Kaʻanapali Resort** and the fancy **Sheraton**. **Black Rock** will be visible ahead. The action-oriented 1970s surfer crowd dubbed this zone **Dig Me Beach**. Yeah, baby.

Kahekili Beach, north of Black Rock, is not quite the nature stroll, thanks to the addition of behometh time-share resorts in 2005—but you'll still find a run of open sand backed by kiawe trees. The walk begins at a pavilion, set among carefree palms and grassy banks. (Kahekili is also called Ahumanu Beach, or Old Airport Beach, or, at the south, Ka'anapali Beach.) You can walk left on the beach for about .5-mile to Black Rock, with the **Royal Lahaina Resort** looming on the bluff above. To the right, is open beach for about .75-mile, with ironwoods buffering the slopes and Molokai beckoning offshore.

More Stuff: Joggers and excercise walkers will want to know that the **Wahikuli Interpretive Trail** extends south for nearly a mile from Hanako'o Beach Park. The route hugs the coast through several beach parks ending near Lahaina.

SNORKEL: The south end of **Hanako'o Beach Park**, by the lifeguard platform, is a calm area with sandy bottom, suited for novice snorkelers. This park is also called **Cemetery Beach**. Most snorkelers in the area head for **Black Rock**. *Other parking:* For the closest access to Black Rock, take Ka'anapali Parkway toward the Sheraton and use Shoreline Access 213 in the 20-space parking garage, just south of the hotel. Another 12-space public lot is next door at the Ka'anapali Beach Hotel; enter the hotel lot and turn right. You can also park at Whaler's Village for a few dollars per hour ('free' validated parking requires a purchase of $20 or more). Signs notwithstanding, beach access is easy from Whaler's. Okay, out of the car! A paved walkway leads to the beach. Then head right to the sand just south of the point. Swim out along the steep walled **Keka'a Point**, where spirits of the dead were said to leave the island in ancient times, and where intrepid swan divers launch themselves these days. Fish are abundant, but visibility can be reduced by wave action. Bring your own shade, since Black Rock is a scorcher.

Black Rock

SURF: Boogie boarders and surfers like the area just south of **Hanako'o Beach Park**, sometimes called **Sand Box**. Winter rides are available, though summer is better, and this is not in the top ten Maui surfing beaches. But try the mellow right-breaks.

15. KAPALUA BAYS   HIKE, SNORKEL, SURF

WHAT'S BEST: Nature has scooped a series of sandy bays out of the rocky coast—providing surfers, snorklers, strollers, wave-watchers, and sun-bathers with lots of choices to hang out amid the buzz of condos and resorts. Or, select a mountain hike from among the free, private trails offered by Kapalua Resort.

PARKING: Go north past Ka'anapali on Hwy. 30, the Honoapi'ilani Hwy. Near mm29, turn left on Napilihau Rd. Then turn right on Lower Honoapi'ilani Rd. *Note:* Additional driving directions follow from this point in the activity descriptions.

HIKE: Coastal hikes: Napili Beach to Kapalua Beach (1.25 mi.); Kapalua Beach to: Hawea Point Shoreline Conservation Area (1.25 mi.), or Oneloa Bay (2 mi.); D. T. Fleming Beach Park to Dragon's Teeth (.75-mi.).

Kapalua Mountain hikes: Village Walking Trails (up to 8 mi.); Maunalei Arboretum (3 mi..); Mahana Ridge (5.75 mi.)

Talk Story: Once the domain of Chief Pi'ilani, who controlled six bays and the three islands—Molokai, Lanai, and Kahoolawe—that are visible from the shores, this 5-mile coastline today might well be called the Condo Coast. Creative site planners have blocked light from squeaking between the buildings in places, but these older places now seem folksy in view of some of Maui's larger resorts and timeshare "beach villas."

The coast walk from **Napili Beach to Kapalua Beach** is on a scenic path hidden in plain sight. The hard part is finding Napili Bay. *Driving:* Continue north on Lower Honoapi'ilani and, at about mm29.5, go left on Hui Drive; look for a Shoreline Access sign, and signs for Hale Napili. The access path is where Hui Drive bends right. Park at will, amid weekend car jams. From the beach, walk to your right around the pretty crescent of sand, and hop up to the railed path with paved stones that goes in the direction of the point. Before the point, the path ends, and you'll need to step down to a route that is plainly visible on a lava shelf. This fisherman's trail hooks around the point, passing tide pools. Notice footprints carved into the lava. After rounding the point, step up to a lawn area of a resort, from which your route to Kapalua Beach will be visible. *Be Aware:* Don't try this walk during high surf.

In spite of its scenic charms, the hike from **Kapalua Beach to Hawea Point and Oneloa Bay** is taken by few people—though the route's popularity increased with the opening of the 4-mile **Kapalua Coastal Trail to Honolua Bay**. *Driving:* To get to Kapalua Beach, go north on Lower Honoapi'ilani Road and turn left after an uphill

Kapalua Beach

S-turn near mm30, and just past the Napili Kai. A Shoreline Access sign points to a large parking lot (if arriving later, you will have to park on the shoulder before reaching the beach lot). Walk down the lot through a short tunnel to the beach and continue to your right along the sand, or on the grassy fringes of the huge new condos that sit above it. Round the coastal bluff, turning slightly uphill to your right. You'll cross a road amid condos and then go left at a Public Shore sign, pointing toward the low-lying **Hawea Point Shoreline Conservation Area**—the most *au naturel* spot around these parts. Tide pools on its north side make for soaking tubs, when the conditions are right. Double back from the point and head north on the lawn at the margin of nicely spaced condominiums. A boardwalk makes for easy walking to **Oneloa Bay** (Ironwoods Beach).

The **D. T. Fleming Beach Park to Dragon's Teeth** walk is a wave-watcher's special, leading from beach to the buttresses of **Makaluapuna Point** below the golf course at the **Ritz Carlton Hotel**. *Driving:* Take Highway 30 past both Napilihau Road and Office Road, which leads to Kapalua and the Ritz. At the bottom of the grade at mm31, turn left at a Shoreline Access sign, onto Lower Honokahua Road. A .25-mile drive takes you to Fleming Beach Park. *Driving alternative:* You can also reach Dragon's Teeth by beginning from the lower end of Office Road, where it makes a left turn below the Ritz. From the parking lot, cut across the golf course fairway at the edge of the burial site.

Dragon's Teeth

From **D.T. Fleming Beach Park**, go left along the sand, staying away from the shore break, until it peters. Then make your way up to the low bank along the golf course, following the out-of-bounds markers beside the trees. The **Honokahua Burial Site**, dating from 850 AD, covers some 14 acres to your left. Respect for this site, and years of legal haggling, is what caused the Ritz to be set back so far from the coast. Cut through scraggly ironwoods, and pass the **Dragon's Teeth**, a line of sharpened tufts of whitish trachyte, four- or five-feet high. Beyond the teeth are lava flats and a grassy area, where on most days you can watch waves explode. *More Stuff:* A shaded, paved path connects the Ritz grounds to the beach park.

Other shoreline spots: Driving north from the beginning of Lower Honoapi'ilani Road, you will see a few of Shoreline Access points with fair-to-good recreational values. First up, going from south to north, is the minor gem of **Honokowai Beach Park** (see *Snorkel*). After that, as the road gets curvy, past Akahele Street that leads to airport, is **Pohaku Park**, or **S-Turns**, a scenic turnout in view of the Kahana Beach Resort. A very good access is just north of here. Go left on **Hui Road E** at mm 28.7, to the end of the cul-de-sac. A tree-tunnel trail leads out to small **Haukoe Point** with tide pools; you can make your way north to a sweet sandy cove.

D.T. Fleming Beach

The **Kapalua Mountain hikes** are on the 22,000 acres owned by venerable Maui Land & Pineapple Co., which owns Kapalua Resort. *Be Aware:* Free hiking and shuttle bus reservations must be made in advance; 808-665-9110. *Driving:* Take Highway 30 to near mm30 and turn left on Office Road, toward Kapalua and the Ritz Carlton. Make your second right (past the Golf Academy) toward the red-painted Kapalua Resort Center. A free trail guide with maps is available. **Village Walking trails** encircle a nicely treed golf course that is just north of the center, on Plantation Estates Drive. The Master Loop Trail covers 3 miles with 400 feet of elevation.

For the **Honolua Ridge Trail**, with a side loop of **Maunalei Arboretum**, hop the free shuttle to another trailhead. The arboretum loop trails total about 1.5 miles, with 1,400 feet of elevation. The trails meander through the 1928 plantings made by D. T. Fleming. Hawaiian flora mingles with plants from around the world. The Honolua Ridge Trail, 2.5 miles, round trip, begins at the same place and climbs 1,700 feet past a sugi pine grove to the top of Pu'u Kaeo. From there, you'll have an option of hiking down the **Mahana Ridge Trail** nearly 5.75 to the Kapalua Resort Center. Or double back on the Honolua trail. For all Kapalua hikes, make sure you get the pick up time straight with the driver. *More Stuff:* Ever seen an ancient Hawaiian village being uncovered from a jungle valley? You can volunteer to help in the effort. Contact Malama Honokowai, a nonprofit group that is unearthing ruins: See page 234 in *Resource Links*.

SNORKEL: Go to the right at **Kapalua Beach** for easy entry and good snorkeling, as you stroke out toward the point. People also swim and snorkel below the bluffs on your left, as you come out of the pedestrian tunnel. Experienced snorkelers will want to check out the cove that is down to the left from the coastal trail to Hawea Point. Once dubbed "America's Best Beach" by travel mags, over development has bumped Kapalua from among even Maui's best beaches, in the opinion of some. **Napili Beach**, Kapalua's kissing cousin to the south, also has great swimming and decent snorkeling—to the right as you face the water. See Hike descriptions for driving directions.

Honokowai Beach Park is a bright spot at the south end of the Condo Coast. Go left from Highway 30 after mm25, and continue on Lower Honoapi'ilani Road for .5-mile. The park's protective reef makes for decent snorkeling and forms a very good keiki pool, with sandy entry. Bring the family and a cooler full of hulihuli chicken.

SURF: During the winter, surfers ride the tiers rolling into **Oneloa Beach**, a.k.a., **Ironwoods**. This is a big curve of white sand, not known for swimming, but it scores high marks among beach strollers. To get there directly, go north on Honoapi'ilani Road; pass mm30.5 and the Kapalua Resort, and take the left turn lane at the low sign for Ironwood Lane. You should see a sign for Shoreline Access (unless it's still missing). From the 20-space parking lot an improved path leads a short distance to the beach. You can also get here by turning left off Highway 30, towards Kapalua and the Ritz, on Office Road. Go downhill past the rows of ironwood trees, turn left, and then make a right on Ironwood Lane. Bodysurfing and bodyboarding is sometimes good at **D.T. Fleming Beach Park**, but the shore break and undertow can be dangerous when surf's up; lifeguards post hazard signs.

16. HONOLUA MARINE PRESERVE   HIKE, SNORKEL, SURF

WHAT'S BEST: At the beginning of Maui's wild north coast are a snorkeling sanctuary, a dramatic bluff walk, and world-class surfing waves—watch 'em or ride 'em.

PARKING: Take Hwy. 30 (the Honoapi'ilani Hwy.) north of Kapalua. The road narrows. *Mokuleia access:* Just before mm 32, look for a Marine Conservation District sign and paved turnout on your left at a chain-link fence. *Honolua access:* About .25-mi. past the Mokuleia access, on your left as the road curves right, is an overflow parking lot for Honolua Bay; from this overlook you can also observe conditions in the bay. Down the road from this lot (about .25-mi. past mm32) on a sweeping left bend, are marginal on-street parking spots for Honolua; more parking is on the left at a one-lane bridge just before mm33. *Lipoa Point access:* Continue to mm33.5 and look for a dirt road on your left, just past the guardrail at the top to the hill. *Be Aware:* Leave your car free of valuables at all these parking spots.

HIKE: Honolua and Mokuleia Marine Conservation District (up to .75-mi.); Lipoa Point (1.75 mi., 175 ft.); Windmill Beach (up to .5-mi.)

Railed concrete steps help on the short walk down to the small sand beach at **Mokuleia Bay**, which is known to surfers as Slaughterhouse Beach. To the right is Kalaepiha Point, the protuberance that separates this bay from its twin, Honolua, to the north. From the on-street parking for **Hononolua Bay**, a .25-mile trail within a dense forest that includes banyans and dripping vines takes you across a stream to the boulder shores. You'll find a concrete boat ramp, small patches of grass and sand, but no real beach. In 1976, re-created Polynesian sailing canoes took off from this bay and proved that the trip back to Tahiti would have been possible by the ancient voyagers.

Ironwoods

With weird formations, crashing surf, and offshore views, **Lipoa Point** is a place you'll long remember if you sit for a while. From the highway, a rutted but passable dirt road curves down and right to where it's blocked by a gate and berm. Normally, surfer's cars will line the road. If you drive this part, subtract .5-mile from the round-trip walk. From the berm and gate, walk down the dirt road, keeping to your left. A agricultural field will be on your right on this gradual descent. In the 1940s the field was a golf course, and this point is sometimes called **Golf Links**. You'll pass a grove of palms and then one of Norfolk pines, where a lava wall marks the remains of the old golf clubhouse. Bear left toward the point, through ironwood trees, and drop down through grassy patches and a rock-bordered path to the tip of the point. A smooth shelf is low enough to catch sea spray, but you can scramble up to perches on the craggy wall of trachyte that forms the point to get a point-blank view of Molokai. Below, little coves are pocked with caves, and you'll also see smooth tide pools that invite soaks.

Windmill Beach, officially called Punalau Beach, is north of Lipoa Point. Look for a gate and road to your left, near mm34.5. A path leads a short distance down an embankment through a stand of nicely spaced ironwoods to a long run of sand that is punctuated by sharp lava boulders. This is the last sandy beach going north, and its quiet, scenic shores are right for a picnic. *Be Aware:* Leave your car free of valuables.

SNORKEL: In spite of having a rocky shore, **Honolua Bay** offers some of the island's better snorkeling. Enter at the boat ramp and swim out channels in the coral both left and right. Snorkeling tour boats often anchor farther out in the bay. **Kalaepiha Point**, to your left, hosts lots of fish but be mindful of choppy waters on days when surf is breaking. **Mokuleia Bay** is usually wavy and only suitable in the summer; flipper out to the point on your right. The northwest side of **Lipoa Point** has snorkeling pools awaiting for trailblazers willing to do the rock hopping it takes to find them. Also, at the outset of the hike as described above, look for a small coco palm beach down a ravine to your left, where snorkeling is good. *Be Aware:* Avoid Honolua after a heavy rain, when the stream muddies the waters. Outer points will have current.

SURF: Surfers like the right-break at **Slaughterhouse Beach**, that is, **Mokuleia**, just off the point on its north side. Bodysurfers also like Mokuleia, but rock hazards are present. The real action at this trailhead is at the north side of **Honolua Bay**—reachable via the **Lipoa Point** access—where fabulous right-breaks draw intermediate to advanced surfers. This is one of Hawaii's best breaks. The overlook is a magnet for surf photographers; a short, steep trail leads from turnout to an ideal viewing perch. **Windmill Beach** is less crowded. Scope out the offshore rocks before paddling out.

17. NAKALELE BLOWHOLE   HIKE

WHAT'S BEST: A sea geyser erupts from a multicolored shelf on a rugged coast.

PARKING: Take Hwy. 30 (the Honoapi'ilani Hwy.) north of Kapalua. At mm38, look for a turnout on the left with a gate, from which a Coast Guard light is visible. *Alternate:* Some people take a slightly shorter, but much steeper, trail that is .5-mi. beyond this parking area. The blowhole is visible from the bluffs near beginning of this trailhead. *Be Aware:* Car break-ins have occurred at both parking spots.

HIKE: Nakalele Blowhole (1.5 mi., 200 ft.)

The **Nakalele Blowhole** is a 3-foot circular opening in the roof of an underwater cave beneath a lava reef, where wave action compresses air with a hollow whooshing sound, followed by towering blasts of white water. Bursts can rise 50 feet or higher. From the parking area, head down the red cinder road through the eroded grassy area, bearing right of the **Coast Guard light**. Then go down the gray-rock gully to the right of the light, to a sandy spot at the bottom. The blowhole is about .25-mile away, to your right, on a trail leading though sea-scoured rocks that may remind you of a Nevada desert—gray, black, and red; pock-marked and smooth; swirled together at their seams, or lying about in cobbles and boulders. You'll cross a large sandy area, make passage through a tuft of these rocks, and come to the blowhole—set to your left, maybe 40 feet from the sea and 15 feet below on a broad, smooth reef. You can view from above or circle around inland to drop down to the lava shelf for an eye-level perspective. Unless you'd like a shower, get a fix on the spray's direction and magnitude before circling the hole. *Be Aware:* Stay well away from the actual opening. Anyone slipping into that foamy maw is not coming out. Deaths have occurred.

Nakalele blowhole

More Stuff: On the way to the blowhole, **Honokohau Bay** is at the big bend north of mm36. An intriguing wide stream flows into a rocky surfer's beach. Most locals are friendly, but a few Bad Boys may be hanging around giving the stink eye to tourists.

18. OHAI LOOP & EKE CRATER TRAILS   HIKE

WHAT'S BEST: Take a trekking journey from the grassy upsweeps of the north shore to the fringes of the jungle at the wet heart of the island. Or forget that and opt for a nature stroll along the coastal bluffs.

PARKING: Take Hwy. 30 (the Honoapi'ilani Hwy.) north of Kapalua and continue as the road narrows along the north shore. *For the Ohai Loop Trail:* Begin at a signed trailhead on the ocean side of the highway at mm40.5. *For the Eke Crater Trail:* Turn right on dirt Poelua Rd., at mm40.7 and just before a speed limit sign. Drive in a short distance on a rutted road and park at the small hunter check station. *Note:* Hunter's gate is open to vehicles on weekends and holidays.

HIKE: Ohai Loop Trail (1.5 mi.); Poelua Road-Eke Crater Trail (6 mi., 1,600 ft.)

The **Ohai Loop Trail** is a chance to get out of the car and go looking for whales (in the winter), soaring seabirds, and low-lying native plants, such as the trail's namesake ohai naupaka, and other species that thrive in salt air on the windswept bluffs. Less than .5-mile into the hike is a sea-viewing bench between two grassy hillock, the hike's scenic highlight. Sit down for awhile and watch the sea crash into **Papanalahoa Point**. A sign midway in the loop says, "end of trail." Whatever. You can easily continue on an inland loop, though backtracking is more scenic. *More Stuff:* The highway sweeps down to **Hononana Bay**. Near mm41, after a one-lane bridge, a path leads down to the boulder shores. If you rock-hop for about .5-mile to your right at the coast, you may find a seldom-seen blowhole. Watch for high surf.

Talk Story: **Eke Crater**, also called Mount Eke, is in the wet center of West Maui, at an elevation of nearly 5,000 feet, getting some 30 feet of rainfall each year. You can't walk there—too dangerous, with tangles of greenery, and lava tubes ready to slurp up a wayward hiker. But you can hike a few miles to where the jungle laps at your knees.

For **Poelua Road to Eke Crater Trail**, walk up the road to your left. You'll soon cross a metal gate, and curve to the right. Avoid two right-hand options as you arc around a red-cinder amphitheater, staying on the main road. The route climbs on a switchback amid koa trees, and then ascends straight up a ridgeline, with green **Poelua Gulch** down to the left. A little over a mile from the trailhead, you'll cross a grassy area—to the left across the field is a game-watering station—and reach a second gate. Then ascend a long straightaway through a tunnel of planted pine trees. The view up from here is of a knoll at the head of the gulch, where the trail will take you if you're willing.

After the steep walk to the top of the knoll, you'll be greeted by a garden of several kinds of ferns, and a forested bench that affords a view from the high rim. After this point, the plants that have been slapping shin-high start to reach crotchward. Continuing upward, you lose Poelua Gulch on the left, and start picking up views of a deep valley to your right, which contains **Honokohau Stream**. Through the greenery that chokes the trail, look up to head of the drainage to see a portion of inaccessible **Honokohau Falls**, which is one of the highest in the nation. Pick your own turnaround point. On the way back you'll enjoy the seaward views as you drop to the airy slopes that lead to the trailhead. *Be Aware:* Prepare for a full-fledged day hike, with both rain and shine.

19. WAIKALAI PLATEAU & BELLSTONE POOLS   HIKE, SNORKEL

WHAT'S BEST: Embark on a getaway hike, from the cliffs of the north shore to the grassy plateau and pine forests high above them, with close-ups of the peaks at Maui's interior. Or make your way down to swimming pools carved into a dramatic shoreline.

PARKING: Take Hwy. 30 north of Kapalua, as road narrows around the north shore. After mm42, Hwy. 30 becomes Hwy. 340 (the Kahekili Hwy.) coming around the other way, from Wailuku. *For Bellstone Pools snorkeling:* Pass mm42. About .6-mi. later, after a signed "dip" in the road, look for a dirt turnout on the ocean side. A "danger" sign marks the spot. *For the the Waikalai Plateau:* Continue past mm16 (the markers start descending), and at mm15 .5-mi. later, park on the left at a dirt turnout, across from the gate for Waikalai Game Management Road. *Note:* Hunter's gate is open to vehicles on weekends and holidays.

Bellstone Pools

HIKE: Bellstone Pools (.5-mi., 125 ft.); Waikalai Plateau (5.75 mi., 1,400 ft.)

For the **Bellstone Pools** (a.k.a. Olivine Pools), head down the red-dirt trail through dwarf ironwoods and make a little curl right at a second "danger" sign. The pools are visible on a shelf below, a straight-on descent. The tide pools are well worth exploring even if you won't swim—but watch for big waves. See *snorkel* for more on the pools.

For the **Waikalai Plateau** hike, start up from the gate and pass the hunter check station. You're headed into **West Maui Forest Reserve** to the lip of the **Kahakuloa Natural Area**, home to the endemic dwarf greenery that sprawls northward from the center of the West Maui Mountains. After ten minutes you'll hook around to a view of Kahakuloa Head, the shark-fin-shaped landmark that rises above the village. About a mile into the hike, after a switchback up and a straightaway beside koa trees, you'll reach a grassy field. A wildlife watering station provides a viewpoint to the coast, and inland you get a first look at **Mount Eke**, which lies far inland. From above the watering station, walk a narrow shoulder inland, and then dip down across a land bridge spanning a gorge. Atop the other side is a freshly scented pine forest. A little more than 2 miles in, the road leaves the ridgeline, alongside a cut bank that reaches the stream. You then embark on a serious uphill segment, which leads to a grassy tableland that is planted with pines. From here is a commanding view seaward, but press on as the route snakes gradually up and in. In a few minutes you'll see a plateau, the green hillock that is your destination, rising just above the tablelands.

Take the road to the top—spurs lead elsewhere—and you'll get a view of green, stepped ridge that climbs to flat-topped Mount Eke, a.k.a. Eke Crater. **Puʻu Kukui**, is also visible, to the right. Notice that the vegetation changes here, transitioning into the West Maui Natural Area Reserve, which is home to many plant species unique to Hawaii. At this end point, you may feel the hike is just beginning, such is the allure of the view. Go, if you must. *Be Aware:* Prepare for both hypothermia and heat stroke. Bring a hiking pole and plenty of water.

SNORKEL: The **Bellstone Pools** (a.k.a. Olivine Pools), are several natural tubs scooped into a sea shelf about 8 feet above wave-battered northeast coast of Maui. Greenish olivine is a semi-precious gemstone that is sluiced by wave action from the surrounding soils and comes to rest on the surface. To the left below the cliff, an intimate pool is tucked into a rocky point. The largest, sweetest, and easiest entry is the pool on the flat to the right, the most seaward. More fish reside here. When the waves cooperate, this is one of Maui's best experiences. *Be Aware:* High surf can make swimming dangerous. People have died here. Watch the waves for many minutes before getting in, and don't assume it's safe because people are in the water. *More Stuff:* The ancient **Bellstone**, or Pohaku Kani, lies at the roadside near the trailhead. Striking the stone on its mountain-side achieves a hollow, metallic sound.

20. KAHAKULOA VILLAGE   HIKE

WHAT'S BEST: Although wood-frame homes with electricity belie the image of "my little grass shack," this tiny village, with its dramatic location, is the island's best example of how Hawaiians lived in ancient times. And getting there is part of the thrill.

PARKING: Take Hwy. 30 north of Kapalua as road narrows along the north shore. Continue past mm42, when route becomes Hwy. 340—and road *really* narrows. Dip into the valley and park after steel bridge near mm14.5. *Note:* You can also get here by taking Hwy. 340 north of Wailuku; that option involves more narrow-road driving.

HIKE: Kahakuloa Village (up to 1.5 mi.); Kahakuloa Head lookout (.5-mi.)

After enduring the precipitous road into **Kahakuloa Village**, most drivers are anxious about getting out, so not many take the time to stop and appreciate the place—which is a blessing since there are few parking places. But the village is Maui's best example of how people lived in ancient times in an ahupuaʻa—a wedge of land that contained a seacoast with agricultural plain, bisected by a stream that originates in the mountainous woodlands. These were the geographic ingredients for generations of survival.

Backtrack to start your stroll. At the outskirts of the village is the fetchingly sited **Kahakuloa Protestant Church**. Right on the road after that is the village's institution, **Ululani's by the Bay Shave Ice**, where you can talk story with Ululani. Then, from the parking by the bridge, take the dirt road that passes homes, whose stream-irrigated

Kahakuloa Village

gardens display an array of Polynesian fruits. Ubiquitous wild chickens and poi dogs will sound a greeting. The road follows **Kahakuloa Stream** through large trees to the rocky beach—which is not on the list of Maui's most scenic. *Be Aware:* Although the road is public access, be polite and ask permission if you see a local person; tourism creates an impact on this quiet village. Then, backtrack and continue up the main road. On your right will be the driveway leading to the **Francis Xavier Mission**. The tiny church is open to all who want to come in and light a candle.

Kahakuloa Head is the 600-foot "Tall Lord" that presides in his "feather cape" over the northern end of the bay. For a close-up of this angular landmark often seen from afar, you need to drive through the village. After surviving the one-lane road along the cliff, the road bends right. You'll see the head on your left. Pull off on a dirt loop by a fence that provides parking for several cars. *Note:* If you're approaching the head from the south on Highway 340, look for this turnout on the right near mm14, after passing the **Kaukini Gallery**. You'll pass **Pu'u Kahulianapa**, a twin hillock that sits just inland from the head. The turnout is between the two.

From the pullout, walk through an opening in the fence and across the grassy swale between **Kahakuloa Head** and Pu'u Kahulianapa, which is to your right. Social trails lead seaward, down through an eroded area with large pocked-lava boulders. If you continue down to the ledges closest to the ocean, and go left, you'll get a look at **Moke'ehia Island Seabird Sanctuary**. Frigate birds, shearwaters, and tropic birds may grace you with a fly by. You'll also see Haleakala and the east shore. Trade winds are often in your face from this perch, but on quiet days during the whale migrations in the winter, you'll be in a natural echo chamber that amplifies the exhales of the big mammals as they laze by. *Be Aware:* When walking below the head, be mindful of falling rocks.

Windward Coast

Champion Dan Moore rides a 68-footer at Jaws

WINDWARD COAST

The reef-protected beaches and mountain ridges on this working side of Maui are often bypassed by visitors—but not by surfers and windsurfers. Several strolls invite wave-watchers and history buffs, and adventurers will find roads to hidden heiaus, lofty mountain ridges, and sea cliffs where gargantuan waves arrive.

Driving Tour
Picking the Right Day

Select Saturday for this driving tour to see locals at play at the Maui Swap Meet, and avoid the traffic in town during the workaday week. On days when clouds hang in the West Maui Mountains, avoid the high stuff and retreat to the sunnier coast. Featuring some indoor activities, this is a good tour when the weather is not the greatest.

The Roads

You'll at least be on regulation-sized roadways during this drive, although traffic bogs down mornings and evenings in Kahului, like sand going through this hour glass-shaped island. Traffic also clogs headed into Paia late in the afternoons, as commuters head Upcountry. Also respect Mother Nature, by avoiding Highway 340 north of Waiheʻe during or after heavy rains, as flashflooding occurs. For those wishing to circumnavigate West Maui from this direction, one-lane road segments begin about mm8 and continue for some 9 miles—but the only white-knuckle segment is the short stretch through Kahakuloa.

The Course

Follow along on the Windward Coast map, page 84. Refer to trailhead descriptions beginning on page 85 for more details.

Begin early morning. Maui Swap Meet, Kahului. People-watch, souvenir shop, pick up exotic flowers, and expand your art collection at this Saturday morning scene at the **Maui Swap Meet**. Good deals abound. Items range from strictly tourist stuff to some guy selling what's left of his apartment before moving back to Des Moines. A good time to arrive is about 8:00 a.m., after the early birds. Think about picking up some homemade bread, organic veggies and fruits for a fresh picnic lunch.

Mid-Morning. Take Kaʻahumanu Avenue, which is Highway 32, to Iao Valley State Park. Every day is a weekend at Iao, and you're bound to see a tour bus or two in the parking lot. The **Iao Needle** is Maui's signature landmark, and it deserves its reputation. Stop at **Kepaniwai Heritage Gardens** and **Hawaii Nature Center** on the rebound. After that, if you feel like getting high on an out-of-the way trail, try Kapilau Ridge.

HEAD UP THE COAST ON HIGHWAY 330, WHICH BECOMES HIGHWAY 340. This route takes you up **Market Street** in **Wailuku**, where you can pop out of the car to take some of the old-town stroll. Then continue north on the highway. You can use pullouts or the short trails to check out the coast at **Hulu Island Seabird Sanctuary**. Hikers might also take side trips for the stream walk at Swinging Bridges (probably closed), or the uplands of Waiheʻe Ridge. But the best bet for a daylong tour is the short walk to the **Kukuipuka Heiau**, a big-mana viewpoint for the Kahului coastline. It's at the same parking for Waiheʻe Ridge.

NOON. HEAD BACK DOWN HIGHWAY 340. In a few minutes you can take a side-trip in Waiheʻe to see the town's hidden, pleasant beach park. Then roll the wheels south, making sure to keep left on Highway 340, which is **Waiehu Beach Road**. This will give you a chance to pull in to see the **Halekiʻi-Pihana Heiaus State Historical Monument**, hiding in plain sight.

Kepaniwai Heritage Gardens, Iao Valley, Bailey House Museum

HUG THE COAST AS THE ROUTE BECOMES KAHULUI BEACH ROAD, AND KEEP LEFT AT A MERGE WITH HIGHWAY 32. Keep left, turn left on Hobron, and turn right on Amala to get to **Kanaha Beach Park**. Here you can enjoy your picnic and be entertained by kite-boarders and windsurfers. This place is a never-ending action movie. Across the street is the Kanaha Pond Wildlife Sanctuary.

AFTERNOON. DOUBLE BACK AND GET ON THE HANA HIGHWAY, HIGHWAY 36. You'll want take to a few minutes to do a drive-by at the locals' beaches mentioned in the **Spreckelsville** trailhead—and, hey, nobody's going to sue you if you decide to flop back for the rest of the afternoon at one of them. Or, continue driving, through **Paia** to check out some country scenery, either by taking the fairly long walk to **Pauwela Point**, or a shorter one to **Halehaku Heiau** and Kahuna Point. The Halehaku option is a respite among tropical trees, before you backtrack to Paia.

SUNSET. PULL IN AT THE HO'OKIPA LOOKOUT. The world has few better places to finish out the day than from **Ho'okipa Lookout** of the surfer and windsurfer scene. You can follow up with a meal and stroll of **Paia** after dark. Don't worry about a dress code. Or, if you need to get back to another part of the island, cruise down the road to **Baldwin Beach Park** for sunset. Coco palms fringe a long sand trip, giving way to a view of the Iao Valley and, far to the north, Kahakuloa Head. It's easy to pop a whole chip of images here—big sky, ultra-aquamarine water, perfect light. Island-style rules, as locals gather to savor another day in paradise.

Iao Theater, Baldwin Beach

Map 3
Trailheads 21-34
WINDWARD COAST

Mokeëhia Seabird Sanctuary

Iao Valley State Park

Waihee

Waihee Beach Park

Waiehu Beach Park

Wailuku

Kahului

Kahului Bay

Kanaha Beach Park

Spreckelsville

Baldwin Beach Park

Paia

Hoökipa Beach Park

WAILUKU & KAHULUI

to Waihee

Kahekili Hwy

Waiehu Beach Rd

N. Market

to Iao Valley

Halekii-Pihana Heiau State Monument

West Main

City Offices

to Lahaina

Honoapiilani Hwy

Kaahumanu Ave.

Wahinepio

Swap Meet

Wailuku

Kahului Beach Rd

Kahului Harbor

Kamehameha Ave.

Wakea

Kanaha Pond

Amala

to Lahaina

Kuihelani Hwy

Dairy Rd.

to airport

Hana Hwy

Puunene

Kahului

to Kihei

Hansen Rd.

MAUI

WINDWARD COAST

TRAILHEADS
21-34

TH:	TRAILHEAD
HIKE:	ALL WALKING, FROM SHORT STROLLS TO FULL-FLEDGED DAY HIKES
SNORKEL:	BOTH FISH-VIEWING WITH MASK AND FINS, AND PLACES TO SWIM
SURF:	BOARD, BODYSURF, BODYBOARD, WINDSURFING, KITEBOARDING
MM:	MILE MARKER, CORRESPONDS TO HIGHWAY SIGNS

All hiking distances in parentheses are ROUND TRIP.
Elevation gains of 100 feet or more are noted.

21. SEABIRD BLUFFS   HIKE

WHAT'S BEST: Wander grassy bluffs above a wild coast and tiny islands that are a sanctuary for seabirds.

PARKING: Take Hwy. 340 (the Kahekili Hwy.) north of Wailuku and Waiheʻe. Look for a white-railed fence beginning at mm5.5, and park at a large turnout at mm5.9, near telephone pole #11A. This trailhead is apparent public access on private property. Use your own judgment. Landowners are not legally responsible for your safety.

HIKE: Seabird Bluffs to Hulu Island view (.75 mi., 150 ft.)

Talk Story: Extending several miles north of Waiheʻe is a roadless coast with cliffs and bluffs that embrace the trade wind's waves. The bluffs were the Western world's first glimpse of Maui, by Captain James Cook in 1778. Offshore the southern end of this coast is Hulu Island, a nationally designated bird sanctuary. Its sister sanctuary, Mokeʻehia Island, is to the north, just offshore of the 500-foot Hakuheʻe Point.

For the **Seabird Bluffs to Hulu Island** hike, pass left of the gate and walk down the wide gravel road amid ironwood trees. Where the road hooks left, continue straight for a couple hundred feet on a weedy path, until you break into the open on a grassy, red-dirt embankment. From there, make your way farther down, veering left. **Hulu Island** will come into view, about 200 feet below in an often churning seas. Several other small islands extend northward, including the farthest north, and largest, **Mokeʻehia Island,** some 4 miles distant. In the winter, trade winds supercharge the flights of seabirds, the giant frigatebird among them. *Be Aware:* Maui is a geologic work in progress. Some bluff edges are precipitous and unstable. Stay back.

Waihee Ridge

22. WAIHE'E RIDGE   HIKE

WHAT'S BEST: Start high and get higher on Maui's best tropical ridge hike to a view of the mountains at the center of the island. Or take shorter strolls: Nearby is a jewel of a heiau with a view, and not far away are two waterfalls with swimming holes.

PARKING: Take Hwy. 340 (the Kahekili Hwy.) north of Wailuku and Waihe'e. *For Waihe'e Ridge and Kukuiipuka Heaiau:* Turn left at mm6.75, across the highway from Mendes Ranch. Drive .75-mi. up a paved road and turn right at a gate across a cattle guard to a parking lot. *For Makamakaole Falls:* Continue northward on the highway to a bridge on the inside turn at mm7.75, and park at a turnout on the left, before crossing the stream. Walk about 100 yards back up the road (watch for traffic) to a turnout that at the top of a rise. (The falls is visible from the road at a turnout near mm8.)

HIKE: Waihe'e Ridge (4.75 mi., 1,500 ft. *Note:* this trail was improved in 2017); Kukuipuka Heiau (.25-mi., 100 ft.); Makamakaole Falls (.75-mi., 200 ft.)

From a cow gate, trudge up the steep concrete ramp that begins the **Waihe'e Ridge Trail**. Part of the state's Na Ala Hele trail system, the route is well constructed and marked. At the top of the ramp, go left through a gate and ascend through a bird-rich tree tunnel that includes Norfolk pines and strawberry guava. After .5-mile, you'll come to overlooks of **Waihe'e Valley**—one has a viewing bench that is a worthy end-point for hikers with less time, or on days when the clouds are hanging on the interior ridges.

From this first overlook the trail climbs with the aid of staircase sections, to a knob and spiny ridge that affords both the big look back toward the windward coast and the ridges that rise inland. The trail then veers away from the valley, across a depression of native scrub, before exacting another climb that is made easier by stair sections. Trail's end is an open hillock at 2,500 feet. A picnic table marks to enjoy the vista and to wave at the occasional tour helicopter. Inland, about a mile away and not much higher, is **Mount Lanilili**. **Puʻu Kukui**, West Maui's highest, is behind that peak, and flat-topped **Eke Crater** is north and inland. *Be Aware:* Prepare for rain and slippery conditions on this hike. The trail beyond the fencing is hazardous and not maintained.

Kukuipuka Heiau is a place that radiates beauty in all directions. Follow a road along a fence in the pasture to an unlocked gate. The trailhead steps begin at the the hill that rises above the meadow. You soon reach an open promontory, and the heiau, whose low, white-limestone walls—about 75-feet square—invite visitors to stop and enjoy. Native flowers and trees accent sweeping coastal views toward the Kahului Bay coast as it sweeps toward Paia, with Haleakala rising above. Be Aware: The heiau has been restored by Leiʻohu Ryder and others; see *Resource Links*. Tread lightly.

Makamakaole Falls are two 'secret' adventures enjoyed mainly by locals on weekends. From the outside turnout, go straight down the steep shoulder to a telephone pole, and continue down little zigzags from the pole (other trails veer left into the gorge). You'll reach the first pool at the top of a 20-foot cascade, where people leap for a chilling dip. Walk-climb down to the right of the pool and then cross left over its outflow. After a hop up to some rocks, the trail continues downstream over mossy bedrock and ferns and reaches the top of the second, 40-foot falls, beside a large banyan. The route down to the second pool is more difficult: you need to back down a 15-foot rocky face with root handholds to the left of the banyan. *Be Aware:* Landowners are not responsible for your safety. Do not attempt this hike during or after rains.

Makamakaole Falls trail

First swinging bridge, Waihe'e Ridge Trail

23. SWINGING BRIDGES   HIKE

WHAT'S BEST: Take an adventure hike over plank suspension bridges that lead upriver in a tropical canyon—to where waterfalls drop from on high. **The bad news:** Landowners have prohibited access. Call for the latest information; see page 235.

PARKING: Take Hwy. 340 (the Kahekili Hwy.) north from Wailuku. Pass the school in Waiheʻe and turn left at mm4.8 on Waiheʻe Valley Rd., before the bridge at mm5. Drive in .4-mi., turn right on a paved road (now gated), and continue a short distance to the check-in station for Waiheʻe Valley Plantation. *Notes:* Probably still closed. Admission formerly was around $6. Permission to enter is also required from Wailuku Water Co.

HIKE: Swinging Bridges (3.5 mi., 250 ft.)

This inviting trail follows the river up Waiheʻe Valley, which is nearly 3,000 feet deep. Waiheʻe means "slippery waters," made so by algae, so be extra careful with your footing on wet rocks. For the **Swinging Bridges** hike, walk the dirt road from the concession stand at the trailhead, passing a decrepit cable gate. The road starts up through dense subtropical forest, with the river and taro patches down to your right. After about .25-mile, the road begins a contour alongside an irrigation ditch, which periodically disappears into dripping tunnels. Just after .5-mile, you'll drop to the first bridge, a plank-and-cable strand some 125 feet long and 10 feet above the water. Just after the first bridge is the second, set in a profusion of jungle greenery. The second span is maybe 175 feet long, with a slightly uphill grade nearly 20 feet above the river. Both bridges were originally built to ease the way for agricultural workers.

Okay, you made it. From the second bridge, the trail follows the water amid a garden of bamboo, ti, and ginger and then crosses the river on rocks. After that, you weave up the other bank in a hau and banyan thicket, drop down, and cross the stream again. Continue up through rocks and ferns. The trail forks—either way works, but the left fork follows an interesting concrete ditch. After a short distance you'll reach a decrepit dam and spillway, with an 8-foot waterfall and swimming pool. Upstream is a view of the 3,000-foot-high amphitheater carved by the Waiheʻe River, often draped with a waterfall. *Be Aware:* Flash floods in this valley present a significant hazard. Stay out during rains. If you get stuck on the wrong side of a torrent, wait it out.

24. WAIHEʻE BEACHES   HIKE, SNORKEL, SURF

WHAT'S BEST: This long, scenic beach offers a quiet relief from resort strips. Nearby heiaus are a historical surprise, hidden above the neighborhoods.

PARKING: *For Waiheʻe Beach Park:* Take Hwy. 340 (the Kahekili Hwy.) north of Wailuku. In Waiheʻe, just after the ball field and before mm4, turn right on Halewaiu Rd. At the bottom of the hill, veer right toward Shoreline Access sign, and then turn left just before the golf course into the beach park. *For Haleki'i-Pihana Heiaus:* Take Highway 340, or Waiehu Beach Rd., south from its junction with Highway 330; Or, approach from Kahului Harbor, going north Hwy. 340. From Waiehu Beach Rd., turn inland on Kuhio Pl. (across from Ka'ae Place). Then turn left on Hea Place; park at Akulikuli Way.

HIKE: Waihe'e Beach Park (up to 4 mi.); Haleki'i-Pihana Heiaus (up to 1-mi.)

At **Waihe'e Beach Park,** the 600-foot-high walls of the northeast shores have tapered down to sea level. This long curve of tree-fringed sand and coral reef is seldom visited by tourists. Tall ironwoods surround a spacious lawn, creating a choice beachside picnic spot. From Waihe'e Beach Park, you can walk about a mile north, or left, on the sand, but rocks make the going tough before reaching Waihe'e Point—site of **Kealakaihonua Heiau**, located just south of where the **Waihe'e River** joins the Pacific. *More Stuff:* Hundreds of coastal acres are part of the **Waihe'e Coastal Dunes & Wetlands Refuge**; to explore natural and cultural sites, or to volunteer, call 808-244-5263.

Going to the right, is a pretty walk for about a mile to **Waiehu Beach Park**, which abuts the other side of the golf course. The sand dwindles along the fairways, and you may have to skirt margins of the golf course. You then hit the sandy, open beach at Waiehu Beach Park (see *Surf* below for driving directions to this beach).

The huge **Haleki'i-Pihana Heiaus** are a **State Historical Monument**, with some ruins dating from the late 1500s. The monument is on 10 weedy acres atop the hill, with views of the Iao Valley and Kahului coast—as well as the warehouses and modest suburbs that engulf the site, providing visual irony. The **Pihana Heiau** remains are farthest from the parking lot. The **Haleki'i Heiau** ruins spread from the lot's interpretive signs. *Talk Story:* Kamehameha the Great made human sacrifices here in 1790 to prepare for his conquest of Maui in the Iao Valley. Both these heiaus were partially dismantled when kapus against sacrifice and other decrees were made in the 1800s.

SNORKEL: A coral reef offshore **Waihe'e Beach Park** limits shore break and provides for colorful swimming, the best on this coast when conditions are right. Local spear fishermen love this place. The park is an excellent picnic choice. *Be Aware*: Waves breaking on the reef mean rip currents may exists. Waters will be shallow at low tide.

SURF: In recent years, both kiteboarders and windsurfers have discovered little **Waiehu Beach Park**. Take a seat on the little lawn and check out the colorful scene—but be sure to give them plenty of space. Short-board sufers will also be around. *Driving directions:* The park is located at the end of Lower Waiehu Beach Road. Take Highway 330 north from Wailuku, turn right at the junction with Highway 340 (Waiehu Beach Road), and then turn toward the ocean .25-mile south of this junction on Lower Waiehu Beach Road. *Alternate:* Take Highway 340 north from Kahului and then turn right on Lower Waiehu Beach Road, before you reach the junction with Highway 330.

Kepaniwai Heritage Gardens

25. IAO VALLEY   HIKE

WHAT'S BEST: The Iao Needle is Maui's signature spire. And surrounding tropical ridges, cascades, gardens, and ocean panoramas woo hikers and strollers alike.

PARKING: *For all hikes,* take Hwy. 320 (Iao Valley Rd.) from Wailuku. Iao Valley Rd. is where Hwy. 32 meets Hwy. 30, near city hall. *For Tropical Gardens of Maui:* Look on the right before mm1. *For Kepaniwai Heritage Gardens-Hawaii Nature Center,* look for the gardens at a bend in the road near mm1.5. Turn left into a lot that is a little farther up the road; the nature center sits above the gardens. *For Iao Valley State Park hikes,* continue 2 mi. to a paved lot. Don't leave valuables in car. A fee of about $5 is charged to park. *Note:* A 2016 flood closed the park for major repairs; work may continue through 2018.

HIKE: *Before the state park:* Tropical Gardens of Maui (about .25); Kepaniwai Heritage Gardens (about .25-mi.) and Hawaii Nature Center (up to 2 mi.); *Iao Valley State Park to:* Botanical Gardens and Iao Needle Overlook (.75-mi.), or Iao Tablelands vista (1.5 mi., 250 ft.), or Iao Stream (1.25 mi.)

Featuring a bridge over wide Iao Stream and a pond-side gazebo, privately owned **Tropical Gardens of Maui** is worth a look on your trip to the park (admission is about $5). Concrete paths swerve through several acres of plantings that are at once manicured and profuse—a result of 25 years of hands-on care. A plant export nursery near at the entrance allows you to send some of the greenery home.

The **Kepaniwai Heritage Gardens** sit at the gateway to Iao Valley, where steep green ridges rise alongside rushing **Iao Stream**. The county park features banyans, coco palms, taro, and a variety of Polynesian flora, growing amidst a stone-foundation grass hut and other exhibits that recreate village life on Maui. A Japanese garden and Chinese pagoda also grace the park, along with the architectural styles of Portugal, the Philippines, and New England—all meant to pay tribute to the many people who have called Hawaii home. If you're headed to the state park, these gardens are the best spot to stop for a picnic on the way back. *Talk Story:* On a less harmonious note, Kepaniwai means "damming of the waters," in reference to the mounds of fallen warriors that virtually stopped the flow of Iao Stream during the great battle of 1790.

Some 35 acres of streamside rain forest surround the nonprofit **Hawaii Nature Center**, a place for the family to enjoy both the botanical and historical bounty of the island. The center's gift shop is worth a browse. The attached museum features a large sun room, burbling stream, and touchy-feely exhibits that will elicit giggles and impart knowledge. Guided hikes (distances vary to suit the group) explore the rain forest. *Note:* An admission is charged to the museum. Hikes are about $30 per person.

Most tourists, some in buses, visit **Iao Valley State Park** to pay homage to the phallic Iao Needle, the poster-boy for Maui travel brochures. Nonetheless, you'll find room to roam. For the hike to **Botanical Gardens and Iao Needle**, take the paved path past the restrooms, and go left down the stairs before the bridge. You can wander around among the signed plants, both indigenous and Polynesian-introduced, and ponds. At the far end of the gardens, face upstream to observe the confluence. **Kinihapai Stream**, which flows under the bridge from the Needle, joins **Iao Stream**, which comes from the valley to the left. Then retrace your steps out of the garden, cross the footbridge—a Kodak moment—and take the paved path to the right. After hopping up a few dozen stairs, you will come to the small covered viewing area for the 2,250-foot Iao (rhymes with "meow") Needle.

The boundary for the 6-acre state park is the railing at the **Needle Overlook**. To continue to the **Iao Tablelands vista**—the choice hike for the valley and one of the best on Maui—you need to step over the railing at the overlook, thus entering a state forest reserve, and continue up the well-used trail. *Note:* Signs at the rail ask that you "stay on designated walkways" and warn that cars left after park closure will be towed. The trail is hiked frequently. Use your own judgment.

The **Iao Tablelands** is the area between and above the two streams, which join below at the botanical garden. The trail at first is cut into the side of a narrow ridge, with an embankment rising to your left and a steep valley on the right. As you climb, during the first .25-mile, you'll rise above the Needle and be able to observe that the backside of the spire is anchored up high to a ridge, eliminating the needle effect. After another .25-mile, the trail climbs so that there is no rise to your left. Double-back to your left here, amid strawberry guava saplings, and continue a few hundred feet down the trail that runs along the ridge, parallel and slightly above the main trail.

Iao Valley Botanical Gardens

You'll come to a little clearing with astounding views: Inland is the the Iao Valley and seaward is the Kahului Coast. Both streams are visible. On the north is the **Wall of Tears**, a 3,000-foot fissured cliff that at times will have a half-dozen silvery falls; at times, water vapor falls down the cliff faces. And then turn around. The craggy green **Kapilau Ridge** is equally captivating. *Be Aware:* Stay back from trail edges, where greenery disguises dangerous drop-offs. *More Stuff:* From the vista point, the trail continues into the tablelands for more than a mile, and gradually up. Although flora encroaches at times—ferns, koa, ti, bananas, guava—the route is easy to walk. You won't achieve a view comparable to the vista point, and forget about taking the ancient route to the Olowalu Valley: It's overgrown and washed out. *Be Aware:* Make sure to memorize your trail junctions, as coming back can be confusing.

For the **Iao Stream** walk, cross the bridge at the stream on the improved path. At the stairs leading to the Needle, go to your left on a path and stairs down to the forested banks of Iao Stream. A social trail leads upstream. The improved trail makes a loop downstream, passing near the confluence across from the botanical garden. *Talk Story:* The Iao Valley has become known for the gruesome battle. But for centuries is was also the place on Maui where the Makahiki was celebrated in the fall—when the god Lono returned to bring peace and renewal, and to bless the land's bounty.

26. KAPILAU RIDGE-MAUI TROPICAL PLANTATION HIKE

WHAT'S BEST: A little-used trail takes you up to a sweeping view of the isthmus' two coasts and a goat's-eye look toward Iao Valley. Or, a nearby old-style garden and visitors center offers families a more leisurely options, plus a chance to buy organic produce.

PARKING: *For Kapilau Ridge:* Take Hwy. 320 (Iao Valley Rd.) from Wailuku. After about .5-mi., veer left toward Wailuku Heights on W. Alu Rd. Continue about .25-mi., to where guardrail ends and the road makes a big left. The trail is on the right at telephone pole #5. Park at a shoulder on the left *before* reaching the turn. *For Maui Tropical Plantation-Kumu Farms:* Take Hwy. 30 (S. High St.-Honoapi'ilani Hwy.) about 2 mi. south from Wailuku; it's off the highway just south of Waiko Rd.

HIKE: Kapilau Ridge to: Wailuku Cross (1.5 mi., 850 ft.), or Pu'u Lio (4.5 mi., 2,100 ft.); Maui Tropical Plantation-Kumu Farms (up to .75-mi.)

Talk Story: Around 1960, parochial school students from Wailuku erected a large cross on the Kapilau Ridge, which is the one to the left as you look toward the Iao Valley. The white cross is visible from highways north and south of Wailuku. For **Kapilau Ridge hikes**, step up the grassy embankment to the right of telephone pole #5 and begin the steep climb through trees. Roots help with footing. The trail flattens before you reach the wooden **Wailuku Cross**, contouring along through koa, ironwoods, and even paperbark trees. For the aerial views from **Pu'u Lio**, continue past the cross. The trail makes several steep rises, followed by flatter segments on knolls. Not far above the cross, century plants may block the trail in one spot, but good passage follows. The first big pitch from the cross reaches a clump of ironwoods. From there you'll ascend two eroded, red-dirt ramps. The more forested Pu'u Lio is above these; a small grassy area, which is often at cloud level, lets you look through leaves and century plants, down at the Iao Needle, and the Kinihapai Stream side of the valley.

Maui Tropical Plantation's 60 acres sprawl from the base of the West Maui Mountains, planted with an orchard of tropical fruit trees and flowering shrubs, and surrounding a large pond that is home to feedable fish and quacking ducks. On the grounds are a large gift store, a minimalist zipline, and a monkey cage. Kids will love it. You can see it all on an outrigger cruise or a 40-minute tram ride (about $16 for adults, $6 for children), or by taking a stroll of the central grounds. It all adds up to an old-timey, relaxing visit. **Kumu Farms**, next to the plantation's entrance, has an open-air organic produce store set next to 15-plus acres of lush garden. This is the place to stock up at the beginning of your vacation. Herbs, spices, cheeses, and exotic fruits are in the mix.

27. WAILUKU TOWN   HIKE

WHAT'S BEST: Do some quirky souvenir shopping while you get a sense of small-town Maui, circa 1950. Or roam other buildings that date from a century earlier.

PARKING: Go north toward Wailuku on Hwy. 30, which becomes S. High St. At a traffic signal, S. High St. meets Hwy. 32, which is also Main St. *For the Historical Buildings:* Park at public lot across the street from the library, just before reaching Main. *For the Old Town Stroll:* Turn right on Main St. and then turn left on N. Market St. Park on-street, or in a public lot that is on the left before reaching Vineyard St.

HIKE: Historical Buildings Tour (up to .5-mi.); Old Town Stroll (.25-mi.)

Talk Story: At the opening to the Iao Valley, Wailuku's site was the chosen spot for the kings, or ali'i, of ancient times. This is also where Kamehameha I's forces won the final battle that united the islands as a kingdom, where the missionary movement and educational reforms were centered, and, finally, the capital for sugar industry's growth during the late 1800s and well into the 1900s. All of these historical threads are braided together within a few blocks on the Historical Buildings Tour, featuring some 10 buildings listed on the National Register of Historic Places.

The **Historical Buildings Tour** begins at the **Old County Building**, under the huge monkeypod trees at the parking lot, dates from 1925. Next door, the **Circuit Courthouse**, was built 18 years earlier. Both are National Historic Places. So are the Wailuku Public Library across High Street, and the **Territorial Building**, which sits with a lawn buffer just above it. At the corner of High and Main streets are the **Ka'ahumanu Church**, built in 1876 to honor Hawaii's favorite queen, and a small cemetery in **Honoli'i Park**, where Hawaiian ali'i and missionary families lay side by side.

Walking to your left, toward Iao Valley, on Main Street, you'll see the **Alexander House**, built in 1836. And just up the street is the stone-and-stucco **Bailey House Museum**, one of the better small museums in Hawaii. Built on lands donated to the missionaries by Hawaiian royalty, the plantation-style structure was home to the Wailuku Female Seminary from 1832 to 1932. Today, you'll find native Hawaiian artifacts and paintings by Edward Bailey, who also made much of the furniture. Displays tell the story of Maui's golden era, when educational and cultural reforms took place in the 1800s. Outside is an exotic garden with inviting benches and a view of Haleakala, and the entrance to the gift store, which is run by the Maui Historical Society. *Note:* The museum is open Monday through Saturday, 10 to 4. Admission is around $5.

Although the county seat since 1905, the high tide of commerce has been receding from Wailuku since the 1960s, as evidenced in the 'charming,' art deco-meets-Old West buildings along the **Old Town Stroll**. Antique stores, bonifide junk stores, Hawaiian crafts, used records, galleries, second-hand clothes, old books, and espresso cafes, are strung along one block, all set around the crown jewel of funk deco, the **Iao Theater**. Old Wailuku is gradually being spruced up, and some brochure writers have dubbed Market Street, "Antiques Row." On side streets, are neighborhoods with sugar shacks covered with sprays of flowers and tropical greenery.

28. KAHULUI HARBOR   HIKE, SURF

WHAT'S BEST: On Saturdays, catch the gargantuan Maui Swap Meet, an open fruit stand, flea market, and art gallery. Then see if there's a canoe race or big surf at the harbor.

PARKING: Take Hwy. 311 (the Mokulele Hwy.) north to Kahului. Mokulele becomes Hwy. 350 and Puʻuhene Ave. Follow Puʻuhene Ave. .75-mi. to Kaʻahumanu Ave., Hwy. 32, and turn left. Continue another .75-mi. and turn right on Wahinepio Ave. Parking is .25-mi. farther, next to Maui Community College and across from the Maui Art Center. *Alternate route:* While driving along the water on Kahului Beach Rd., Hwy. 340, turn inland toward the Maui Art Center on Wahinepio Ave.

HIKE: Maui Swap Meet (about .5-mi.); Kahului Breakwater and Keopualani Park (up to 2 mi.)

Locals gather before 7 a.m. on Saturday for the **Maui Swap Meet**, in search of good deals on fresh flowers, sunglasses, island art, T-shirts, books, jewelry, ethnic snacks, native crafts, castaway junk, baked goods, trinkets, and a mind-boggling assortment of locally grown fruits, herbs, and vegetables. The booths are set along asphalt paths and lawn medians, a uniform ambiance with few places to find shade or sit down. But most visitors will be entertained and few will depart empty handed. The event closes up around 1 p.m.

Driving: To get from the swap meet to the **Kahului Breakwater** drive toward the ocean on Wahineipio Avenue and turn left on Highway 340, which is Kahului Beach Road. Then turn right into a paved lot at the foot of the wide breakwater that forms the west side of the harbor. Park near the gate and walk about to view the big ships, incoming surf, fishermen, and surfers. *Driving:* To reach **Keopualani Park**, home to the **Maui Art Center**, spacious play areas, and **Maui Nui Botanical Garden**, turn right from the breakwater on Kahului Beach Road and then make your first left on Kanaloa Avenue. The state-run gardens are slowly growing into one of the better exhibits of Polynesian and native plants. Hours are Monday through Saturday, 8 to 4. *More Stuff:* The Hawaiian Canoe Club puts in at the grassy shores of **Hoaloha Park** for paddles out Kahului Harbor. *Driving:* Take Highway 32 (Kaʻahumanu Avenue) in the direction of the airport, but turn left on (unsigned) 2nd Avenue toward Shoreline Access—just past Lono Avenue and just before the light at Puʻuhene. The small park offers a view of Pier 2, where the cruise ships and container vessels dock.

SURF: The breakwater at **Kahului Harbor Park** presents a choice for surfers: a left-break inside the harbor, or a larger, right-break outside on the ocean side. The outside break is often better reached from the **Paukukalo** neighborhood. *Driving:* Take Highway 340 north as Kahului Beach Road veers right and becomes Waiehu Beach Road. Several Shoreline Access points are on dead-end roads: Kainalu, Linekona, Kaikoʻo, and Kailana. The Paukukalo neighborhood is very local.

29. KANAHA BEACH PARK   HIKE, SNORKEL, SURF

WHAT'S BEST: Beach walk while trade winds froth the waves inside a long coral reef, supercharging the sails of windsurfers and kiteboarders. You can find both action and or a private beach. Or take an even calmer stroll at the nearby historic wildlife pond.

PARKING: *For Kanaha Beach:* Go east from Kahului on Hwy. 32, Kaʻahumanu Ave., and continue straight at the jct. with Hwy. 36 (the Hana Hwy.) as that road goes to the right. Turn left on Hobron Ave. (32A), and then turn right on Amala Pl. Continue for 1.75 mi., as Amala becomes Alahao St. The beach park covers more than a mile along the street; the primary entrance is the second paved road on your left. *Alternate:* Go to the airport, loop around the terminal, and turn right toward the rental car returns on Kaʻa St. Kaʻa joins Alahao St.; turn right for beach park. *For Kanaha Pond:* From its jct. with Hwy. 32, take Hwy. 36. Veer left toward the airport on Hwy. 36A. Then veer left off 36A toward the airport on Keolani Pl. and make the first left on Palapala Dr.

HIKE: Kanaha Beach stroll (up to 1.25 mi.); Kanaha Beach to Spreckelsville Beach (2 mi.); Kanaha Pond Wildlife Sanctuary (up to 1.75 mi., permit required)

Try the **Kanaha Beach stroll** in the afternoon, when the kiteboarders are airborne and dozens of colorful windsurfer sails accent the breaking waves. Many visitors overlook this scenic park because it is off main roads and near the airport. About .5-mile after making the right on Amala, on the left before a bridge, is the pipe gate for the **Kaʻa Point** section of the beach park that is the kiteboarders' hangout; a second access is about .4-mile beyond the first. These athletes from around the world stand on a short board with

Maui Swap Meet, Maui Zipline at Maui Nui Botanical Garden, Hoaloha Park toe clips, while harnessed into a kite—which has just enough lift to swing them into the air, but not enough to yank them into the wild blue yonder. Farther down Alahao Street, at the farthest lot for **Kanaha Beach Park**, is the take-off spot for the windsurfers. Stroll down the beach to your left and continue past the rounded point to reach the kiteboard beach. On the way you'll weave through the expansive picnic and camping area, shaded by ironwoods and tall broadleaf trees.

Start the **Kahana Beach to Spreckelsville Beach** hike from the farthest last parking lot at the beach park. This is one of Maui's pleasant surprises. Head to your right along the coarse sand, at the edge of a backshore of ironwoods, palms, and

Kanaha Beach Park

kukui trees. You'll pass a little black-rock jetty and reach a nice run of sand, from which Kanaha Park will no longer be visible. Cross a second black rock point, leading to another, smaller beach. Nice beach homes are set back from the beach, and you'll have to walk the tops of the bulkheads of their yards to round the point. One last section, with Spreckelsville Beach now visible, is easiest wading—and not that easy at high tide.

The **Kanaha Pond Wildlife Sanctuary** walk covers 150 fenced acres. Paths encircle four ponds, creating a walking track with options. Wandering these tree-shaded land patches between still waters will be a memorable experience for bird watchers. *Note:* You'll need a permit from state wildlife (available from September through March, when birds are not nesting). Hikes are possible Monday through Saturday, 8 to 4; call 808-984-8100. The free permits can be processed on the day of your request. *Talk Story:* The pond was built to raise fish and waterfowl, more than 200 years ago by King Kapi'ioho'okalani. Today this National Natural Landmark provides habitat for native Hawaiian species, such as the coot, stilt, and duck—all endangered. Migrating waterfowl and shorebirds also touch down here in the winter.

SNORKEL: The long Spartan Reef offshore **Kanaha Beach Park** provides for colorful snorkeling on calm days, but windsurf action makes swimming iffy. A roped-off pool near the lifeguard station is a safe place to take a dip; or, show up before 11, the start time for the wind worshipers. Your best bet for a beach day is to take the walk toward Speckelsville, described above. Bits of seaweed and wave-borne sand detract from water clarity, but you won't find a more private and pretty beach scene on Maui.

SURF: Kanaha Beach Park is a windsurfing and kiteboarding Mecca, both for those who take part and those who want to kick back and watch the spectacle (see *Hike* above for directions). These guys and wahines are among the world's best.

30. SPRECKELSVILLE   HIKE, SNORKEL, SURF

WHAT'S BEST: Three beaches present different ways to get away from it all, without having to go far to do it.

PARKING: *For all beaches:* Take Hwy. 36 toward Hana past its jct. with Hwy. 37 and mm3. *For Spreckelsville Beach:* As Hwy. 36 bends to the right (before the senior center), turn left at mm4.4 on Spreckelsville Beach Rd., a.k.a. Stable Rd. *For Sugar Cove and Baby Baldwin:* Continue as Hwy. 36 bends right, pass the senior center, and turn left at mm5 on Nonohe Pl. *For Sugar Cove:* Drive .2-mile to the bottom of Nonohe Place, turn left on Pa'ani Place, and continue for .2-mi. Park at road's end, near a sign for Shoreline Access 302 (though this sign may be missing). *For Baby Baldwin:* Stay to the right on Nonohe at the bottom, and then immediately turn left toward Shoreline Access, on Kealakai Place—instead of going to the golf course.

HIKE: Spreckelsville Beach (up to 2.5 mi.); Sugar Cove (up to 1.25 mi.); Baby Baldwin Beach (1.25 mi.)

Talk Story: Claus Spreckels came to Maui already a millionaire in 1877. He left 20 years later a multi-millionaire known as the "Sugar King" of Hawaii, after he bought up thousands of acres and built mega-irrigation ditches that captured stream flows on the north slope of Haleakala. Known also by some as a robber baron, Spreckels' former compound, Spreckelsville, was where the Maui Country Club is today.

You'll see several potholed spur roads to **Spreckelsville Beach** after you pass coco palms. Dunes and beach succulents appear on your right. A few rough access roads are within .75-mile from the highway turnoff, before reaching homes at road's end. The best access is at a yellow pipe gate, .6-mile in. Drive in through the pinkish sand dunes to unimproved parking the beach. To your right you can walk about 1.25 miles, passing rounded **Papaula Point**, to **Sugar Cove**. Small black-rock points intrude into the sand along the way. *More Stuff:* To your left, alongside the road, is the bike path that goes to **Kanaha Beach Park**. You can also beach walk to Kanaha.

Baby Beach, Kanaha

To **Sugar Cove**, A short sand trail leads along a lava seawall to a good-sized cove set below unobtrusive, high-end condos. You can walk left to Spreckelsville Beach—the reverse of the hike described above—but this beach is more a place to catch a few winks or count grains of sand. If you get antsy, try walking right up steps and taking a marginal trail along a seawall (watch for waves) to Baby Baldwin. The parking for **Baby Baldwin Beach** is at Wawau Point, where a mosaic of red banks, black rocks, and white sand make for an interesting stroll. The beach hike seamlessly connects with **Baldwin Beach Park**.

SNORKEL: A finger from Wawau Point's reef curls just offshore for several hundred feet at **Baby Baldwin Beach**, making a sandy-bottomed oval that can accommodate large numbers of swimmers. The beach is a well-known dipping pool for families, safe even during trade winds—although be mindful of the current flowing to your right as water returns out the open end of nature's pool. Sand dunes and ironwoods buffer the shore. Not many fish are in the pool, but this is a five-star swimming spot. You'll also find a very good **baby beach at Spreckelsville**. Go to the access road that is .6-mile in from the highway, just before the private road begins. A long oval is carved out of the shelf, open to the sea on its left side, which also opens to the big look at Iao Valley. Soak and stare. *Be Aware:* Wave action will bring current, usually right-to-left. It's normally safe. Local families will show up on weekends, but not many tourists will find this sweet place.

SURF: Windsurfers catch the breeze off **Wawau Point**, near Baby Baldwin, but offshore rocks make this less popular than other spots not far away, both up and down the coast. The offshore tiers at **Sugar Cove** occasionally attract local shortboard surfers and kite-boarders.

31. BALDWIN BEACH PARK   HIKE, SNORKEL, SURF

WHAT'S BEST: Baldwin is one of Maui's sweet spots, where coco palms fringe golden sand and turquoise waters—the perfect place to enjoy life on a waning afternoon.

PARKING: Take Hwy. 36 (the Hana Hwy.) past the Maui Country Club to mm6. Turn left into signed beach park lot. Hours are from 7 to 7.

HIKE: Baldwin Beach to: Baby Baldwin (.75-mi.), or Paia via State of Mind Beach (1.5 mi.)

Talk Story: The beach park is the former home for families who worked the sugar cane for Harry A. Baldwin—whose grandfather Dwight Baldwin was one of Maui's original missionaries in Lahaina in the early 1800s. Harry furthered the efforts of his father, Henry P., and the family by the 1930s was one of the Big Five, who controlled more than 90 percent of the state's sugar production—and virtually ran Hawaii's govern-

Baldwin Beach Park

ment. Local mills have shut down, but some of the workers and their descendents still gather at the park. If you're lucky, you'll arrive on a day when blade-wielding Tongans are climbing the park's willowy coco palms to trim.

Late afternoons are a good time for **Baldwin Beach**, as locals gather to frolic in the surf and unwind. **Baby Baldwin Beach** is a sand-and-surf walk. In the background is the jade tunnel of the Iao Valley, and to the right in the distance you'll see the shark fin of Kahakuloa Head. A trail also parallels the backshore through a dune planted with ironwoods and beach shrubbery. Going to your right from the pavilion, toward **Paia**,

State of Mind Beach

you'll cover a stretch of sand and then hop up to a dirt fisherman's path, protected by riprap. After rounding a point, you'll reach isolated **State of Mind Beach** (a.k.a. Montana Beach). The path continues just above its narrow run of sand, a couple hundred yards long. After a copse of ironwoods—where at shore a large, washed-up concrete block is spray-painted with "state of mind"—come the sands of **Lower Paia Beach Park**, which is on the outer edge of the town.

SNORKEL: **Baldwin Beach** is not known as a snorkeling beach, but you will find spots to take a dip. The best is to the right a hundred yards from the pavilion. A curve of rocks creates a fairly protected pool. Ample sands and shade trees lure locals and a smattering of kicked-back tourists. Ask lifeguards about surf conditions.

SURF: The shore break to the left of **Baldwin Beach** parking draws bodysurfers and bodyboarders in the winter. But be careful, as head plants can be scary at times. The lifeguards normally post hazard signs, but you shouldn't rely on them. Board surfers head for the reef break, to the right of the pavilion in the direction of Paia.

32. PAIA-HOʻOKIPA   HIKE, SNORKEL, SURF

   WHAT'S BEST: Shop for surf shoes, espresso, or island art in this back-to-the-earth beach town. Then just down the road is the world capital of windsurfing.

   PARKING: *For both hikes,* from Kahului take Hwy. 36 (the Hana Hwy.) past mm6. *For the Paia stroll:* As you approach the first buildings, at the first crosswalk and reduced

Paia, Hookipa

Paia

speed sign, look for public parking sign on your right. On-street parking is also available. *For Ho'okipa Beach walk:* Drive beyond Paia. At about mm8.5, pass the first entrances to the beach park and turn left past a sign for Ho'okipa Lookout. Park at the upper lot.

HIKE: Paia stroll (.75-mi.); Ho'okipa Beach walk (1 mi.)

For the **Paia stroll,** wander up the Hana Highway to its T-intersection with **Baldwin Avenue.** All the action is a block or two on either side. If you need a beach break, begin by doubling back a short distance to the **Lower Paia Beach Park,** at the Paia Youth Center. The scene amps up on weekends with surfers and sunbathers.

Paia reinvented itself in the 1980s, when the studly new sport of windsurfing married the fetching waves of nearby Ho'okipa Beach. The fading Old West wood-frames, plantation cottages, and sugar shacks got new coats of pastel paints, as the sandy-footed set created a demand for a host of low-key tourist shops—boutiques, hemp-reggae wear, surfer-Joe outfitters, espresso internet cafés, seafood grills, and some of Maui's best art galleries. The with-it epicenter for Paia is **Mana Foods**—up Baldwin Avenue on the left—where tribe members of organic enclaves and other low-key locals seek whole-grain goodies and stimulated conversation. If dining out in Paia, don't bother to shave or blow dry, since this is a dress-down place, even for island-style.

Surfers catch the right-break at the point below the **Ho'okipa Beach Lookout**, riding in toward the shore as spectators view from a pipe railing. At the far end of the railing, a social trail curves down a grass embankment to the smooth lava shelf. You can get a board's eye view on the action. *Be Aware:* Big surf can be a hazard at this lower area. Then, for a closer look at the beach scene, take the road down to the pavilion. Late in the day, the long parking lot along the beach is filled with surfers enjoying their day at Hookah, er, Ho'okipa. The lower part of the beach extends for about .25-mile, with a reef close in on the east end below the lookout. Windsurfers from around the globe gather off the point extends on the west end of the beach. Grassy bluffs are designed for photographers and gawkers.

SNORKEL: Paia and Hoʻokipa, with reefs close in and wave action, aren't good for swimming, particularly in the winter. To take the plunge, try **Mama's Cove**. Driving toward Hoʻokipa from Paia, turn near mm8, into the Mama's Fish House; a dozen shoreline access parking places should be on the right, marked by blue cones. *Alternate parking:* Turn toward the ocean on **Kaiholo Place** at mm8 (close by on the Paia side of Mama's) and park at Poho Place; then walk up Kaiholo on a grassy drive toward cottages, up steps, and then right on another street to a shoreline access path. Either way, you'll pop out to this sandy cove, on the beach fronting Mama's. The cove has a reef close in that creates a keiki pond, normally safe for swimming—but don't expect lots of fish. *Be Aware:* Low tide brings poor swimming conditions.

SURF: Body boarders ride the tiers of fast-breaking near-shore tubes at **Lower Paia Beach Park**, which is on the left as you come into Paia. Lots of friends and onlookers hang out on the few hundred yards of fine sand. **Hoʻokipa** has been home to the world championships of windsurfing; they normally gather at the west end of the beach, where the **Spartan Reef** begins. Much of the sport's equipment, including Simmer, is designed in Paia. Some of Maui's best board surfing waves are off the lookout, several tiers of wedges that break to the right. In the little settlement of **Kuau**, about .5-mile from Paia, are two Shoreline Access spots that host a lower-key surf scene. *Driving:* The best spot is at mm7.4, down dirt cul-de-sac that is just past Kuau Beach Place.

33. JAWS   HIKE, SURF

WHAT'S BEST: Behemoth, perfect waves form off the bluffs above the pineapple fields. When Jaws goes off, big-wave surfers come fast. On other days, take a sea-view hike.

PARKING: Take Hwy. 36, the Hana Hwy., past mm11 and the turnoff to Haiku. *For Pauwela Point:* After another .8-mi., park on right near the Haiku Community Center, which is between Pauwela Rd. and Pili Aloha. *Note:* On dry days, you may be able to drive the first mile of the hike, on Lighthouse Rd., marked by a stop sign. *For Jaws:* At mm12.5, park at an ocean-side turnout at a gate; it's just before the memorial park cemetery—across the highway from a fruit stand and where a sign notes that W. Kuiaha Rd. is coming up. *Alternate:* 4WD vehicles can go to mm13.5 and turn on Hahana Rd., which turns to dirt after .25-mi. When the surf's up, too many cars make this road tough.

HIKE: Jaws (2.5 mi., 275 ft.); Pauwela Point (up to 3 mi., 200 ft.)

Talk Story: Maybe a couple times each winter, waves 25- to 70-feet high form off **Peahi Point**, attracting intrepid surfers from all over the world—including the king of big-wave surfing, Laird Hamilton (star of American Express ads). Check the forecast or, better yet, head to the decrepit county boat ramp at **Maliko Bay**: On an inside bend

Jaws

at mm10, turn inland and then turn right again before the old bridge, driving under the highway. Jet skis transport surfers from here, and when Jaws is going off, the lot fills with trucks and jet-ski trailers. (The spoil-sport County of Maui is thinking about closing Maliko and making the guys come from Kahului.)

To walk to **Jaws**, head down the road to the left from the gate, but then make sure to jog right directly toward the ocean across the pineapple fields, and not stray down the gulch to the left. After crossing the field, go left along a treeline with another gulch on your right. About 15 minutes into the hike, go right at a berm into the gulch on a road. You'll drop down and then curve left and up. At the top, go right for a short distance. Then go left, on a long straightaway sloping down, now with a gulch on your left. This road curves right at bluff's edge and comes to a 100-foot dirt circle that is the lookout for Jaws. *Be Aware:* The road from Hahana reaches Jaws from a different direction. Access to this hike may be limited; landowners are not responsible for your safety. *More Stuff:* To get down for a sea-level look at **Jaws**, go right from the lookout down a spur road through ironwoods to where the road ends amid a tree filtered view. To the left is an easy-but-steep trail down 100 feet; a rope aids the way in places. You reach the bouldered beach and stream where the white foam of Jaws' waves reach shore.

For **Pauwela Point**, walk across the highway from Pili Aloha. An unpaved and perhaps unsigned **Lighthouse Road** skirts the east end of the broad wedge of pineapple fields that slopes downward. The field will be on your left, while on your right, bananas and tropical trees will give way to a steep gully that eventually falls to tiny **Kuiaha Bay**. Keep heading seaward toward a white light beacon, which is on the point. Acres of grassy bluffs surround the light beacon. Loop left along the edge for a view West Maui and Molokai, and then peel off right, following decrepit concrete stanchions along a path with the view toward the Hana Coast. The path eventually comes around to the road you walked in.

SURF: Jaws breaks a couple hundred feet offshore, farther out as wave size increases. Most guys tow in to take the right-break on the perfectly formed monsters, since the left-break presents a rock hazard. Jet skis are needed to get enough speed to ride these big boys, which appear to be moving in slow motion from land. The jet ski partners also whiz in to pick up surfers after a wipe out. Head to **Maliko Bay** (mm10) to watch surfers coming back in and to listen to war stories told with an adrenaline rush. The lookout is a good spot for photographers, but the spur road to the right also presents perches for shutterbugs. On days when Jaws breaks, this place is jumpin'.

34. HALEHAKU HEIAU   HIKE

WHAT'S BEST: Contemplate the sea overlooking this secluded bay, or take a short walk that leads centuries into the past, to the ruins of a village.

PARKING: Take Hwy. 36 (the Hana Hwy.) past the Haiku turnoff. Just after mm16, turn left on Haumana Rd. Continue on a country lane for .4-mi., veer right on Kulike Rd., and follow 1 mi. to its end, where it becomes unpaved. Park near guardrail.

HIKE: Kahuna Point (.25-mi.); Halehaku Heiau (1 mi.; 200 ft.)

Halehaku Heiau is a place you may not think much of as you go on your merry Maui way, and then two weeks later you won't be able to get it out of your mind. **For both hikes**, take the trail that leads from the left of the guardrail, and walk straight out the visible perch that sits about 200 feet above the west side of Halehaku Bay. **Kahuna Point** affords both details and a panorama of the wild bay and the steep, lush walls that frame its opening to the sea. You're bound to see whales offshore in the winter, and down below don't be surprised if sea turtles swim by.

To get to **Halehaku Heiau**, double back 50 feet from Kahuna Point and take the trail that traverses inland. You'll veer down through koa, kukui, and hau trees, which provide hand supports when this trail then drops straight down. Cross the stream at the bottom, and make your way across the grassy bench that sits just above a boulder beach. After a few hundred feet, hook right and walk in to see the big heiau and wall remains, built under a canopy of trees. *Be Aware:* The stream crossing can be dangerous during rains.

Talk Story: In 1790, King Kamehameha, having ventured from Hana during his invasion of Maui, won a decisive battle near here, bolstering his flagging confidence on his way to the final victory at Iao Valley. Trees grow through places in this landmark, but its terraces and enclosures are fundamentally intact. Built of beach rock, its duel platforms each measure roughly 125 feet square. Some remains in this area date from the 1500s. *Be Aware:* As with all such sites, be careful not to disturb anything.

Hana Highway

North from Keanae Peninsula

HANA HIGHWAY

More than 50 one-lane bridges allow passage on a squiggly blacktop that hugs the cliffs and valleys of a rain forest—and in typical Hawaiian fashion, each has a name, such as, "open laughter," "heavenly mist," "land of deep love," and "lightning flash." Waterfalls are strung like confetti. The coast is wild, with waves doing battle with sculpted lava. Then you reach Hana and its hidden beaches, pastoral slopes, historical strolls, and freshwater pools. After Hana, the twisting highway takes a curtain call, offering more waterfalls and forest, as the journey continues to the Kipahulu section of Haleakala National Park, at the Pools of Oheo.

DRIVING TOUR
PICKING THE RIGHT DAY

Every day is a weekend on the Hana Highway, although you'll see less local traffic on the real weekend. The main concern is to avoid this tour during and right after tropical storms, when mud slides and flash floods present a hazard. Of course, a safe time after storms is when the road's greenery sparkles and waterfalls are most plentiful. Overcast weather will not spoil a day here, since this is not a fun-in-the-sun adventure, and the rain-forest greens deepen under cloud cover.

The wisest advice is to depart early, if you would like a more private experience. Rental cars seem to form a train beginning from about 8 a.m. to 10 a.m. If you are taking the half-trip—see below—you could also opt to depart after the rush.

THE ROAD

Provided the weather is fair, the Hana Highway is not in the running for Maui's most dangerous drive. Cars tend to plug along in a mellow samba line. The one-lane bridges have clearly marked yield lines. Although some publications say that cars headed toward Kahului yield to cars headed toward Hana, this etiquette is rarely practiced. The car that gets to the bridge or one-lane road segment first goes through, along with the cars in the same posse. If you arrive behind that stream, pull over and yield to the oncoming traffic from the other side of the bridge.

Exceptions to the yield rule are surfers hell-bent on catching the next wave down the road, and pick-ups and other commuters who drive the highway with a certain reckless abandon. *Give the locals a break. If cars are on your tail, pull over.* Everyone will be happier. Also remember to fill up on gas before leaving Paia. You also want to cart any garbage you produce back with you, since the Hana landfill is nearly full.

THE COURSE

Follow along on the Hana Highway map, page 118. Refer to trailhead descriptions beginning on page 119 for more details.

Note: Visitors who have an extra day on Maui can consider breaking this tour into two trips: The first would end at Nahiku, where the highway leaves the rain forest, and the second would begin there, and continue around to the pasturelands of Hana and the Pools of Oheo. If you want to do two trips, then take advantage of the side trips and hikes. Otherwise, take the side trips sparingly. The times outlined in the course below are for the longer tour.

BEGIN EARLY MORNING. TAKE HIGHWAY 36 PAST MM16 TO WHERE IT BECOMES HIGHWAY 360. Consider grabbing a steaming caffeinated beverage and baked goods to-go in **Paia**, just before sunrise. Just before the road narrows, you'll pass **Twin Falls**, which is one of the better, and longer, inland hikes on the coast. After that, the road starts living up to its reputation.

Over the next 10 or more miles, you weave in and out, on the fringe of the **Ko'olau Forest Reserve**, where the **Waikamoi Ridge Nature Trail** and Garden of Eden, as well as several state hunter's roads, lead into a rain forest that gets denser the farther you go. Waterfalls appear at inside bends, beginning around mm6.

MID-MORNING. After mm12 you come to the **Kaumahina State Wayside**, an excellent rest stop that received a complete makeover in 2005. A short path leads to a view that previews the **Keanae Peninsula** that lies just down the road. Beyond the wayside, down in the next valley, is rugged **Honomanu Bay**, the only place the

St. Augustine Shrine, Wailua

Hana Highway cascade

highway reaches the water until you get to Hana. After climbing out of this valley, you reach the **Keanae Arboretum**. If you were to take just one short walk along this stretch of the highway, this is it. Just after the arboretum are the side trips to **Keanae** and **Wailua**, both of which impart a sense of Old Hawaii.

NOON. After Keanae, the Hana Highway really does the hokey-pokey, offering cascades and steep hillsides dripping with flora in a constant turn of the wheel. Inland is the **Hanawi Natural Area Reserve**, one of the wettest places on earth. A side trip to mysterious **Nahiku** awaits at mm25. After rounding the bend in Nahiku, fruit stands and occasional homesteads appear, as the highway changes character. The overhanging jungle lifts, giving way to bucolic slopes, pocketed by tropical woodlands.

Just before Hana, at mm31, is one side-trip that is tough to pass, to **Kahanu National Tropical Botanical Gardens** and **Pi'ilanihale Heiau**—where you can appreciate the Hawaiian culture at its zenith. And just down the road from these attractions is the Blue Pool, unsurpassed in scenic beauty by any of the island's other pools. Beyond the turnoff to the gardens is the road to **Waianapanapa State Park**. You could easily spend the day here, and the park's picnic grounds are the best around. If you're looking for a long coastal walk next to exploding waves, this is the place.

Travaasa Hana

AFTERNOON. If you're on a day trip, and plan on doing some walking around at the Pools of Oheo, you might have to give **Hana** short shrift. But make time for the **Hana Cultural Center** and a stroll around wharf area—and for that matter, the .25-mile hike to Kauiki Head and the Queen Ka'ahumanu Birthplace is a bell ringer. For an overview of Hana, hump up to **Fagan's Cross** on Pu'u o Kahaula. Come to think of it, **Red Sand Beach** isn't that far, and it is a sight you'll never forget; although the trail can be hazardous, this beach is unique.

Keanae

Koki Beach

As you head out of Hana—and Highway 360 becomes Highway 31—you'll have time to hook seaward and see **Koki Beach Park** and **Hamoa Beach**. Haneoʻo Road loops back out to the highway. Unless you bypassed all the stuff early in the day, you may have to skip Venus Pool. About five miles later—passing waterfalls through deep forest on some fairly hairy one-lane segments—you reach **Kipahulu Visitors Center** at the lower part of **Haleakala National Park**.

At Kipahulu are the **Pools of Oheo Gulch**, formerly known as the Seven Sacred Pools, scooped out by Pipiwai Stream before it enters the ocean. Fantastic as they are, the pools are not the epitome of the Hana Highway tour. In fact, they may play second fiddle in this neighborhood to the trail that leads inland to the **Falls at Makahiku** and **Waimoku Falls**—up a jungle crevice and bamboo forest, over a hard-rock stream on bridges. If pressed for time, do the falls walk to the bridges—for a big scenic payoff. Darn it, we wish we were there now instead of writing this book.

SUNSET. Unless you left yesterday, your waning hours will be spent behind the wheel going home. But that's good news, no matter which route you select. One choice is to continue around on **Highway 31**, past **Kaupo**. The road is actually an easier drive than the Hana Highway—with the exception of a mile-long segment about three miles from Kipahulu, near mm39 at **Lelekoa Bay.** It's narrow, but you can find marginal turnouts and the traffic, what there is of it, is almost all headed the same direction (clockwise). If you go back this direction, you can dip in to see **Charles Lindbergh's grave**, before that narrow stretch. Look at the Haleakala driving tour for more on this route. You'll see sunset on the backside of the big volcano, as well as have a sunset ocean view. *Be Aware:* This route can be dangerous after and during heavy rains.

An equally good choice is to retrace your route on the **Hana Highway**. You may need to do this just to believe all the sights you beheld earlier in the day. Certainly, you can drive the Hana Highway a dozen times and see fresh sights. The place is overflowing with them.

Ko'olau Forest Reserve

Hana Highway, Kipahulu Campground, Waianapanapa State Park, Kipahulu Fruit Stand

MAP 4
TRAILHEADS 35-44
HANA HIGHWAY

MAUI

35 Twin Falls

360

KO'OLAU FOREST RESERVE

Waipio Bay
Huelo Pt.

36
Waikomo Ridge Nature Trail

Kaumahina Wayside Park

Honomanu Bay

Keanae Arboretum

Keanae
37

Wailua

Pua'a Ka'a Wayside Park

Waihue Bay
38 Nahiku

360

HANAWAI NATURAL AREA RESERVE

Blue Pool

Kahanu Garden
39 Pi'ilanihale Heiau

Waianapanapa State Park
40

Haleakala National Park

Hana
41

Hana Bay
Red Sand Beach

44 Kipahulu

43 31 42 Hamoa Beach

Lindbergh Grave

Pools of Oheo

Venus Pool

118 | HANA HIGHWAY MAP

HANA HIGHWAY
TRAILHEADS 35-44

TH:	TRAILHEAD
HIKE:	ALL WALKING, FROM SHORT STROLLS TO FULL-FLEDGED DAY HIKES
SNORKEL:	BOTH FISH-VIEWING WITH MASK AND FINS, AND PLACES TO SWIM
SURF:	BOARD, BODYSURF, BODYBOARD, WINDSURFING, KITEBOARDING
MM:	MILE MARKER, CORRESPONDS TO HIGHWAY SIGNS

All hiking distances in parentheses are ROUND TRIP.
Elevation gains of 100 feet or more are noted.
Please pull over for locals when driving the Hana Highway.

35. TWIN FALLS   HIKE, SNORKEL

WHAT'S BEST: A half-dozen waterfalls tumble into swimming pools amid tropical flora. Amazing, but don't try to fit this adventure in with the long drive to Hana.

PARKING: Take Hwy. 36 (the Hana Hwy.) beyond mm16, where route becomes Hwy. 360 and mile markers restart from zero. *For Twin Falls Botanical Preserve:* At mm2, pull out to the right on the shoulder of a wide bridge at the Twin Falls Farm Stand.

HIKE: **Twin Falls Botanical Preserve (up to 2.5 mi., 275 ft.)**

Talk Story: The preserve is where two streams with waterfalls, pools, and very long names join together, fall some 20 feet over a lava ledge, and depart as one: Hoʻolawa Stream, which then descends over two more falls-with-pools before reaching Hoʻolawa Bay. Trails are on lands of the Twin Falls Botanical Preserve—*please* make a donation. Their organic produce is a deal in both price and quality.

People meander on the various trails through the **Twin Falls Botanical Preserve.** *Be Aware:* Wear shoes that you can get wet. Here's a semi-loop option: Immediately after the gate, leave the road and go left on a trail that soon reaches the stream, where you go right, upstream (a left forking trail here leads to the top of Lower Twin Falls). Then immediately take a left-bearing trail that drops, with one brief hands-on section, to a beautiful, 100-foot oval pool with a **25-foot cascade** falling through basalt columns under a huge banyan tree. Then backtrack to the trail and continue upstream, above this cascade and near the main road. Within minutes, the trail drops to and crosses the streambed, reaching a wide, **10-foot falls**. Roots line the walls of a cavern and a rope swing invites swimmers to take a ride and plunge. From here, backtrack to the main preserve road and you go left. (On the way out, stay on this road and enjoy its floral delights—papayas, hibiscus, ti, guava, bananas—that rival the falls as this hike's main attraction.) The road crosses the stream at a spillway (dangerous at high water) and, a few minutes later, reaches a **three-fork junction at painted rocks**—your gateway to both 'Left Twin Falls' and 'Right Twin Falls.' For both falls, go left at the faded painted rocks and, a few hundred feet later, go right. Then, for **Left Twin Falls**, take an mmediate left and walk for several minutes over a rooty trail. A rope aids the easy 30-foot descent to the pool and ferny amphitheater. You can swim behind the sheet of water or take a tame rope swing ride.

To **Right Twin Falls**, the most popular, backtrack on the rooty trail and go left, as if you had not visited the Left Twin Falls, that is, the first right fork after the three-way

Twin Falls

at the painted rocks. The road dips through paperbark trees and reaches an irrigation channel. Cross a plank 'bridge' and go left along the rock wall of the ditch, then across roots and rocks, and you'll reach the Right Twin Falls—cascading 35 feet from a curved cliff into a pool, all of it under a leafy ceiling. To reach the top to of the falls, take a steep route that is to the right at the edge of the pool. Only the first part requires hands. *Cool tip:* Stay on the trail from the top of Right Twin Falls, through lovely paperbark and pandanus trees. to reach the jewel of the preserve: 'Upper Right Twin Falls,' a sunny, 12-foot waterfall into a private pool! *Be Aware:* A sign notes that hiking about the falls is not is advised. Hike Maui guides visitors in this area; see page 235.

SNORKEL: Bring your swimsuit and camera. After school and on weekends, zany high school kids and locals leap from overhanging rocks and branches, with the premier show at Right Twin Falls. Left Twin Falls will better suit tourists. The most attractive for visitors may be the basalt-column falls, that is to the left off the main road, immediately after the entrance gate. *Be Aware:* Submerged rocks and shallow waters are a hazard. Get advice and test the waters. Don't dive.

More Stuff: You can access the bottom **Lower Twin Falls** from the old highway. *Driving:* Backtrack on Hwy. 360 about .1-mi. and turn right on unpaved Ulalena Loop. Continue .4-mi. to an old concrete bridge and park. Walk upstream (you have to cross) a short distance to the 15-foot cascade. Also, trekkers will want to note **Lupi Road** which climbs several miles into the pleasant treed birdlands and flowering shrubs of the **Ko'olau Forest Reserve**. Look to the right and up, as you face the fruit stand.

Another attraction nearby: Built in 1853, on a grass clearing in a jungle setting, **Kaulanapueo Church** is poetically situated. The church's thick walls are plaster-covered basaltic boulders that rise to a steeple. Palms and Norfolk pines accent several acres of lawn. Sitting next to the building is a historic cemetery. *Driving:* Continue to mm3.6, as the Hana Highway narrows. Turn left toward **Huelo** at a bus stop with a public phone. After .25-mi., turn left on a short, rough uphill driveway.

36. KO'OLAU FOREST RESERVE   **HIKE**

WHAT'S BEST: Pick a tame or wild adventure from among these walks into the rain forests and waterfalls just off the Hana Highway.

PARKING: Take Hwy. 36 toward Hana past mm16; route becomes Hwy. 360 and mile markers start at zero. This trailhead covers mm 6 to mm11. Continue to mm6. *For Bamboo Forest Falls:* Park at a turnout near an opening in a bamboo hedge at mm6.6. Leave car free of valuables. *For Waikamoi Ridge Trail:* Park at a signed turnout at mm9.5. *For the Garden of Eden:* Use a turnout at mm10.5 and proceed up a signed entranceway. *Note:* Some Ko'olau Forest Reserve lands are leased by East Maui Irrigation Company. To enter, you may need a waiver from the irrigation company. Waivers normally are

Koʻolau Forest Reserve

granted only to members taking hikes with the Sierra Club or Mauna Ala Hiking Club. See page 235 for contact information.

HIKE: Bamboo Forest Falls (.75-mi., 150 ft.); Waikamoi Ridge Nature Trail (1.25 mi., 200 ft.); Garden of Eden (up to 1 mi., 125 ft.)

Talk Story: The **Koʻolau Forest Reserve** runs for about 10 miles along the highway, extending inland to an elevation of about 4,000 feet. Roads connect an elaborate system of tunnels and irrigation ditches, many dating from the late 1800s, a remarkable engineering feat led by Henry P. Baldwin. Son of missionary Dwight Baldwin, Henry gained fame in 1876—one month after losing his arm in a sugar mill accident—when he belayed 120 feet down a gorge after his work crews balked at the precipice. The massive water conveyance project was completed in the nick of time to prevent a takeover by the rivals of Baldwin, and his partner and boyhood friend, Samuel T. Alexander.

For the quick, well-used jaunt to the **Bamboo Forest Falls**, duck through the rabbit hole in the bamboo and head right. Cross a small stream and continue on either fork. Then cross the main stream on rocks (when flow rate allows) and go left on an upstream trail. A first falls and pool is only 10 minutes into the hike. To see the second falls, continue for about 5 minutes upstream on the trail through a bamboo tunnel. *More Stuff:* After the bamboo forest, at mm6.75, a gate is on your right marking **Papaʻaea Road**, which passes a large reservoir at the outset and leads over several streams to an immense hillside of ferns.

Featured in many brochures, the **Waikamoi Ridge Nature Trail** attracts a fair number of visitors stopping midmornings on the way to Hana. The hike climbs through native and planted trees, many identified, with view benches along the way. You'll find picnic areas at the trailhead and at the top. To start, go to the left as you face inland, and keep left to the first lookout. From there the trail makes a long switchback among pandanus at eye level. Then comes a second lookout, above the dense flora of a bend in the highway. The trail levels through a lovely paperbark and bamboo tree tunnel, at the end of which is a picnic hut. To your right is the **Kolea Road**, a route that descends through bamboo to trailhead parking to make this a loop hike.

The 26-acre **Garden of Eden**, begun in 1988, has family walking trails, one of which features a look at Keopuka Rock, which appeared in the opening sequence of *Jurassic Park*. At several picnic tables you can commune with coco palms, mangoes, ti, bananas, and a host of flowering botanicals. A few of the plants were contributed by the late Beatle George Harrison, friend of owner (and musician) Alan Bradbury. On the way out, visit the small flock of exotic birds who pose for snapshots. *Note:* For what you get, admission is pricey, about $15 per person. For free you can visit the beautifully sited Garden Gallery.

More Stuff: To the right at the Garden of Eden turnout is **Wahinepe'e Road**, leading through 'Little Jurassic Park' to **Wahinepe'e Falls**, as pretty as any in Hawaii (3.5 miles round-trip, 300 foot climb). Head up the road, which skirts the garden. Stay left at a fork, and then left again, going up a double road. At a main, contour road, go left

Garden of Eden

Wahinepee Falls

again. You'll swerve through a lush gully of ferns. Keep right, following a stream up to the 100-foot double free-fall and cascade, which flows under an artful 1925 concrete bridge. Not many visitors see this baby. *More Stuff:* For an easier .25-mile walk to **Puohokama Falls**, a 30-footer into a pool, begin at an inside turnout near the bridge at mm11 past the garden. *Note:* Heed signs and use these trails at your own risk.

37. KEANAE **HIKE, SNORKEL, SURF**

> **WHAT'S BEST:** Wild seascapes, village taro fields, historic churches, pools, falls and a tropical arboretum: Old Hawaii lives on.
>
> **PARKING:** Activities take place over a 6-mile section of Hwy. 360 (the Hana Hwy.) taking in both sides of the Keanae Peninsula—from near mm12 to mm18.

HIKE: **Kaumahina Wayside Nature Trail (.25-mi); Honomanu Bay (up to .5-mi.); Keanae Arboretum (1.25 mi.); Keanae village and pools (up to 2 mi.); Wailua Valley State Wayside (less than .25-mi.)**

Driving: At mm12.2, pull off at an outside bend into the **Kaumahina State Wayside**, which is more than a great comfort stop. Head up the railing of the park's nature trail to a view straight down to Honomanu Bay and toward the low lava peninsula that is Keanae. An unofficial trail at the top loop through forests and back to the parking. Wild **Honomanu Bay**—the only place the highway reaches sea level between Paia and Hana—features a wide jungle stream, trees dripping with vines, and a smooth-rock beach, all enclosed by high cliffs drilled with sea caves at water level. *Driving:*

At mm14.1 (after the bridges at the bottom) veer left and drive steeply down (paved at the top) .25-mile to a beachfront flat area. At the boulder-and-black-sand beach, walk right to the sea caves beneath the cliff.

The **Keanae Arboretum** is the best family leg-stretcher on the coast, featuring a wide path alongside **Piʻinaʻau Stream**, in the shade of huge trees brought here from both sides of the equator. A wide, paved trail slopes to a grove of tropical trees from around the world, extremely large considering the arboretum dates only from 1971. A giant bamboo is inspiring. The paved path becomes dirt as you continue upstream and enter the native Hawaiian and Polynesian species—including taro, papaya, bananas, and ti. From here the path becomes a trail that crosses a tributary stream and then deteriorates while heading into the rain forest along a second tributary. *Driving:* Use a signed turnout at a gate on your right near mm16.6, not far past the YMCA camp. Additional parking is on the left side of the highway, just past the gate on a sweeping left turn.

Talk Story: The Keanae Peninsula came into being after one of Haleakala's more recent eruptions, when lava flowed out the Koʻolau Gap and fanned out into the Pacific. *Driving:* For the **Keanae village and pools** hikes, turn left just down the hill from the arboretum, before reaching mm17. Continue on the sleepy road for almost .75-mile, and park at the big turnout on the left across from the church and ball field. Start out by walking to the point toward lava stacks, nature's statuary that fight a losing battle against oncoming waves.

Keanae Arboretum

Village life centers around a little church with a big name—ihiʻihioiehovaona Kaua—sitting dreamily below green ramparts and on the edge of taro fields. The edifice dates from 1860, but it was rebuilt in the 1900s. From the church, walk over to munch a petite loaf of Aunty Sandy's righteous banana bread at the **Keanae Landing Fruit Stand**.

The **pool** is a large lagoon formed where **Keanae Stream**, hemmed in by the cliff above the peninsula, meets a gravel bar at the beach. From the ballfield parking, walk with the ocean on your left, and keep left as the road forks passing by houses. (Ask permission if you see someone; the public is normally permitted.) You'll reach a turnaround and gate. Continue on the grassy road. Veer left before reaching the ironwoods and palms, and descend several feet to lagoon level. Under most conditions, you'll be able cross the stream or just walk onto the gravel bar that separates the lagoon from the ocean. At the far end of the long pool, is a cascade of Keanae Stream. *More Stuff:* On the way south from Keanae, for the **supreme view of the village**, look for a turnout near mm17, at a guardrail, where a tidal wave siren hangs above telephone pole #41.

ihiʻihioiehovaona Kaua

Keanae Peninsula

More Stuff: The scenic **Wailua** churches and taro fields get far fewer visitors than Keanae. *Driving:* Veer left from the highway near mm18.25, on Wailua Road. Just down the blacktop on your left are **St. Gabriel's Church** and, in the gardens behind it, **St. Augustine Shrine**—both cared for by some big-hearted local folks. Across the road, taro fields carpet the rich valley floor, encircled by green cliffs rising a thousand feet. Down the road is a big look inland at **Waikani Falls**, where you can park near a 'local traffic only' sign and walk to a rocky beach at **Wailua Bay**, where two streams converge.

More Stuff: Leaving Wailua, look for the **Wailua Valley State Wayside** on the right climbing the grade, just before mm19—and before the turnout on the left where most people stop. The parking is through a cut bank. The overlook is up a mere 40 steps to an on-high view of Wailua. From the wayside parking, a road leads into the **Keanae Valley**. Trees occlude an inland view initially, but after a short downhill grade, the road swerves right into rich birdlands. Then, not far past the wayside (at the bridge near mm19.5) is **Upper Waikani Falls**, a standout beauty even among the Hana Highway's darlings.

SNORKEL: You can get a swim in at the lake-sized **Keanae Pool**. Higher upstream are several popular swimming pools, locally known as **Sapphire Pools**. *Driving:* Continue a short distance toward Hana from Keanae and park after the second bridge (where Pi'ina'au Road goes inland). Scramble down from the bridge and you'll find clean, pure tubs. *Be Aware:* Flash floods make this a bad choice during or after rains.

SURF: Surfers who want to get away from it all ride the tiers of offshore wedges at **Honomanu Bay**. Winter swells of 4- to 8-feet break within the mouth of the bay.

38. NAHIKU   HIKE

> **WHAT'S BEST:** Subtropical sunbeams strike rich soils moistened by 300-plus inches of rain per year. See the green results at the dramatic, remote coast at Nahiku.
>
> **PARKING:** Take Hwy. 360 (the Hana Hwy.) past Keanae. Highlights for this trailhead take place over a 4-mile section from near mm21 to mm25.

HIKE: Nahiku (up to .75-mi.)

Talk Story: The Hana Highway climbs inland from Keanae and zigzags through a botanical crescendo over a 4-mile run that crosses some 10 streams. Botanists counting species will hit triple figures in no time. Prominent among them are huge banyans and rubber trees. Some 25,000 rubber trees were planted near the coast, launching the Nahiku Rubber Company in 1905, which failed in spite of fabulous production due to geographic isolation. In more recent times, the Nahiku environ gained fame as a retreat for former Beatle, the late George Harrison.

To explore **Nahiku**, veer left from the highway after the bridge at mm25. A narrow, but well-paved road descends 1,000 feet over 2.5 miles before ending at ocean-scoured Opuhanu Point. About .5-mile from the top is a cavelike lava tube, which is near **Big Spring**, the largest on Maui. As the road levels, .25-mile from the ocean, you'll see a 4WD road to the right that invites further exploration, among tin-roofed sugar shacks and the occasional honor-system fruit stand. The Catholic church near the school dates from the early 1867s, a time when Catholics were persecuted on the island. You'll cross a stream and bridge, snap a picture, and come to road's end at big-bouldered **Honolulunui Bay**. The **Opuhanu Point's** lava tongues extend into the powerful seascape, accented with heliotropes, palms, and pandanus. Walk to the right along the shore to see a waterfall entering the sea at a decrepit bridgeworks. Swimmer like the pool here, in benigin conditions. *Be Aware:* Big waves are a danger at the shoreline.

More Stuff: Look for **Wailuaiki Road** near mm21.25, just after an uphill grade and sharp right turn; the gate sits above the road making it difficult to see. A fabulous waterfall and gorge lie less than .5-mile in on Wailuaiki Road (permission to enter may be required by State Department of Fish and Wildlife). Farther along is **Pua'aka'a State Wayside**, a 5-acre developed park at mm22.5. It can be dreary in rains, but absolutely idyllic when sun shines on the lush greenery, 20-foot waterfall, and swimming pool; an excellent picnic stop. Just before the bridge and turnoff to Nahiku at mm25 is **Makapipi Road**. It leads toward the **Hanawi Natural Area Reserve**; showered yearly by more than 30 feet of rain, the reserve is nature's storehouse of endangered plants. Finally, just after the road to Nahiku, at mm25.3, is the **Kuhiwa Bamboo Forest**, a chance for quick immersion into greenery, but going gets rough early for hikers.

39. PI'ILANIHALE HEIAU-KAHANU GARDENS   HIKE, SNORKEL

WHAT'S BEST: A huge temple dates from the 1500s and now resides within a National Tropical Botanical Garden. A nearby blue pool rests beneath a waterfall next to crashing surf—but its popularity has made access iffy at best.

PARKING: Take Hwy. 360 (the Hana Hwy.) almost to Hana. At mm31, turn left on Ulaino Rd. *For Kahanu Gardens and Pi'ilanihale:* Continue 1.5 mi. on the partially paved road to the entrance on the right just after a stream crossing. *For Blue Pool:* In dry conditions, you will be able to drive nearly to the beach. Park at one of the signed, private lots ($2 or $3) that are 1.25 mi. from Kahanu Gardens. *Be Aware:* Locals have discouraged visitors by claiming that this coastal access is closed. Best to stay away.

HIKE: Pi'ilanihale Heiau-Kahanu Garden loop (1.25 mi.); Blue Pool (.75-mi.)

Kahanu Gardens is a 123-acre living exhibit of Hawaiian culture, and also one of only five National Tropical Botanical Gardens set up by an act of Congress to preserve and study endangered plants. From the entrance station you drive almost .5-mile across a

Nahiku

sprawling lawn, through a grove of 200 breadfruit trees, as well as other species. On your left is one of Hawaii's last pandanus forest ecosystems. You can backtrack to roam this grove later on. *Note:* Admission is about $10; Monday through Saturday, 9 to 2.

From the parking area, cross left across a lawn and come upon kamani trees and a "canoe" garden, so named because it replicates the growing cycles for some 27 plants the voyaging Polynesians brought with them across uncharted seas nearly 2,000

Kahanu Gardens

years ago. But you may not notice this garden at first because, across the grass field, **Pi'ilanihale Heiau** looms out of the jungle foliage. This 'House of Pi'ilani' is named for a beloved king of the 1500s, a time that in many ways was the zenith of Hawaiian life. The platform stone structure—roughly 300 feet by 300 feet, with walls terraced about 50 feet high—will remind some of the ancient civilizations in the Americas. It was refurbished in the late 1990s. The path continues toward the heiau, dipping in and out, and then up a short distance to an interpretive hut. *Be Aware:* Visitors are not allowed to use trails that circle the structure.

From the interpretive hut, the path loops away from the heiau, along low lava cliffs at the ocean's edge, before reaching a cabin, Hale Ho'okipa. The cabin was part of the area's former life as **Kaeleku Plantation** in the 1800s. Old Hawaiian and homesteader gravesites are nearby. Several families, and the Hana Ranch, donated property to form the gardens in the 1970s. Complete your loop by circling right to the lava ledges behind the hale, and continuing through the **Wishard Coconut Grove**, back to the parking area.

SNORKEL: To see the **Blue Pool**, walk down the road from the parking lot, a perfumed and shaded journey that ends about 100 yards in from the surf at a green lagoon of Heleleikeoha Stream. Follow the stream to the boulder beach, cross, and go left for less than .25-mile. You'll see whitewater sheeting down about 100 feet of ferny cliff—known as Blue Angel Falls—and into Blue Pool. From the lip of the 30-foot oval, the ocean's waves are a short throw away. *Be Aware:* Unless attitudes have changed, access to Blue Pool has been blocked by angry locals. If it is open, don't cross the stream during high water. Nudity is not allowed.

40. WAIANAPANAPA STATE PARK   HIKE, SNORKEL

WHAT'S BEST: The ancient King's Trail hugs a sea-sculpted lava shelf, which features fountains of whitewater and historical sites. Enjoy the tropical flora, caves, and Black Sand Beach at one of Hawaii's top state parks.

PARKING: Take Hwy. 360 nearly to Hana. At mm32, turn left at sign to Waianapanapa and follow the road .4-mi. to the state park. Go left and park at the picnic area.

HIKE: Waianapanapa Caves (about .25-mi.); North coast: Kipapa O Kihapi'ilani Trail (2.75 mi., 150 ft.); South coast: Ohala Heiau (1.5 mi.)

Talk Story: Coco palms, pandanus, heliotrope, hala, and a wealth of other flora soften the sharp lava that paves the coast at the 122-acre **Waianapanapa State Park**. Burial sites and ruins hint at the history. The picnic grounds are picturesque, and the park's 12 coastal cabins, though not exactly cheap or clean, offer the better rustic lodging on Maui. The campground is also very good.

The **Waianapanapa Caves** trail dips down from the parking area and loops through a lush streambed, where caves are carved at the base of mossy rock knobs. *Talk Story:* Legend proclaims these dripping caverns were the tryst site for a Princess Popoalaea and her lover, until her husband found out and killed her here. In the spring, the waters turn red with the memory of her blood—or from tiny shrimp hatching, take your pick.

Wainapanapa cabins

Black Sand Beach

For the **Kipapa O Kihapi'ilani Trail**, which crosses the **Kapukaulua Burial Site**, take the trail from the railing at the picnic area, which drops to the **Black Sand Beach**, a.k.a., Pailoa Bay. Trod the sand-slash-pebbles and climb up to the low point at the far end of the beach. Part of the **King's Trail**, circa 1550, the rocky path weaves through a lovely grove of pointed-leaf pandanus and passes two small, black-boulder coves—Pokohulu and Keawaiki. The path heads across the sharp lava to the north side of **Pukaulua Point**, where the burial mounds and heiau remains are located, about 20 minutes into the walk. After that you will pass a large lava tube (down left) and then reach an orange, blank sign that marks the remains of a heiau. *Be Aware:* Take care not to disturb sacred ruins. Wear sturdy shoes, as many trail sections are on unstable rocks. Prepare for harsh sun. Concrete walkways in the park were improved in recent years.

To see the **Ohala Heiau** remains and breaking waves do battle with tufts of lava, walk right along the railing at the picnic area from the signed trailhead. You'll pass the park's buildings as the trail hugs a frothing coast and passes a natural arch. Within .25-mile you'll pass the cabins, set back from the trail; a road to the right just after them leads back to the park, making for a .75-mile loop option. Next comes a blowhole and a lava bridge and, a distance farther, are the the walls of the Ohala Heiau. *More Stuff:* Stay on the trail, hugging the coast over lava, to continue to Hana, several miles away.

SNORKEL: Black Sand Beach is the best snorkeling spot along a coast with few choices. On the right day, it's something to write home about. If surf is small, under 2 feet, you can swim out to the right toward the natural arch, and also to the left toward **Pokohulu Cove**. *Be Aware:* Rip currents may exist in the bay, especially when surf is up. Due to safety concerns, the **Waianapanaha Caves** may be closed to swimmers.

41. HANA   **HIKE, SNORKEL, SURF**

WHAT'S BEST: After the precipitous curves through the rain forest to get here, Hana's sloping pasturelands and open bay will come as a surprise and a relief. Pick from several short walks—a cultural stroll, powerful seascapes, or a panorama.

PARKING: Follow Hwy. 360 (the Hana Hwy.) to mm33.7. *To Fagan's Cross:* Keep right on Hwy. 360, pass Keawa Pl., and park at mm34.5 in a lot across from Travaasa Hana (formerly Hotel Hana Maui). *For all other hikes and activities:* Veer left on Uakea Rd., continue 1.5 mi., and park at the bay, which is just past Hana Cultural Center.

HIKE: Fagan's Cross (1.75 mi., 400 ft.); Hana Bay stroll (.75-mi.); Kauiki Head-Queen Ka'ahumanu Birthplace (.25-mi.); Red Sand Beach (1 mi., 200 ft.)

Don't come looking for action in Hana. Low-key aloha rules here, with quiet cottages set above the harbor, and a few Hawaiiana shops and cultural sites spread about. **Fagan's Cross** is atop Pu'u o Kahaula, visible from the parking lot. Follow the paved path as it takes a gentle rise through the pastures of Hana Ranch. As you near the base of the pu'u—also known as Lyon's Hill—the trail curves around to the right and does its serious climbing. The view from the top is a geography primer for Hana and its coastline. *Talk Story:* The cross is a memorial to Paul Fagan, who introduced cattle in the 1940s to found the ranch, and later started the Hotel Hana Maui. Across from the trailhead parking, the hotel is now Travaasa Hana. Check out the open pool near the sea cottages. *More Stuff:* In the pasture not far from the trailhead, the **Hana Maui Trail** takes

Travaasa Hana

Hana Wharf

off to the left, a 4-mile, round-trip exercise jaunt through the ranch. It comes out near the highway before Haneoʻo Road; see TH42.

Begin **Hana Bay stroll** by backtracking the road to the **Hana Cultural Center and Museum**. The small center is an educational work of love, with artifacts, crafts, quilts, photographs, and exhibits that reflect both ancient times and contemporary. Outside is a re-creation of a village, including a Hawaiian Ethno-Botanical Garden that grows all the essential plants from ancient times and changes seasonally. Also on the grounds is the Old Historic Courthouse and Jail, dating from 1871.

Hana Beach Park rims the bay, where visitors are released from shuttle buses to sit under coco palms and ironwoods and enjoy the food of the Barefoot Cafe. At the far end of the bay is **Hana Wharf**, a T-shaped intrusion several hundred feet onto the water. *Note:* Damaged by a storm in 2004, the wharf will most likely still be closed.

The **Queen Kaʻahumanu Birthplace** is at a sheltered rock near the tip of **Kauiki Head**, which is the furry 400-foot rise that frames the south end of Hana Bay. Begin at the wharf and take a red-cinder trail that skirts the shoreline among ironwoods. Stay near the shore. At the beginning, one eroded spot requires handholds and will dissuade some hikers, as will mini-slides of red cinder that tend to cover the trail (danger signs are posted). But the payoff is big. *Talk Story:* In the 1700s, the Kauiki Head was a stronghold for warriors during the ongoing battles between Maui and the Big Island—typically these Hana slopes were controlled by the Big Island's forces, since open sea was easier to cross than the terrain of East Maui. Near the tip is a plaque commemorating Queen Kaʻahumanu, who was born in 1768 and went on to become Kamehameha the Great's favorite wife, as well as a beloved and enlightened ruler. A tiny island with a light beacon, **Puʻukiʻi Island**, lies a long jump from the tip—too long when the big seas are galloping in. This ten-minute hike gets you a million miles away.

Red Sand Beach, officially called Kaihalulu, is on the other side of the head from the bay. *Driving:* To get to the trailhead, continue a few blocks on Uakea Road, past Hauoli Street, and park on-street near the Hana Community Center. The striking cove is scooped out of a towering red cinder cliff, protected by the jagged teeth of a black-rock reef that is just offshore. Traverse the county park lawn just beyond the cultural center, and drop down through ironwoods—a cemetery will be on your left, and the sea cottages of the Travaasa Hana on the right. Stay right at the end of the lawn and drop down to the right of a knarled ironwood tree, reaching a coastal trail. A slide in 2008 took out a section of the trail, and you need to hop down to the beach for a segment. You then climb a little to a ledge above the water and reach a point. Around this corner is the eye-popping view of the beach. The trail is cut into the cliff (watch your step) as you descend to the red sand. *Be Aware:* Although the trail is used frequently by the public, it is on property of Hana Ranch; use your own judgment. Avoid this trail during heavy weather. Once on the sand, don't sit under the crumbly cliff at the far end.

More Stuff: To see some of the dozen churches and other sites in town, stop by the **Hasegawa General Store**, which is on your left at the edge of town as you continue south. A free Hana Visitors Guide with map should be available. The venerable general store is also one of Hana's main attractions, run by the same family since 1910, as well as being the best place to buy snacks, trinkets, and supplies.

Red Sand Beach

SNORKEL: The best snorkeling at **Hana Bay** is between the base of the wharf and the light beacon on Puʻukiʻi Island. Currents sweep out the bay during higher surf, so stay close to shore and avoid swimming when the surf's up. Due to natural silt, the bay is not known for clear near-shore waters. Your best chance is during the winter, **Red Sand Beach** is a spectacular swimming hole, inside the black-rock breakwater. Lots of fish reside. *Be Aware:* Waves indicate rip currents may be present. Also, in spite of the bare bottoms you may see, nudity is not permitted on Hawaiian beaches.

SURF: Mostly during the summer, you'll find the wave riders off the **Hana Wharf**, a nice deep-water break.

Hamoa Beach

42. HAMOA BEACHES HIKE, SNORKEL, SURF

WHAT'S BEST: A short side trip from the Hana Highway passes two beaches, including the south shore's most luxurious swath and one with an offshore bird sanctuary.

PARKING: Take Hwy. 360 through Hana. After mm33, the road becomes Hwy. 31. You begin at mm51, with numbers *descending* as you travel away from Hana. Turn left on Haneoʻo Road, .7-mi. past mm51. Haneoʻo loops back to the highway at mm49.2.

HIKE: Koki Beach Park (up to .5-mi.); Hamoa Beach (.25-mi.)

Koki Beach Park, a tranquil place with an exciting view, will be on your left, .4-mile from the highway. From the shoulder parking, an ample strand of sand leads left toward a red cinder cliff. A natural arch is near the point. Walk to the right, by a thatched hut, and cross a small stream to a grassy area shaded by palms, ironwoods, and an occasional Norfolk pine. Offshore the tip of land is small **Alau Island Seabird Sanctuary**, with a few fronless coco palms pointing askew from its crest like wayward hairs.

Koki Beach

Hamoa Beach is around the point on Haneo'o Road, a little more than a mile from the highway. Look for a bus stop and low lava wall on the left. Concrete steps and ramp lead down to a good-sized white sand crescent—the beach used by guests of the Travaasa Hana (formerly Hotel Hana Maui). A lawn and garden, part of the hotel's private beach facilities, border the sand. From the shore is a spot-on look at the Big Island, rising from the far horizon. From Hamoa Beach, Haneo'o Road travels .5-mile through the quiet homes of Hamoa and loops back to Highway 31.

SNORKEL: Enter **Hamoa Beach** to the left as you face the water, and swim out the lava tongues and submerged rocks. *Be Aware:* Shore break and rip currents may present hazards. Avoid swimming at Koki Beach except on the calmest of days.

SURF: The conditions are often good for bodysurfing and bodyboarding at both **Koki Beach** and **Hamoa Beach**. The same is true for **Lehoula Beach** (turn toward the ocean at mm51, before the Koki turn) although public access may be iffy.

43. VENUS POOL   HIKE, SNORKEL

WHAT'S BEST: Freshwater pools await at ocean's edge, a short walk in from the highway. *Be Aware:* Landowner's may have restricted access to this pool.

PARKING: Take Hwy. 360 through Hana. After mm33, the road becomes Hwy. 31 coming from the other direction. You begin here at mm51, with numbers *descending* as you travel away from Hana. Cross a bridge at mm48, and park off the road on the shoulder to the right at telephone pole #88 (don't block driveways).

HIKE: Venus Pool (.5-mi.)

To reach the **Venus Pool**, walk back across the bridge and hop through a gatelike opening in the fence. A path leads down the sloping pasture, with Waiohonu Stream on your right. A few minutes into the walk you'll come upon a dome-shaped rock kiln, where the path curves right toward the stream. Fringed with greenery, the pool reveals itself only when you come upon it from about 15 feet above. *Be Aware:* Although this trail is used by the public, a Hana Ranch sign at the trailhead warns of trespassing.

The waves from a rocky nook in the coast mingle with the leading edge of Venus Pool, while upstream of the 75-foot oval, freshwater enters from bedrock ledges that are carved out in places, forming smaller pools. Pool conditions will vary depending on both the surf and runoff. The pastures above the pool extend seaward toward the black-rock point, providing room to roam with a Big Island view.

More Stuff: Significant cultural sites at **Muolea Point** in 2005 were conveyed to the county, thanks to Trust For Public Land and others. Nonprofit Na Mamo o Muolea are stewards of some 73 acres that include King David Kalakaua's summer residence. *Driving:* About .75-mile past mm47, look for an access just after a one-lane bridge. Public access may not yet be established, so heed posted signs.

SNORKEL: On sunny days, **Venus Pool** is ideal for swimming around.

44. POOLS OF OHEO   HIKE, SNORKEL

WHAT'S BEST: The Hana pilgrimage leads to a series of terraced pools scoured in bedrock. Inland are two of Maui's highest waterfalls, alongside a trail that penetrates a bamboo jungle. Farther down the road, a shorter hike leads to a more secluded falls.

PARKING: Take Hwy. 360 through Hana. After mm33, the road becomes Hwy. 31 at mm51—with numbers *descending.* After mm43 you'll pass Haleakala National Park boundary, and then a bridge over Oheo Gulch. Just after mm42, turn left into the parking for the Kipahulu Visitors Center. *Notes:* An entry fee of about $10 per car is charged; the fee is good for a week, and also applies to the summit area of Haleakala National Park. Additional directions follow for Lindbergh and Alelele Falls hikes.

HIKE: *National Park:* **Pools of Oheo loop (.75-mi, 150 ft.)**; **Pipiwai Trail to: Falls at Makahiku (1.25-mi., 300 ft.), or Waimoku Falls (4.25 mi., 850 ft.);** *Other hikes:* **Kipahulu Point Park-Lindbergh Grave (.25-mi.); Alelele Falls (1 mi.)**

Talk Story: Just when you thought it was safe to get back in the car … the pasturelands of Hana give way to a rolling rural area, lush with gardens and blue-water vistas, which in turn transition to a narrow, twisting road that is punched through steep rain forest and across eight streams over five miles. Then comes the visitors center for the **Kipahulu section of Haleakala National Park**. This portion of the park is located on the ahupua'a of Kipahulu, a village of antiquity that was one of the largest on Maui. *Be Aware:* The Pools of Oheo can be a zoo during peak hours on sunny days. Get there early.

For the **Pools of Oheo loop**, walk to the low-key **visitors center** and take the signed **Kuloa Point Trail**. You'll meander in the shade of a huge banyan before reaching the stream and its pools (formerly dubbed the Seven Sacred Pools). When nearest the ocean, jog right a short distance to see the ruins of **Kipahulu Kauhale** heiau and its four-star view bench. Then take the path upstream to the highway bridge before looping back to the visitors center. *Be Aware:* All the pools present a danger due to

Pools of Oheo, Pipiwai Trail

flash floods. Normally, a gate will close access during flood conditions. Oceanfront waves are also a potential hazard. *Note:* A 2017 landslide closed the pools; work to reopen was scheduled for completion in 2018.

The **Pipiwai Trail** is one of Hawaii's best waterfall hikes. Begin by taking the trail to the left of the visitors center, or backtrack on the highway toward the bridge, to where the trail crosses. On the leg to the **Falls at Makahiku** you cross a pastureland and then climb the forests above the stream, lying steeply below to your right. You'll come to a falls overlook sign, where the 200-foot watery ribbon is visible. Fine, but be sure to take the spur to the right just afterwards that leads to the top of the falls and a view down the gulch. *Be Aware: S*tay back from drop-offs, especially during rains.

To continue to 400-foot **Waimoku Falls**, ascend the trail past a gate and under the boughs of a huge banyan. The trail levels as you get a first glimpse of the higher falls from a stand of guavas. Stream overlooks will be to your right. About a mile from the trailhead, the stream narrows as it crashes through a rocky gorge, falling in cataracts and pools that are spanned by **two footbridges**—one of the hike's highlights. During much of the hike's final run, you'll be on long sections of boardwalk and stairs, through towering bamboo forests straight out of Borneo. The trail ends with two crossings at a stream confluence, just before the skyscraper amphitheater of Waimoku Falls. Walk up the rise opposite the falls for a point-blank view.

More Stuff: For a mile-long coastal stroll away from the crowds at the pools, go right as you face the visitors center, driving toward the campground. A grassy shoreline trail loops around small **Kukui Bay** to **Puhilele Point** and the ruins of the heiau.

Kipahulu Point Park and **Charles Lindbergh Grave** are a mile away from Oheo, well worth the trip. *Driving:* Continue past **St. Paul's Catholic Church** and mm41. Then turn left on a lane lined with century plants (at Maui Stables' sign) and left again to Palapala Ho'omanu (Kipahulu) Church, dating from around 1860. At the small cemetery next to the church is the grave site of the most famous American of his time. Lindbergh was laid to rest here in 1974. Down the lawn from the church is the small county park with shaded tables and a big view back across the wide channel to the Big Island. *More Stuff:* When you leave this area, turning right on Highway 31, look on the left for the big smoke stack and other ruins of **Kipahulu Sugar Mill**, which shut down in 1922. If you turn left on the Highway 31, about .25-mile away, is **Laulima Farms**, an organic smoothie and espresso shack whose surrounding gardens grow virtually everything they serve. You may not want to leave. Lastly, for guided cultural hikes, contact the **Kipahulu Ohana**; see page 235.

The **Alelele Falls** trail is several miles from the Kipahulu visitors center, heading toward Kaupo on Highway 31. It's about a 15-minute walk, under kukui trees and over some rocks, to the 100-foot falls—one of Maui's more hidden treasures. *Driving:*

Highway 31 drops into the hairy, narrow section between mm40 and mm38 at Lelekea Bay. Park near the middle, one-lane bridge (inscribed 'Alelele') and take the trail upstream. *Be Aware:* Rockslides in 2007 closed the road near mm39.5 for two years. Stay clear of this area during rains, when flash floods are a hazard. Also, don't linger on the roadway sections near cliffs: falling rocks have caused at least one death. *More Stuff:* **Alelele Falls** and **Lelekea Bay** are part of a finger of **Haleakala National Park** that extends down from the volcano. At the next bridge (Kalepa) a rough trail heads inland and makes an undulating contour for almost 4 miles, and comes out to the road near Lelekea Stream. Experienced hikers only—and on sunny days.

More Stuff: Going back toward Hana from the Pools of Oheo—between mm44 and mm45—are the double bridges of **Wailua Falls**, with a view turnout normally frequented by craft vendors. Additionally, on the uphill grade after the first bridge is the marker for the so-called trail to **Helio's Grave**. The route is a precipitous butt-slide 300 feet down an overgrown embankment to Wailua Cove. A 20-foot cross memorializing Helio is on high ground. Helio and his brother, Peterto, led a Roman Catholic movement on Maui in the 1840s.

SNORKEL: You'd look silly with a mask and fins in the **Pools of Oheo** but not swimming around. Between the highway and the ocean are five pools, with waters up to 40-feet deep. The middle two are most popular. *Be Aware:* Flash flood hazard exists here, so dip only when skies are blue. Some days these pools are brown, even when it's not raining. For a secluded dip, try a small black-sand beach on **Lelekea Bay**, near the Alelele bridge.

Waimoku Falls

Haleakala

Sliding Sands Trail, Haleakala National Park

HALEAKALA

You don't need to leave Maui to cure tropical malaise, just drive up 5,000 feet to the rolling hills and pine forests of Kula. Or, put on the outerwear and head up 10,000 feet to leave the planet altogether on a journey into the Haleakala crater. As a third choice, go to the unexplored Kaupo coast for a trip to Arizona with an ocean.

Driving Tour
Picking the Right Days

Seeing sunrise from the summit of Haleakala is a quest for many Maui visitors, and if you're one of them, bring every stitch of warm clothing you have. *Note:* You must make reservations (www.recreation.gov) in advance to enter the park between 3 and 7 a.m.; extra fee is $1.50.) Perhaps this quest has derived from the myth surrounding the volcano's name "House of the Sun." In ancient times, the demigod Maui snared the sun with his fishhook, thereby insuring a longer planting season and well-being for the people. The sunrise expedition, aside from being cold and crowded, also must begin in darkness, meaning you can't reliably check out visibility on the summit. When clear, the Haleakala summit is an eye-popper. Consider leaving just after sunrise, which will put you ahead of the tour buses and allows you to enjoy the scenery on the way up in daylight. Sunset is also a good choice, when the summit offers solitude.

Regardless of what your watch says, when the weather appears clear at the top is the time to head for Haleakala. Bear in mind that Kula clouds often hang at about 5,000 feet, making the peak appear socked in when it's not—you wind up with an airplane's view of these clouds. And, aside from full-on storm conditions, clouds get tossed around up there, so be patient. Cloudy days have clear moments.

Kula is a scenic drive any day, but it doubles as a fallback alternative when weather forces a retreat from the summit. The Kaupo coast is Maui's least visited region, and therefore is a good choice if seeking quietude on a busy weekend. In the shadow of Haleakala, it's also the most arid, and the most likely place to find sun, even when rains are lashing West Maui and the Hana coast. During droughts, and mostly in the summer, the Kaupo coast will be dry grasses, save the coastal Kiawe trees and the upper reaches of the Kahikinui Forest Reserve. But during normal winters and springs, a green carpet of low-lying vegetation fills in around the lava formations.

The Roads

The Haleakala Highway has the most elevation gain per horizontal mile covered of any paved road on earth. But it's built on the mountain's relatively gentle north slopes, and using long switchbacks without vertigo-inducing hairpins. Provided your brakes hold out on the way down, and you avoid the stream of downhill bicyclists as you go up, the road is a snap. Kula is made for convertibles. Along several miles well below the summit, the Kula and Haleakala highways run on parallel contours—with old Lower Kula Road between them—providing loop options for touring the Upcountry.

The southern Kaupo coast—where Highway 37 circles around to become Highway 31—is also an easy one to navigate. New steel and concrete bridges appear to have been built in advance of commute traffic, and the county crews are extending the pavement toward Kaupo. But currently, the smooth pavement ends before the road reaches sea level at Nuʻu Bay, and becomes pothole-patched and dirt-graded after that, but no problem for passenger cars. Lack of shoulders present hazards in some areas. Just follow the yellow-paint line. Traffic is wonderfully sparse, increasing only in late afternoons when the Hana commute comes through on the clockwise circum-navigation. The only dicey, narrow section is past Kaupo, near mm39 when the road narrows to one lane at Lelekea Bay on its 8-mile finale to Kipahulu. Even with this challenge, you might consider visiting the Pools of Oheo from this direction, rather than coming around from Hana. Go in the morning, and double back to visit the Kaupo coast in the afternoon.

THE COURSE

Follow along on the Haleakala map, page 152. Refer to trailhead descriptions that follow on pages 153 for more details.

From Puu Maneoneo, Kaupo Coast

Note: Three tours for this trailhead section: Haleakala, Kaupo coast, and Kula. The Kula tour can be combined with either of the others, or done independently, but to do all three would be more like work than a vacation.

Haleakala Tour. Begin early morning. The Haleakala Highway starts as number 37, changes to 377, and finally becomes 378 as it makes its switchbacking ascent into the Haleakala National Park. The highway segment, after Pukalani, is through rolling horse country, sensu-

Haleakala, Kaupo Coast

HALEAKALA DRIVING TOUR | 145

Haleakala Visitors Center

ous hills dotted with eucalyptus as well as native Hawaiian trees. The tight turns of Highway 378 at first cut through the flower farms and gardens, and then the road tops out on the broad shoulders above the tree line. Keep your eyes peeled, because you pass through different biological zones in minutes.

You enter **Haleakala National Park** at mm10, where an entrance fee is charged. Consider saving **Hosmer Grove**—to the left after the park entrance—for the return leg of the tour, but a visit to **Park Headquarters** is a recommended stop for an introduction to the visit. Then, push the wheels toward the top. The **Kalahaku Lookout**, after mm18, can only be accessed on the downward trip.

Must-do stops include the **Red Hill** observation area at the summit, and the **White Hill** walk at the **Haleakala Visitors Cente**r, just before the road's end. The intimate center hangs right on the edge of a cliff. At the summit, observe the sinking phenomena described by author Jack London when he rode a horse up here: Since you see more of the horizon as you climb, the summit of Haleakala can be perceived as a downward journey. After taking in the summit, energetic travelers will want to immerse themselves in the red cinder of the crater, by descending the **Sliding Sands Trail**. Save some energy for climbing back up.

On the way down, check out at the **Leleiwi** and **Kalahaku overlooks**. Highly recommended is **Halemau'u Trail** to the **Ko'olau Gap** overlook—a place that exceeds imagination. You'll be able see most everything on this tour, since Haleakala is the right size for a full-day visit. And you'll feel like you've been gone for a week after descending to the sandy beaches and coco palms.

KAUPO COAST TOUR, BEGIN EARLY MORNING. TAKE HIGHWAY 37 PAST KULA AND CONTINUE AS IT BECOMES HIGHWAY 31. Traditionally, people see this area on the last leg of a long day, coming around from Hana. Consequently, it's passed over as an "eerie moonscape" you pass by on the way back to the resort for the evening's Mai Tai. For many visitors, however, the **Kaupo coast** will be Maui's most pleasant surprise—gulches becoming canyons along a rugged wilderness coast rich with archeological sites, and all of it under the towering relief of Haleakala.

After rounding the bend at **Kula**, you may wish to take a first rest stop at **Sun Yat Sen Park** at mm18. But save a refreshing wine-tasting and historical tour at **Tedeschi Winery**, just down the highway, for the homeward leg. Don't miss it—the sublime, parklike grounds were a favorite stop for Hawaii's last king, David Kalakaua, as well as author Robert Louis Stevenson. Normal hours are 10 to 5:30.

Makawao, Huialoha Church

A couple miles past Tedeschi, which is on the grounds of **Ulupalakua Ranch**, the road narrows, and you start to pick up views down to the lava flow on the Kinau Peninsula at La Perouse Bay. Cinder cones rise from the desert flora of the slopes. The road begins a long descent, passing the **Lualailua Hills** and reaching near sea level at **Manawainui Gulch**. From the turnout at Manawainui, you can walk a short distance to see the natural arch and fishing shrine ruins on a remote portion of the **King's Trail**.

The highway stays near sea level for the next several miles. Stop at will. Along this coast, you truly can explore. You will most likely want to see the petroglyphs at **Nu'u Bay**, as well as the view of Haleakala you get from the boulder beach there. After Nu'u, the highway climbs to **Pu'u Maneoneo**, where you can hop out of the car for a perspective on where you've just been. This is one of Maui's eye-popping scenes.

For the next several miles, the partially paved road winds through ranchlands, passing **St. Joseph's Church**, and reaching the sanctum sanctorum of this coast, the **Kaupo Store**. That this country-funk place is the center of commerce for the entire coast speaks wonderful volumes. Sit a spell. From here, adventurers wanting the area's best hike can try the **Kaupo Trail**, that scales Haleakala and reaches the park through the Kaupo Gap. Beyond the store, the remaining 8-mile trip to the Pools of Oheo is one of Maui's most scenic. But even if you don't go that far, be sure to check out **Huialoha Church**, which is about a mile from the Kaupo Store.

KULA TOUR. ADD ON TO THE HALEAKALA OR KAUPO TOURS, OR DO SEPA-
RATELY. The **Kula**, or **Upcountry**, portion of Maui runs along a contour at several

Haleakala downhill biking

Hosmer Grove

thousand feet in elevation on the west slope of Haleakala. Cool temperatures, moderate rainfall, and trade-wind clouds prevail here, an ideal environ for gardens, forests, and arboretums. Put Bruddah Iz Kamakawiwoʻoleʻs version of John Denver's *Country Road* on the CD player and roll.

TAKE HIGHWAY 37 TO HIGHWAY 377. A horse's life may seem appealing as you see them grazing up here on the rounded hillsides, with enough shade and windbreak offered by eucalyptus and native tree groves. Near mm5 is **Kula Lodge**, a venerable eatery with an art gallery downstairs and **Upcountry Harvest** gift store nearby. But seekers of all-things-Maui should head next door for the **Kula Marketplace**, set just below its on-highway parking lot. You'll find local art, jewelry, books, a wealth of souvenir ideas, and a totally tempting array of island baked goods, fruit and veggies, sandwiches, and local delectables. Guys, buy a newspaper, you'll have a long wait.

Farther down the road, on either side of the junction with Highway 378, are **protea flower farms**, and then the entrance to the old-timey **Kula Gardens**, Maui's oldest garden. It's ambitious plantings are backed by a great view. Kids will love it.

If you're doing a full day in the Upcountry, you'll want to take a spin up **Waipoli Road** to the **Kula Forest Reserve**; the road will be on your left before Highway 377 joins Highway 37. At least drive up about .5-mile to check the scene at **Aliʻi Kula Lavender** (turn right from Waipoli at a dragonfly sign just before the cattle guard).

From there, Waipoli Road wiggles upward to about 6,000 feet, over hillsides favored by model airplane buffs and parasailors, before becoming unpaved and entering the sublime trails of the **Polipoli Springs State Park**. It's the relatively secret side of Haleakala.

FROM THE JUNCTION OF HIGHWAYS 377 AND 37. Take Highway 37 around the mountain for some 7 miles to **Tedeschi Winery** that is within **Ulupalakua Ranch**. On the way you'll pass through the historic Chinese settlement of **Keokea**, just past which you can veer left up the hill to see the movie-like setting of the **Kula Sanatorium**. Also on the way, near mm18 is Sun Yat Sen Park, where views of Makena open up. And down the road from the park is Uluapalakua Ranch and the Tedeschi Winery—offering tasting and a history tour of its arboretum.

BACKTRACK TO JUNCTION OF HIGHWAYS 377 AND 37. JUST PAST THIS JUNCTION, TURN RIGHT ON LOWER KULA ROAD. You don't want to miss this slice of old Maui, left intact since bypassed by the newer highways. At the turn is **Rice Park**, with rolling lawn and a commanding overlook toward West Maui. Down the road is **Calasa Service**, built in 1932, where gassing the car will be an experience. Down the street from the service station is the **Morihara Store**, a throwback to a time when these mom & pops were just about the only place to shop. Farther along from these establishments is the centerpiece of Kula, the **Church of the Holy Ghost**, an octagonal edifice built in 1894.

Note: Beyond the church, Lower Kula Road pops back out to the highway. You can take another section of the road—a right turn shortly after coming out to the highway—to

Tedeschi Winery

Makawao Forest Reserve

see the **Mormon Pulehu Church**, built in 1851. This segment of Lower Kula becomes roughly paved and joins Highway 37 again a few miles ahead.

CONTINUE ON HIGHWAY 37, TURN RIGHT ON HIGHWAY 377, AND TURN LEFT ON KEALALOA HANAMU ROAD. This maneuver takes you through dairylands and joins up with **Olinda Road**. *Note:* You could also continue on Highway 37 to Highway 365 and reach Olinda Road a little farther down the mountain in Makawao. Either way, you can turn right on Olinda for a spin to the upper Upcountry, ending at the **Waihou Springs Forest Reserve**.

On the way down Olinda are big views toward the Kahului coast. **Makawao**, the Upcountry's cowboy town is well worth a walk through; turn left at the stop sign on Highway 365—across from which Olinda Road becomes Baldwin Avenue. You can then return to the lowlands via rural **Baldwin Avenue**, which is Highway 390, down to Paia. On the way are the venerable **Baldwin Estate** (now Hui Noeau Visual Arts Center) and the Father Damien memorial at the **Holy Rosary Church**.

Church of the Holy Ghost

HALEAKALA DRIVING TOUR | 151

Map 5
Trailheads 45-52
HALEAKALA

HALEAKALA
TRAILHEADS 45-52

TH:	TRAILHEAD
HIKE:	ALL WALKING, FROM SHORT STROLLS TO FULL-FLEDGED DAY HIKES
SNORKEL:	BOTH FISH-VIEWING WITH MASK AND FINS, AND PLACES TO SWIM
SURF:	BOARD, BODYSURF, BODYBOARD, WINDSURFING, KITEBOARDING
MM:	MILE MARKER, CORRESPONDS TO HIGHWAY SIGNS

All hiking distances in parentheses are ROUND TRIP.
Elevation gains of 100 feet or more are noted.

45. OLINDA UPCOUNTRY-MAKAWAO   HIKE

WHAT'S BEST: Take a walk around Maui's cowboy country town, or choose an exercise hike on two trails into higher-elevation forest reserves where few tourists venture.

PARKING: Take Hwy. 36 to Paia and turn right on Hwy. 390, Baldwin Ave. Follow about 5 mi. to Makawao. *For the Makawao stroll:* Park on-street, near the T-intersection of Baldwin and Makawao avenues. You can also get to Makawao from the Hwy. 37 (the Haleakala Hwy.): turn left at Pukalani on Makawao Ave. *Waihou Springs Forest Reserve:* Continue straight at jct. with Makawao Ave., as Hwy. 390 becomes Olinda Rd. At mm11.9, park at a sign for Tree Growth Research Area. *For Makawao Forest Reserve:* Turn left on Makawao Ave., go .25-mi. and turn right on Pi'iholo Rd. (Hwy. 394). After 1.4 mi., veer left on Waiahiwi Rd. Then continue .4-mi., turn right on Kahakapao Rd. and drive about 1 mi. to signed, on-street trailhead parking.

HIKE: Makawao stroll (up to .5-mi.); Waihou Springs Forest Reserve (up to 2.25 mi., 450 ft.); Makawao Forest Reserve (6.5 mi., 475 ft.)

Makawao (rhymes with 'wow') is Maui's dark-horse contender for best walk-around town, where love-the-earth locals and the low-key Hollywood types mingle at galleries, eateries, boutiques, and upscale gift stores—but place retains an Old West look that reflects its paniolo (cowboy) culture. Follow your instincts, or get the lowdown at **Gecko Trading Company**, which hosts the art of Deybra. Chow down at **Makawao Steakhouse**, and get down to Upcountry tunes at **Casanova Restaurant**.

Olinda Road winds skyward from Makawao. **Waihou Springs Forest Reserve**, part of the state's Na Ala Hele trails system, was test-planted with pines and other species in the 1920s. Head down the needle-cushioned road through the orderly pine grove. After about .25-mile, turn right toward the overlook, and then, to reach **Waihou**

Waihou Springs Forest Reserve

Springs, go right again, amid spindly ash trees (you will backtrack to this junction). You reach an overlook with a bench among sugi pine, where the springs trail drops steeply on switchbacks. The springs seep from a 200-foot mossy wall that is bored with cavelike irrigation tunnels— in wet conditions a mysterious Hobbit-land. Backtrack to the trail junction and go right. The trail continues on an undulating circle, through a variety of trees that include cypress and koa, as well as some good-sized pines. Then you reconnect with the main path back to trailhead parking. *More Stuff:* Olinda Road ends about .25-mile past mm12. From just above the road's gate is the lower part of **Waikomo Ridge Trail**, which descends from Hosmer Grove. Permission to hike may be required from The Nature Conservancy; see page 235.

Enter the **Makawao Forest Reserve** for a bird-lover, tree-hugger exercise jaunt on the peaceful and pretty **Kapahakapao Loop Trail**. You start down a wide paved road. After .5-mile (before the reservoir) go right on a dirt road at a trail sign, and then, .5-mile later, go right again on the **West Loop Trail**. The trail ascends beside a drainage and loops left, ever upward. A new drainage will appear on your left, above which the trail crosses, through lovely ti and tree ferns. You'll reach a junction for the **East Loop Trail**; go left. You're now on the downward leg, which swerves through baby ferns and tall Norfolk Pines, before returning to the start of the West Loop Trail. *More Stuff:* In 2017, a 3-plus-mile leg of the ancient **Haleakala (Ranch) Trail** was declared by courts to be public land. For the latest on access, contact PATH Maui, a nonprofit; see page 235.

More Stuff: Head down **Baldwin Avenue** from Makaweo (to below Hali'imaile Road at mm3.75) to take a 15-minute walk around **Hui Noeau Visual Arts Center**, set on groomed acreage of the former Ethel and Harry **Baldwin Estate**. Pastoral serenity and towering trees are a backdrop to the 1917 Mediterranean buildings. On site now are a gift shop, photography studio, jewelry and ceramics workshops, and art gallery.

Makawao Forest Reserve

46. HALEAKALA NATIONAL PARK   HIKE

WHAT'S BEST: A journey to a volcanic planet two-miles in the sky in the middle of the Pacific. Choose from hikes that will suit every energy level: forests, craters, and overlooks with aerial views of Maui and beyond.

PARKING: Go inland on Hwy. 37, the Haleakala Hwy. After Pukalani-Makawao jcts., turn left on Hwy. 377. Follow for 6 mi. and turn left on Hwy. 378. The national park boundary is near mm10. Additional directions follow, beginning at the boundary. Admission is $25 per car, good for three days. *Note:* Advance reservations (www.recreation.gov; fee $1.50) are required to enter for sunrise, between 3 and 7 a.m.

HIKE: FROM BOTTOM GOING UP: Hosmer Grove Nature Trail (.5-mi.); Halemau'u Trail to: Ko'olau Gap-crater overlook (2.25 mi., 250 ft.), or Holua Cabin (8.25 mi., 1,200 ft.); Leleiwi Overlook (less than .25-mi.); **NEAR VISITORS CENTER AT TOP:** White Hill (.5-mi, 150 ft.); Sliding Sands Trail to: cinder cones overlook (2 mi., 400 ft.), or Ka Lu'u o ka O'o (5.25 mi., 1,400 ft.), or Kapalaoa Cabin (11.5 mi., 2,500 ft.), or Bottomless Pit (11.25 mi., 2,600 ft.); Red Hill Summit (less than .25-mi.); Skyline Trail (1.5 to 15 miles mi., 200 to 3,200 ft.)

Talk Story: Climbing to 10,000 feet over a few horizontal miles, the **Haleakala Highway** is the steepest roadway in the world. Yet its sweeping curves are a mellow drive, by Maui standards, unless your brakes fail coming down. The crater (19 square miles and 3,000-feet deep) is not technically a crater, but an eroded valley, whose moonscape is dotted with about a dozen red cinder cones. These mini-craters, called pu'us, are vents from separate eruptions. Haleakala is an active volcano—it will erupt again, say the experts. Clouds bring wintry conditions to the summit. Weather changes rapidly. Frequently, clouds hangs near Kula, near 4,000 feet, making the top appear socked in from below when it's actually rising into the sun—Haleakala, "House of the Sun."

The **Hosmer Grove Nature Loop** through native shrubs will be of most interest to botanists and ornithologists. *Driving:* The trailhead is at the campground, a .5-mile drive on a left turn just after entering the park. The first part of the loop goes through cedar, spruce, and other conifers planted in the early 1900s by forester Ralph Hosmer. The second part is through native shrubs, where our feathered friends live. *More Stuff:* The **Waikomo Ridge Trail** is near a restroom a few hundred feet from the end of the road into the campground. The catch: Call The Nature Conservancy for permission to enter; see page 235. No catch: The **Supply Trail**, which climbs 500 feet over 2.5 miles to join the Haleamu'u Trail, a wonderland of low-lying native plants and a good choice when fog lingers higher up. It begins on the right, before Hosmer Grove. For other hiking information, stop at the **Park Headquarters**, just up the road near mm11.25.

The **Halemau'u Trail** hike to the **Ko'olau Gap** and **crater overlook** reaps a big return for the investment of energy. *Driving:* The parking lot is at an elevation of 8,000 feet,

Holua Cabin, Silversword, Sliding Sands Trail

just after mm14. After descending through low shrubs you reach a precipice. On your right is the west side of the Haleakala Crater, a jumble of black lava here, speckled with greenery. You walk the spine of the precipice toward the gap, where a lava fall created the Keanae Peninsula off the Hana Highway, down to your left.

To reach the **Holua Cabin**, the trail takes a herky-jerky descent of nearly 1,000 feet down a weirdly formed escarpment. On the bottom, your feet briefly are comforted by a grass patch, before the trail again ascends up a lava bench. Atop the bench, on a small lawn below the towering Leleiwi Pali, is the cabin. Often waddling around this rustic oasis are the endangered nene, or Hawaiian goose, the state bird. Please don't feed them. A trail leads south from the cabin, eventually connecting with trails coming down from the top of the crater (see *More Stuff* below). *Be Aware:* Caves formed by lava tubes in the area can be dangerous; venturing inside of them is inadvisable.

The kiosk **Leleiwi Overlook** offers a view from the high cliffs above Holua Cabin, as well as the entire crater. *Driving:* Look for a signed turnoff after mm17. Late in the day at the overlook is a good time to observe the surreal ho'okuaka effect: With clouds in the crater and the sun at your back, your shadow sometimes will appear in the mist, illuminated by a halo of color. Another variation of a sky-high view, can be seen at the **Kalahaku Overlook**, which is up the road on the left, but only accessed when coming down from. Below the overlook, clouds often gather and vanish like wisps of smoke.

The stone **Haleakala Visitors Center** features a fabulous view from its perch on the edge of the crater, the place to chat with rangers, or wait for clouds to clear. *Driving:* It's almost to the top, at mm20. A graded trail from outside the center winds to the top of

From Kalahaku Overlook

White Hill, a.k.a. Pa Kaʻoao. The exquisite view is a prime destination for short-walk specialists. This site ancient Hawaiian celestial observation huts also serves a big view of the Big Island.

The **Sliding Sands Trail**—the premier trail at Haleakala—departs from the right as you enter the visitors center parking lot. Descending with long

From Sliding Sands Trail

traverses over red sand, this trail has many options and a way of drawing visitors deeper than they intended, so begin prepared for a long hike. Austere beauty envelops hikers from the get-go. The **cinder cones overlook** will come up on your left, an unmarked spur. The **Ka Luʻu o ka Oʻo** crater will be directly below. To get there, continue down and make a left at the first junction—at a confusing outcropping among some silverswords, the jewel of the Haleakala plant world. When you reach the crater, be sure to take the thrilling trail around its rim.

To the **Bottomless Pit**, a.k.a. Kawilinau, continue on the Sliding Sands for nearly 2 miles past the above junction. The last part will be a steep descent. Then take a left at a trail junction, beginning a moderate fall over about 1.5 miles, keeping two cinder cones to your right. The pit—with a bottom clearly visible—is on the north side of the cinder cones. To reach the **Kapalaoa Cabin**, keep on trekking past the Bottomless Pit-Halemauʻu Trail junction, for 2 more miles. The cabin lies near the edge of the Kaupo Gap, and the 7,000-foot escarpments that fall to the south coast. *Be Aware:* Coming back up the Sliding Sands at this elevation can be a grind. Don't bite off more than you can chew. *More Stuff:* One of the park's best long hikes is a car-shuttle from Sliding Sands, past Holua Cabin, to the Halemauʻu trailhead. The hike is 11.5 miles with 2,800 feet of elevation gain. Hikers without a second car to shuttle commonly hitchhike back to the top. Head toward the Bottomless Pit (Kawilinau) and go left at a signed junction.

At **Red Hill Summit** (elevation 10,023) is covered, octagonal hut with picture windows provides shelter, informative displays, as well as staggering views. *Driving:* It's at road's end, which is at mm21. Red Hill's real name is Puʻuʻulaula—try it, it's easy. For another panorama, don't forget to take the rim trail, which encircles the parking lot.

The fabulous **Skyline Trail** is outside the park boundary and not shown on the visitors maps. *Driving:* Keep left opposite the spur road to Red Hill and park on the left at a locked gate and green cattle guard, which is .6-mile from White Hill. The 'no trespassing' sign refers to the right-veering road to Science City, a defense department and University of Hawaii research center. The trail begins and crumbling pavement and turns to red cinder, giving up big ocean views from an open ridgeline. It continues *way* down to Polipoli State Park, but you can achieve a grand panorama amid sculpted cinder cones with a hike of around an hour. Skyline is a hidden treasure on the volcano.

47. KULA FOREST RESERVE-POLIPOLI SPRINGS PARK   HIKE

WHAT'S BEST: Ascend the green side of Haleakala, where some trails achieve lofty heights with ocean views, while other paths wander misty conifer-and-broadleaf forests that have been battered by nature. Or choose a more relaxing visit in cool Kula: flourishing botanical gardens, a lively lavender garden, or a historic winery.

PARKING: Take Hwy. 37 (the Haleakala Hwy.) up the mountain and keep right as Hwy. 37 becomes the Kula Hwy. *For all Kula Forest Reserve hikes and the two gardens:* Just after Rice Park and before mm14, turn left on Hwy. 377. *For Kula forest and lavender garden:* After .25-mi., turn right on Waipoli Rd. Aliʻi Lavender Garden will be on your right after .5-mi., after crossing a cattle guard. The Kula Forest Reserve is *up* 5.75 mi. on Waipoli Rd. Park after the concrete spillway near end of pavement. *Note:* A 4WD is required to drive the park's dirt roads. The park is ideal for mountain bikes. *For Kula Botanical Gardens:* Pass Waipoli Rd. and .25-mi. later, turn right off Hwy. 377. *Tedeschi Winery* is about 7 miles away on Hwy. 37; the road changes to Highway 31 near mm20.

HIKE: *In the Kula Forest Reserve and Polipoli Park:* **Waipoli Road to: Boundary Trail loop (6.5 mi., 900 ft.), or Haleakala Ridge view (7 mi., 150 ft.); The remaining distances are for visitors with 4WD: Skyline Trail to: Mamane Trail loop (10.25 mi., 950 ft.), or Haleakala Park summit (up to 13 mi., 3,200 ft.); Polipoli Springs-Redwood Trail loop (3.75 mi., 900 ft.,);** *Nearby short hikes not in Polipoli:* **Aliʻi Kula Lavender garden (.25-mi.); Kula Botanical Garden (.25-mi.); Ulupalakua Ranch-Tedeschi Winery (.25-mi.);**

Talk Story: Mother Nature smacked the **Kula Forest Reserve** in 2006 with wildfires, torrential rains, and hurricane-force winds. More than 100,000 seedlings have since been planted. From the yellow posts at the spillway, **Waipoli Road** (graded dirt) maintains a contour through the 12,000 acre **Polipoli Springs State Park**, which is part of the reserve. It's nippy up here, from 6,000 feet on up. Bring warm clothing.

The **Waipoli Road hikes** begin from the parking area (spillway where the paragliders take off). After .5-mi., you'll round a bend and enter the forest and pass the return junction with the Boundary Trail. The road undulates, but basically maintains a contour. For the **Boundary Trail loop**, go right, after about 2.25 miles from the parking area, at the right-hand junction with the Waiohuli Trail. You will drop 900 feet and join the Boundary Trail. Turn right and enjoy views toward the Kihei coast as you return on a more gradual climb. For the **Haleakala Ridge view**, just stay on the road. At 3.25 miles from the parking area, you pass the junction with the spur road that drops to Polipoli Springs. From that junction it's another .5-mile farther up to a big open turnout, where you can look up the **Haleakala Ridge** and down to the vast sheets of lava on the southern coast. The **Skyline Trail** begins its long ascent to the summit here.

Note: Visitors in non-4WD vehicles need to add the *driving distances* to the rest of the hikes listed. For the **Skyline Trail-Mamane Trail loop**, *drive in* about 2.25 miles from the end of the pavement, and park at signed junction for the **Waiohuli Trail**, which crosses the road. This trail gives you a taste of the devastated forest, a cave adventure, as well as big panoramas. You begin with a steep climb for .75-mile to the junction with the **Mamane Trail**—go right. Near this junction you'll find a small volcanic cone used by the ancients as a cave shelter. Over the next 2 miles you traverse native shrub, mainly the mamane trees. You then meet the **Skyline Trail**, above its first set

Polipoli trail

of switchbacks on the ascent up the ridge to Red Hill. To return, go right, down to rejoin **Waipoli Road**. *Note:* You could begin this loop from the Skyline Trail, and descend the Mamane Trail.

The **Skyline Trail** takes you higher and higher, to the Haleakala summit. Begin by *driving in* 4.25 miles in on Waipoli Road. Park about a mile past the junction with the road to Polipoli; about .5-mile past that junction is a turnout with a guardrail, after which the road bends left through forest and reaches an open saddle—where it becomes red-dirt switchbacks that thwart passenger vehicles. Park here. Views open dramatically when you reach the top of the switchbacks. Continue climbing to your left—a right hand junction takes you into a scrub-filled ancient crater on Kahua Road. After about .75-mile, **Red Hill** will be visible up and to your left. The trail continues straight up the ridge, much of the hike rises above vegetation, as the road becomes cinders.

For the **Polipoli Springs-Redwood Trail loop**, *drive in* and veer right from Waipoli Road 3.25 miles after the end of pavement. *Drive* down about .6-mile and park at the picnic area at Polipoli Springs. From the parking area, walk back 100 feet on the road and go left down a short path that leads to the **Polipoli Cabin**. Hang a right at a signed trail when you reach the cabin. The soft-earth trail swerves down, at first through the partial wreckage of cypress and a few sugi pine, and then among redwoods. After a little less than a mile, at a shelter, go left on the **Tie Trail**. You'll drop 500 feet farther through redwoods and then ash trees. If you're quiet you might surprise a wild pig or two. After .5-mile the Tie Trail joins the **Haleakala Ridge Trail**, where you go left. At this altitude, sunlight often mixes with waning fog to produce glowing beams. You'll get ocean peeks at Kahoolawe, as the trail climbs during the next mile. At a junction above a big climb, go left on **Polipoli Trail**—where the Haleakala Ridge Trail continues right to join the road and Skyline Trail. The **shelter cave** is about .5-mile farther up the Polipoli Trail, just off the trail at a signed junction. The wide-mouthed cave, in bedrock, is in a depression in the forest. The Polipoli Trail contours through tattered eucalyptus and pine before reaching the picnic area parking.

At **Ali'i Kula Lavender Garden**, paths meander through about 9 acres of lavender (about 40 species) on open slopes of Kula at 4,000 feet. Culinary lunches and teatime garden tours are available by reservation. Stop by for a scone on the view deck at the Studio Gift Shop, and look inside for dozens of locally made lavender-inspired items—foodstuffs, beauty products, logo wear, and candles. The gardens are the brainchild of the late Ali'i Chang, a personality on Maui. Show up in the morning (hours are 9 to 4) and you'll get a view of paragliders descending from Haleakala and landing just outside the entrance to the garden. *Note:* Admission is $3 per person.

Nearly 40 years old, the family-run, **Kula Botanical Gardens** was Maui's first and will be just the ticket for traveling families. It's groomed paths meander 8 acres featuring a koi pond, love birds, carved statuary, and African cranes, as well as 2,000 species of flowering plants and tropical trees—all of it set at a pleasant slope that affords a bird's-eye view of the ocean and West Maui hanging out there like some far-off land. Admission is about $10 for adults; hours are 9 to 4 daily.

More Stuff: **Thompson Road**, a paved lane closed to traffic, is a favorite dog-walking route among locals, through the high rolling greenery of historic ranchlands that are now owned by Oprah Winfrey. *Driving:* Take Highway 37 past mm16 and veer left just past **Henry Fong Store**. Park at gate where the lane is closed.

Kula Botanical Garden, Ali`i Lavender Garden

Around the mountain from the Kula Forest Reserve is **Tedeschi Winery**, which sits amid **Ulupalakua Ranch**. Tedeschi's staff provide historical tours (normally at 10:30, 1:30, and 3) along with the vineyard's libation. Tasting room hours are 9 to 5 daily.

Talk Story: **Tedeschi Vineyards**, featuring sparkling wines made from pineapple, has been around since 1974, taking over the historic buildings of the James Makee estate. The Hawaiian royal family, including King David Kalakaua, and famous writers, such as Robert Louis Stevenson, frequented the grand estate. Makee planted numerous varieties of trees, now giants, and flowers in abundance. The totems in front were carved from Italian cypress trees that died. The **Ulupalakua Ranch** is still a working operation, and you're likely to see some of the paniolos down the street at the local store. *More Stuff:* Above the highway near the vineyards is the nonprofit **D. T. Fleming Arboretum**, Hawaii's oldest. Views are fabulous, as is the plantlife and grounds of this Maui treasure. Call for free tours; see page 235.

48. GREAT TAHITI-MENEHUNE FOOTPRINTS   HIKE

WHAT'S BEST: Ruins tell the story of migrations from Tahiti 1,000 years ago—to hikers willing to endure sticker brush, beating sun, and high winds on an unmarked route.

PARKING: Take Hwy. 37 (the Haleakala Hwy.) up the mountain and keep right as route becomes the Kula Hwy. After mm20, route changes again, to Hwy. 31. Continue past cinder quarry at mm21.5. At mm22.6, park on left at a shoulder; a 'government property' sign and gate will be barely visible to the left, up and off the road. *Note:* After mm19, as you come down the squiggly highway, note the two Lualailua Hills, lying ahead above the highway. At the saddle between the hills, a contour line of a road goes to the left, toward the upper part of the hill. This is the route to the ruins.

HIKE: Kahikinui ruins-Menehune footprints (3.5 mi., 300 ft.)

Talk Story: **Kahikinui**—or Great Tahiti—was one of Hawaii's earliest settlements, with a population nearing 2,000. Although fishing was primary for the village, freshwater was brackish at the coast and many structures were located near 1,500 feet to trap spring water with small dams. In Hawaiian, Kahiki also means "horizon," and the village was set in a location to observe the cinder cone which they named **Hokukano**, after the star, Hokupukano, which guided the ancient mariners on their 2,500-mile voyage to the Tahitian homelands. The cone is on the ocean side of the highway at mm17.5.

The **Menehune footprints** are the Holy Grail for archeological enthusiasts. A mystery even to the earliest Polynesians, the footprints are etched into a smooth lava shelf about 35 feet in diameter—some 30 prints measuring from 4- to 10-inches in length. They are thought to be a type of petroglyph left by the legendary Menehune, the diminutive precursors to the Tahitians. The prints are difficult to find, and hard to make out—good luck. *Be Aware:* Prepare for wind and sun on this off-trail excursion. Wear long pants if you have them. Footing is difficult, due to lava and brush. Also, respect the boundaries of the homesteads in the area.

For the **Kahikinui ruins-Menehune footprints** hike, head up from the roadway and through the gate that seems to be an entrance to nowhere. But you'll be able to follow a rocky path upward, and, after about 10 minutes, turn left at a right-angle on an old road. The road levels and leads through the saddle between the **Lualailua Hills**, which means "dual tranquility." Benign grasses and weeds will slap your shins as you make your way across the saddle. From the saddle head up to your right, picking your way under some trees just large enough to throw shade. Contour around, ascending a little to stay above the top of a gulch.

From the other side of the gulch—a homestead will be down to the left—you should pick up the trail which contours around the uppermost hill. The trail meets a road, which leads through a rickety, wire gate. Although ruins dot this area, you will find a major site to your left. Walk the smooth lava a few hundred feet and go left out to a promontory marked by a kiawe tree. Here lies the sprawling remains of a **Kahikinui** village site, that was once covered with a wooden superstructure and thatched roofing. *Be Aware:* Use caution to leave the site undisturbed. The **footprints** lie some 500 yards up the slope from this site, on smooth lava, about 300 yards from the base of the hill. Listen for the hushed voices on the wind from the villagers of the past; perhaps they will guide you to just the right spot. Or maybe not. Keep an eye out, too, for lava tubes.

Pahihi Gulch

King's Trail ruins

49. MANAWAINUI GULCH   HIKE

WHAT'S BEST: Explore the fishing shrines on the lost portion of the King's Trail, or take a short but gnarly hike down to heiaus set at a cove in a canyon.

PARKING: Take Hwy. 37 (the Haleakala Hwy.) up the mountain and keep right as route becomes the Kula Hwy. After mm20, route changes again, to Hwy. 31. At the bottom of the long descent, at mm27.5, pull off at a large turnout on the right.

HIKE: Manawainui Gulch heiaus (.75-mi, 300 ft.); King's Trail (1.5 mi. or more, 200 ft.)

From the turnout, walk to the edge and take a gander down the black canyon that is **Manawainui Gulch**, where confused seas meet storm-washed boulders, the alluvium of Haleakala. To reach sea level, walk down the highway to where the guardrail joins the modern concrete bridge. (This steel rail was wiped out by a rockslide in 2007, closing the road for months; chain-link netting was draped on the cliff faces to reduce the rock hazard.) Step over the guardrail—there is no trail—and traverse down toward the bridge. At the bottom, cross the drainage and cut back toward the ocean on the brush-covered bench. Going will be slow. Near the bottom, veer right off the bench, across the boulders to the rough shoreline. There you will find a medium-sized burial platform, built of black rock, and, just behind it, a smaller one built of coral stones.

To explore the **King's Trail**, walk right, as you face the ocean, and down. You won't see a trail or markers on this end of the ancient trail that begins some 6 miles away in La Perouse Bay. You'll see the first fishing shrine about .25-mile from the parking area, beyond the first shallow gully. Along the lava coast, you are likely to see modern fishermen, who drive down, somehow, and use ladders to get out to their favorite casting spots on sharp reefs that stick out into the waves. Prepared hikers can continue, making a true adventure of this little-used route. More ruins, a blowhole, and tide pools are in the offing.

50. HUAKINI BAY   HIKE

> **WHAT'S BEST:** A natural sea arch and a red-rock canyon impart a sense of Haleakala's geologic transformation happening in real time.
>
> **PARKING:** Take Hwy. 37 (the Haleakala-Kula Hwy.) and keep right on the Kula Hwy. After mm20, the route changes to Hwy. 31. Continue to Manawainui Gulch, near mm27.5. *Note:* Further directions from this point are in hiking descriptions below.

HIKE: Natural Arch (up to .5-mi); Pahihi Gulch (2.75 mi., 200 ft.)

Talk Story: Along several miles of the highway, some half-dozen gulches are gouged into the 9,000-foot high wall that is the southern face of Haleakala. The great shield volcano was once about 5,000 feet higher, as over the eons much of its mass has eroded down gulches and fanned out to form this rugged coastline.

To see the **Natural Arch** before walking toward it, walk toward the ocean at the Manawainui turnout, as per TH48, and look down the coast to the sloping arch. *Driving:* To reach the arch from the coast, get in the car again and proceed to the bot-

Natural Arch

*Road to Kaupo trailhead, Nu'u petroglyph, Koa Heiau ruins,
St. Joseph Church, Nu'u highway, Haleki'i Bay fisherman*

tom of the next gulch at **Waiopai Bridge**, another modern feat, at mm28.6. From the black-rock beach, go to your right along the rocky coast to get sort of near the arch. Battered by the sea, it forms an opening some 150 feet in length and about 50 feet high.

Pahihi Gulch is accessible from **Huakini Bay**, where a massive boulder field rings the bay. *Driving:* Park at a shoulder on the left, just as you reach the bay, where the highway crosses a wide wash at sea level, near mm29.5. This gulch is a canyon in the making, as it will continue to deepen over the millennia. A hunter's trail leads through the greenery on the left side of the gulch's wide mouth—above the gravel bed that is the low point of wash, but not next to the cliff either. Stay left, heading toward a slide of yellowish rock. When you reach the slide, keep left of a large stand of kiawe trees.

Another gulch, **Pukai**, joins from the right. About .75-mile into the hike, you'll lose sight of the highway, as the gulch narrows pass to the left of a stand-alone hillock in the middle of the gulch. At this point, look left to see a cave below the cliff; hikers with partners and dual flashlights may want to explore with extreme caution.

Almost a mile into the hike, you'll pass behind the stand-alone hillock, and will be surrounded on four sides by steep, unstable cliffs. Hunters use this area on weekends, and you're likely to find snares made of wire and hear falling rock caused by pigs and goats up high. Birdsong practically echoes in this natural atrium. From here the gulch narrows and curves, and you'll have to pick your way across its rocky bottom, deep-grass, and treed banks. Eventually, it becomes too steep and crumbly to safely walk. *Be Aware:* This is not a hike to take alone. Do not attempt during rains, and avoid falling rock by staying away from cliffs.

51. NU'U BAY HIKE, SNORKEL

> **WHAT'S BEST:** Petroglyphs, a birder's marsh, ruins, Haleakala views, and a snorkeling cove at an old landing: This won't be Maui's secluded secret much longer: In 2008, 4,300 acres of Nu'u Ranch were added Haleakala National Park.
>
> **PARKING:** Take Hwy. 37 (the Haleakala Hwy.) and keep right on the Kula Hwy. After mm20, the route changes to Hwy. 31. Continue to where the road reaches sea level and pass mm30. *Note:* Further directions follow in hike descriptions.

HIKE: Nu'u Bay to: Petroglyphs (.25-mi.), and Nu'u Landing-Kaupo Ranch Wildlife Marsh loop (1.75 mi.); Pu'u Maneoneo (.25-mi.)

At mm30 the highway dips into an oasis of kiawe trees at **Nu'u Bay**, site of an ancient fishing village. From here, the new section of the national park extends inland through ohia-koa forest remnants to the crater rim, bordering with the **Kahikinui Forest Reserve**. A first road leads in to the right very near mm30, and a second road is .5-mile afterward, where the road dips across a spillway. For the **petroglyphs** and the **loop hike**, look for a gate at mm30.7. After a very short distance down the road, curve to your right along a cliff less than 20 feet high. Footing is poor, with tall weeds covering rocks. Petroglyphs will be plainly visible in places, etched into the rocks. Closer inspections will reveal reddish pictographs, drawings on the surface. Anthropologists speculate as to the origins of these recordings. Follow the cliff as it loops out to the boulder beach to find a heiau sitting on a low bluff. *Be Aware:* Take care not to disturb this site.

Nu'u Landing is the low lava point you will see at the far east end of the beach. From the shore is one of the most scenic vistas on Maui: Look inland as the fissured walls of Haleakala and the Kaupo Gap rise some 8,000 feet. To reach the landing, go left when you reach the coast from the petroglyphs; it's easiest to cut inland and take a sandy road along the edge of the trees. At its end, you have to climb up 15 feet. An old concrete ramp leads into the water, the point of departure for cattle in the old days. Take the trail past the landing. You'll come to a right-forking trail that leads down to rugged **Nonou Bay**. You can also stay left on a trail that leads over sharp lava to **Apole Point**, and to tiny **Waiu Bay**, which is on the opposite side of the point from Nu'u.

Once you've explored the point, backtrack on a road that leads from the base of the landing toward the highway. The remains of **Koa Heiau**, a sprawling site, will be on your right, and an ancient salt pond will be on the left. Also on your left, just before the highway, is the tiny **Kaupo Ranch Wildlife Marsh**, a pond fringed by grasses which you can see through the trees. Once you reach the highway, near mm31, walk to the left down the road. After about .1-mile, look closely on your left for a chain-link gate in the fence that leads directly to the pond. If you're quiet, you are likely to see waterfowl and shorebirds taking a break at this tiny wetland on a rocky coast.

For the vistas from **Pu'u Maneoneo**, get back in the car and get the camera ready. After mm31 the road rises inland to a grassy bluff, as the terrain transitions from the arid "dismal coast" to the ranchlands of Kaupo. To the right as the road tops out are a few turnouts and short paths that lead to vantage points. The towering heights of Haleakala will be a crowd pleaser, but don't forget to take a gander up and down the coast. Put a gold star on the map marking this place.

SNORKEL: Experienced snorkelers can find excellent snorkeling and relatively safe waters at **Nu'u Landing**, at times even during the winter. Driving: Use the gate and old road near mm31. Entry is near the landing. An even better spot is small **Nonou Bay,** which is to the right over rocks and down, not far beyond the grass patch at the landing. The walk down to the water is a hands-on affair, but the bay is more protected. This is a deep-water snorkeling area not for beginners—but a highly underrated spot when conditions are right. *Be Aware:* Don't attempt if the swell is high and test the water for currents.

52. KAUPO HIKE, SNORKEL

WHAT'S BEST: Hike high or savor the coast, but don't just drive by beautiful, weather-beaten Kaupo.

PARKING: Take Hwy. 37 (the Haleakala Hwy.) and keep right as the route becomes the Kula Hwy. After mm20, the route changes to Hwy. 31. Continue as Hwy. 31 drops to coast and climbs again, reaching Kaupo Store at mm34.6. *Note:* Further directions follow in the hike descriptions.

HIKE: Kaupo Trail to: **Haleakala National Park Boundary (7 mi., 2,700 ft.), or Kaupo Gap rim (13.75 mi., 5,500 ft.); Huialoha Church-coast (up to 1 mi.)**

The front porch at funky **Kaupo Store** may well be the center of the universe. You'll have to rest a spell with a cold drink, watch the world go by, and draw your own conclusion. It is open 24 hours a day, except when it's not, a tradition that dates from 1925. Inside are antiques and curiosities. The **Kaupo Trail** is the long and wild route into Haleakala. *Driving:* Not far past the store, turn left, before the sign noting that the national park is 8 miles ahead, and before the road drops down to a one-lane bridge. Drive in 1.4 miles on this one-lane, grassy road lined by low rock walls. The signed trailhead parking is on your left.

Heaiu ruins near Halekii Bay

Huialoha Church, Kaupo store, Kahoolawe from Kaupo Road

Walk up the road .1-mile and go left down a left-bearing fork. You'll then see the trail on the right, heading up a grassy gully. For both the **Haleakala Park Boundary** and **Kaupo Gap** rim hikes, follow post markers, set a hundred feet or less apart to mark the trail when the grass gets taller. This trail is all about up. Views are with you from the get go, and they only become better. But many people like this trail for its native koa and ohia forests, which attract flocks of woodland birds.

Ascending on long switchbacks, you reach the park boundary at an elevation of nearly 4,000 feet, with the steep and jungly **Manawainui Valley** down to the right. The frozen wave of ancient lava that poured over the **Kaupo Gap** is to your left. At nearly 7,000 feet, the Kaupo Trail joins the **Sliding Sands Trail** that comes from the top of Haleakala. From here you are .25-mile from **Paliku Cabin**, to the right, and about 9 miles from the visitors center, to the left. For trekkers who can't get enough, the Kaupo Trail is Maui's best wilderness experience.

The **Huialoha Church** is a crown jewel, where nature has conspired to craft perfection. *Driving:* Proceed past Kaupo Store and the one-lane bridge. After about .3-mile (at mm35.3) turn right on a gated, rutted dirt road that drops down for .25-mile (it's driveable, but better to walk down). The church, built in 1859, is set on acres of open grass, accented by coco palms next to small **Haleki'i Bay**. You can also walk to the right as you face the water, on a boulder beach path that actually extends for miles to **Waiuha Bay**. *Note:* The church has received a new floor and other rennovations by local volunteers, including the Aina family, after it was hit hard by vandals. Please leave a donation and or contact **Huialoha Restoration Fund** to help; huialohachurchkaupo.org.

More Stuff: Three hard-to-find heiaus in this region date from Chief Kekaulike's rule in 1730. The **Loaloa Heiau** is upstream to your left just after crossing the bridge beyond Kaupo Store; the **Haleo Kane Heiau** is to the right off the road to the Kaupo trailhead, where the road makes its right-angle to the left; and the **Popoiwi Heiau** is high on a hill off-road to the left, after crossing a second stream past Kaupo Store.

A place of worship of more recent lineage—**St. Joseph Church**, built in 1862—is right on the road before getting to the Kaupo Store; open grounds and a view of Kaupo Gap combine for a pleasant rest stop. *Note:* The highway continuing toward Hana is very narrow in places and bumpy, the road is okay for passenger cars under dry conditions.

SNORKEL: **Haleki'i Bay**, at Huialoha Church, is among the best snorkeling spots along coast from Kipahulu to La Perouse, which isn't saying too much since most of the coast is totally unsafe. You enter deep water, with lots of rocks poking up just offshore, big enough to be called the **Mokulau Islands**. Net fishermen like this bay, as do scuba divers. *Be Aware*: If you see a big, fat, hairy guy sleeping on one of the few patches of sand, keep away: It's probably a Hawaiian monk seal, an endangered species for which the law prescribes a 100-foot buffer zone. Currents here can be strong.

Outer Islands

Molokai from Maui, leaving Lanai

Father Damien statue, St. Joseph's Church, Molokai

*Molokini snorkeler, Hulopoe Beach Park on Lanai,
Royal Grove on Molokai, Lanai Ferry, chapel at Lodge at Koele*

OUTER ISLANDS
TRAILHEADS
53-55

HIKE: ALL WALKING, FROM SHORT STROLLS TO FULL-FLEDGED DAY HIKES
SNORKEL: BOTH FISH-VIEWING WITH MASK AND FINS, AND PLACES TO SWIM
MM: MILE MARKER, CORRESPONDS TO HIGHWAY SIGNS

Take a vacation within a vacation with a day trip to the three islands that beckon from Maui's western shores. Molokini is a half-day snorkeling experience. Although you could spend an entire vacation, or lifetime for that matter, on Lanai or Molokai, a day on either will seem like a week's getaway.

53. MOLOKINI   SNORKEL

WHAT'S BEST: A marine sanctuary awaits only a few miles off the coast, with waters so clear it seems like flying instead of swimming.

TRANSPORTATION: A number of vessels make the short trip to Molokini. Some of the best are those of the **Maui Dive Shop**, which has some half-dozen stores. They offer trained divers who give hands-on help to beginners, and departures from Lahaina and Ma'alaea. If you're looking for a quick trip to the island, select a company that sails from the **Kihei Boat Ramp**. When making a booking, ask your outfitter about boat size, since some of the larger ones are cattle cars. Also get a reading on the weather, since Molokini's crescent shape opens toward the trade winds, which bring big swells during the winter months. Inquire about cancellation policies. See *Resource Links* page 236 for other recommended snorkel companies.

Molokini Island came to be in dramatic fashion, when newly formed Haleakala needed to let off steam. Molten lava pushed up from below, super-heating porous rock of the earth's crust until the steam trapped within the rock burst in a gigantic, circular explosion. When the dust and ash settled— viola!—it hardened and later eroded from a circle to form a crescent. The fish have come, and Molokini is now one of the world's best spots to snorkel. The island is called a tuft cone, the only one formed in this manner on Maui. Aside from being a **Marine Life Conservation District**, Molokini is also a **seabird sanctuary**, and only our feathered friends are allowed to alight on its 70-foot high ridge.

During the winter, waters usually are calmest inside the crescent during morning hours, and the early birds make the 20-minute trip from Kihei starting at 7 a.m. To enjoy warmer sun, take a later departure. Snorkeling boats have their mooring spots inside the crescent, in waters about 30-feet deep near the shore—with better visibility than the air in some cities.

On peak days, a flotilla of boats will be moored and ≠hundreds of fish lovers will be flopping about, prompting stories about oil slicks caused by sun block and lotions. Regardless, there's plenty of room inside the bowl (the outer edge of Molokini's bowl is submerged). On the convex side of the crescent is a world-famous scuba dive, a wall of several hundred feet. Specialized outfitters take tank divers to this side of the sanctuary.

Molokini

Onboard showers, anchored catamaran, Maui Dive Shop's Captain Rae and Michelle, Kihei Boat Ramp

LANA‘I
TRAILHEAD 54

54. LANAI   HIKE, SNORKEL

WHAT'S BEST: Snorkel with spinner dolphin and walk coastal tide pools. Visit two destination resorts, one on the beach and another high in the pines. Then take a stroll around a sleepy former pineapple town that is Old Hawaii. New Hawaii, however, is coming: In 2012 Oracle software king Larry Ellison purchased 98 percent of the land (the government and a few private parcels comprise the rest) and now owns all the hotels. A windmill electrical plant with 200 towers has been proposed, a project that is a holdover of Lanai's previous owner since 1985, tycoon David H. Murdock. Historically, Lanai is the "Pineapple Island," owned by the Dole family. Local groups, including Friends of Lanai, are working to preserve the way of life on this small island. A day trip to Lanai is a vacation within a vacation. Rent a Jeep, or see it on foot with the aid of a the shuttle bus.

TRANSPORTATION: *By Sea:* **Lanai Expeditions** ferries depart early from Lahaina. (Service from Ma'alea Bay will resume when the state okays permits and facilities are ready.) Call 1-800-695-2624, or 661-3756. Advance booking is required; tickets are about $60, round-trip. *By Land:* A shuttle bus is available at the Lanai harbor and makes stops included in the day trip; tickets are $10. Expeditions can arrange Jeep rentals and guided tours, and Dollar rents Jeeps in Lanai City (you have to buy a ticket on the shuttle bus anyway). First-time visitors will be happy with the shuttle bus tour. Repeat visitors may want to rent a car, but the experience may not justify the expense. Advice for Jeep drivers follows the day-trip schedule. Either way, you'll want to take a knapsack with spare food, water, and personal items. If you plan to snorkel, bring your gear.

PARKING: *Lahaina:* Turn toward the ocean off Hwy. 30, on Shaw St., and park at the lot at the corner of Front Street, or continue on Front to Prison St. Parking fees may be charged.

SCHEDULE FOR A DAY TRIP TO LANAI

SAIL THE LANAI EXPEDITION FERRY: 6:45 A.M., LAHAINA HARBOR. The ride takes 45 to 60 minutes. During winter and spring, the cruise doubles as a whale-watching adventure, as the big mammals frolic in **Auau Channel**. You'll enjoy sunrise during the trip. *Note:* Check for current ferry schedules.

LEAVE FERRY DOCK AT MANELE BAY, LANAI, 7:45 A.M. As you look at **Lanai** from Maui, the **Manele Bay** harbor is to the left, just out of sight. The ferry rounds the cliff and pulls into a small marina with a dock just big enough to make the landing. New restrooms, walkways, and covered waiting area have spritzed the place up. Board the shuttle bus to the **Four Seasons Resort at Manele**, where you buy tickets, $10 per day. (You can walk the .25-mile to **Hulopoe Bay**; go up the road and take your first left. You'll reach the lawn of the beach park and see the resort up to the right.)

VISIT FOUR SEASONS MANELE. The resort, whose tiled roofs are slung low over Hulopoe Bay, manages to be grand without being ostentatious. It consistently ranks at the top of tropical travelers' best-places lists among all the world's destinations—six-foot vases, hardwood finish work, floral upholstery, museum quality paintings, and chandeliers the size of playsets hanging in front of towering windows that frame the bay. (Check the shuttle bus schedule before leaving the resort.)

WALK TO HULOPOE BAY BEACH PARK, TIDAL POOLS, SHARK COVE, 8:15 A.M. TO 9:30 A.M. Walk past the resort pool on a path to **Hulopoe Beach Park**. Encircling the park's lawn are tables and campsites, interspersed among ironwoods and palm trees—offering some of Hawaii's best beach camping; call the Four Seasons Manele or Maui County Parks for details. **To walk to the tide pools**, go left (facing the ocean) at the beach and pick up a trail. In a few minutes, you'll see stairs leading down to a long shelf of pools that extend seaward to the point. These aquariums of nature, at low tide, will let you look in on marine life. **Shark Cove** is beyond the stairs and to the left, a sandy nook rimmed by 12-foot high, red cliffs. The cliffs slope up as you encircle Shark Cove, rising to the 200-foot high head that separates Manele and Hulopoe bays. From the top you're above **Pu'upehe Cove** and **Sweetheart Rock**, a.k.a. **Pu'upehe**, the lava stack that is just offshore. Legend tells of poor Pehe, who drowned while hiding in a cave below, and was taken to the top and laid to rest by her distraught lover, Makakehau. This tale dates from around 900 AD.

SNORKEL HULOPOE BAY, 9:30 A.M. TO 10:30 A.M. The spinner dolphin often congregate a few hundred feet offshore at the end of the beach that is closest to the hotel. A stream also enters the bay here, so waters can get murky after heavy rains. Attendants at the beach's snorkel shack can give you a dolphin report. Be sure to view the dolphins passively, letting them come to you, rather than pursuing. At the other end of the beach, snorkeling is also good offshore from the tide pools, perhaps better, although the dolphins aren't as frequent. Since 1976, when the marine conservation district was established, it's been against the rules to feed the fish when snorkeling.

Four Seasons Manele

CATCH SHUTTLE BUS TO LANAI CITY, MIDMORNING. Make sure you get on the right bus at the Four Seasons; others go to the golf course and airport. The 8-mile ride to **Lanai City** takes about 15 minutes, climbing 1,700 feet from the bay— halfway to Lanai's highest elevation—and crossing arid grasslands.

STROLL LANAI CITY AND HOTEL LANAI AND HAVE LUNCH, NOON TO EARLY AFTERNOON. **Hotel Lanai**, built during the pineapple heyday of 1923, has a mountain-cabin feel, a single-story wood-frame under the shade of Norfolk pines. Ellison purchased the hotel in 2014, so things may change. The hotel's rotisserie dining room draws visitors from the island's chi-chi hotels, and it's open for lunch. Uphill from the hotel is a golf course with pleasant walking paths.

Across the street is **Dole Park**, a several-acre lawn planted with Lanai City's trademark Norfolk pines (the ones with curly boughs are the less-common Cook Pine). The town shops, along with quiet residential area, encircle the park. The best thing is to walk the perimeter, wandering to quiet back streets, which are laid out in a grid, as you may be directed by your fancy and the town's humorous signs. You can't get more folksy than **Lanai City**. Try the **Blue Ginger Café**, for its pizza and burgers or **Canoe's** for a hearty all-day menu. Across Dole Park, on 8th Street, **Richards Shopping Center** has been selling groceries and gifts since 1946. Another old-fashioned general store, the **International Food and Clothing Center**, is down 8th Street—behind the **Pine Isle Market**. Next door to the market is **Pele's Garden**, a health food store and juice bar.

Shark Cove, Hotel Lanai, Lanai City

Hulopoe Beach Park, Koele Lodge

Schools and churches are at the opposite end of Dole Park from Hotel Lanai; you get a seaward view from behind them. Many of Lanai City's 2,800 residents have been living in these quiet cottages for 50 years, and to talk to them is a living history lesson.

CATCH BUS AT HOTEL LANAI AND VISIT THE FOUR SEASONS LODGE AT KOELE, 2 P.M. TO 3:30 P.M. The lodge is about .5-mile from Hotel Lanai, walking distance if the bus schedule doesn't cooperate with yours. Head up Lanai Avenue, pass 3rd Street, and go right where it becomes Keomuku Highway. This place is hard to anticipate. Stately Norfolks line the entrance of the **Four Seasons Lodge at Koele**, which resides on green slopes like a colonial plantation manor, a ridge of native forest rising above it. It does not evoke Hawaii to the uninitiated, but this site was the center for the **Lanai Ranch** cattle operations from 1874 to 1951. Inside the elegant 102-room hotel—which is of recent construction—are two-story fireplaces and truss beams.

Behind the lodge is a **40-acre arboretum**, most of it a rolling lawn with large pond, several gazebos, and a **glass conservatory** full of blossoming orchids. Royal palms, towering kukuis, African tulips, and a number of other trees and flowering shrubbery line a path that encircles the grounds. A few structures remain from the ranching days.

CATCH SHUTTLE BUS TO MANELE BAY FOR RETURN FERRY If you have time and energy, you can walk out to the right of the harbor's breakwater, toward **Pail Leino Haunui**, and to watch for the white ship to round the point. The timing is right for a sunset cruise into into Maui, a wondrous sight as you approach from the sea. (Unless the schedule has change, a Lahaina-bound ferries departs at 4:30 and 6:45.)

JEEP TOURS: Rental from Dollar is pricey, about $150 to $180 a day. First-time visitor will be better off relying on the shuttle. If you rent a Jeep, you'll want to take the dirt road north through the **Garden of the Gods** to **Polihua Beach**. (Turn left just north of Koele Lodge, between the stables and tennis courts.) After five rutted miles, you'll pass the dryland forests of the **Kanepu'u Nature Preserve**, with strolling choices for bird-watchers. Soon after comes the mile-long rise of red-dirt strewn with boulders, the Garden of the Gods, a pretty sight though it doesn't quite measure up to its name. The real treat comes after the road snakes down steeply over 4 miles to reach Polihua Beach. Backed by kiawe forest, the deep and two-mile-long run of sand faces open sea—a real out-there experience.

Polihua Beach, Garden of the Gods

Shipwreck Beach is another highlight for Jeepsters. Going north from Koele Lodge, Keomuku Road, or Highway 430, swerves northeast and down about 7 miles to the beaches on the east shore. Go left at the bottom (the road right, often very muddy, passes the spread-out, ramshackle structures of Keomuku Village).

The Shipwreck road becomes sandy, so you may want to walk the last bit. Offshore to the west is the steel-skeleton hull of a liberty ship that the Navy tried to sink after World War II. Across the channel is a big look at Molokai. You can walk your brains out on Shipwreck; to the left is beach-and-bluff route of several miles that reaches Polihau Beach.

Shipwreck Beach, Keomuku Road

The premier hike/drive/bike on Lanai is the **Munro Trail**, which follows the 3,700-foot ridgeline from above the Lodge at Koele. At mm1 north of the lodge, turn right toward the cemetery. After .25-mile you'll reach the trailhead, which is passable via Jeep in only the driest of weather and chancey at that. Better to get out of the wheels and walk, or rent a bike in Lanai City. Mountain biking is a growth industry on Lanai. In addtion to the Munro Trail, three trails take off north from the road to Garden of the Gods: **Kuamoʻo**, **Kahue**, and **Lapaiki**. The best track forks left after the garden, the **Kaena Trail**, which drops to the northwest and then forks several times on a rugged route down to the coast. Be prepared if trying this adventure.

Hulopoe Beach, Lanai City

MOLOKA'I
TRAILHEAD 55

Molokai southeast coast

55. MOLOKAI HIKE, SNORKEL, DRIVING TOURS

WHAT'S BEST: To know what Maui was like in 1950, take a trip to Molokai tomorrow—quiet towns, serrated green ridges, ancient fishponds, open pastures, and expansive white sand beaches. Select from one of three driving tours, or stay overnight to do them all.

TRANSPORTATION: *By Boat passage:* Charter boats visit Molokai (page 236), but your best bet may be **Lahaina Cruise Company (Hawaii Ocean Project)**, which operates a daily schedule: *depart Lahaina,* 7:15 a.m.(except Sundays) and 6 p.m.; *depart Molokai* 5:15 a.m. (except Sunday) and 4 p.m. Round-trip adult tickets are about $150. Call or click to confirm their schedule and prices. Boat travel, compared to flying, is a value, since a sightseeing sea-cruise and whale-watch (winter and spring) are part of the deal. *By Air*: Hawaiian and Mokulele airlines make the short hop from Maui to Hoʻolehua Airport; round-trip tickets will be $150 to $250. *Helicopter:* Blue Hawaiian has a day-trip to take it all in from on high, see *Resource Links* page 235..

PARKING AT LAHAINA: On the south end of town, turn toward the ocean off Hwy. 30, on Shaw St., and park at the lot at the corner of Shaw and Front streets. You'll have to walk a few blocks, but this free lot should have no time restrictions.

CAR RENTAL ON MOLOKAI: You'll want your own wheels or a tour taxi to see Molokai. See *Resource Links,* page 231, for car rentals. Lahaina cruise also offers car rental and day-tour options. If you are taking the ferry, be sure to discuss transportation to and from the airport to pick up your rental car and drop it off. See if your car can be made available at the ferry dock in Kaunakakai.

One Aliʻi Beach Park

The airport is a 15-minute drive from the harbor. **Island Kine Rentals** is located near the harbor in Kaunakakai, and they have a shuttle bus that makes the short drive to their office. Their cars may not be road-weary, but the price is right and they are a local-style business, operating out of a home, with a dog likely to be sleeping on the sofa while auntie is in the corner watching TV. If you use Island Kine, or any of the other rental agencies (see *Resource Links*, page 231), try to get the paperwork done over the phone when you make reservations to expedite things on the day of arrival.

Three Molokai Driving Tours

All three tours assume a morning ferry passage with a return trip that same afternoon, making you feel like you've watched an epic movie on fast forward. Of course, you can stay overnight which will allow time to do it all. *Notes:* All tours include a visit to the Kalaupapa Overlook of Father Damien's leper colony, and a walk through Kaunakakai Town. All tours assume a ferry departure back to Maui at 4 p.m. Check for most recent ferry schedule. Pack snacks and a few bottles of water.

East Molokai Tour, page 192: Begins with mountainous side of the island that has green escarpments, ancient fishponds and heiaus, and churches. Continues to road's end at the rain forest of Halawa Valley and Moaula Falls. Ends with Kalaupapa Overlook and Kaunakakai Town.

West Molokai Tour, page 195: Begins with Kalaupapa Overlook, and then continues on the arid west slopes to a coffee plantation, cowboy country, and the long white-sand beaches on the far coast. Ends with Kaunakakai Town.

All-Island Tour, page 192: Includes all of the above, with the exception of certain portions that will be noted in the tour descriptions. Excludes Halawa Valley. This is a scouting tour for visitors who might be considering spending an entire vacation on Molokai. You might be the only people in a hurry on the island if embarking on this whirlwind.

For all tours: Board Lahaina Cruise Co. Ferry, Lahaina Harbor 7:15 a.m. You'll catch sunrise in the **Pailolo Channel**, which can be choppy when the trade winds are up, but the ride is usually bumpier on the return voyage. The open top deck of the ferry, which doubles as a whale-watching cruiser, allows for an experiential voyage. Waters get calmer about two-thirds of the way on the 100-minute journey, when the ferry gets in the lee of Molokai.

Kaunakakai Wharf is midway on the southern coast of Molokai, which is about 38 miles long. Molokai is really two former islands that are joined now by an isthmus. The mountainous, green side is the higher, with **Kamakou Peak** rising to 4,961 feet, while the red-dirt and grasslands of the west reach an elevation of less than 1,400 feet. Fewer than 7,000 people live on Molokai, most of them in Kaunakakai.

St Joseph's Church, Ualapue Fishpond, Kamakou ridges

BEGIN EAST MOLOKAI AND ALL-ISLAND TOURS, KAUNAKAKAI, 9 A.M. (FOR WEST MOLOKAI TOUR, SKIP TO "BEGIN WEST MOLOKAI" PAGE 195.)

Head east out of town on Highway 450, the **Kamehameha V Highway**. A 28-mile barrier coral reef, one of the longest outside of Australia's, extends offshore along the highway. Although shallow waters limit snorkeling opportunities, the reef provided ideal conditions for a series of fishponds that were constructed by the first Polynesian voyagers. The **Kalokoeli Pond** is offshore the beach cottages, before mm2. Just after mm3 are the **One Ali'i Beach Parks**, two of them, pleasantly decorated with coco palms and fronted by three fish ponds along a mile of coast—Ali'i, Kaoini, and Kanoa. Look for semi-circles of stone that extend into the water.

At mm5, the green relief rises inland, near **Kawela**. In the late 1700s, this is where Kamehameha the Great's seaborne warriors conquered Molokai on the way to his final battle for Oahu. Near mm6, look inland to the east, as **Kamakou**, the tallest peak in the island, comes into view. Look also on the right, amid big kiawe trees and coco palms, for **Kakahaia Beach Park**, which is a National Wildlife Refuge that includes fishpond ruins. Over the next several miles, the straight highway hugs the coast, passing five more ancient fishponds. *More Stuff:* To hike the 2,700-acre **Kamakou Preserve**, contact The Nature Conservancy on Molokai; see page 237.

At mm10, as you enter a reduced speed zone and the highway curves left inland, turn right at spur road to visit **Kamalo Harbor**—you'll see the water from the road. The old wharf here symbolizes several centuries of inter-island commerce, since this was the best natural harbor on the coast. In recent times, the barrier reef was excavated to construct the wharf at Kaunakakai. After making the turns through the Kamalo settlement, you'll come to **St. Joseph's Church**, which was built by **Father Damien de Veuster** in 1876—the Catholic priest had arrived three years earlier from Maui. A statue of the priest and a small cemetery grace the grounds.

The highway swerves inland for the next several miles, as you pass several intriguing roads that lead toward the east ridge of Kamakou. At mm14 are the portrait quality grounds of **Our Lady of Seven Sorrows Church**, Father Damien's first effort, dating from 1874. Across the street is **Ulapu'e Fish Pond**, on the National Register of Historic Places. The next mile or two is the site of one of the larger settlements of ancient Molokai. Past the bridge at mm15, look for a sign and gate noting the **Ili'iliopae Heiau**, more than 30,000 square feet, that lies inland less than .5-mile on a trail that transects the island.

Windsurfing off Pauwalu, Wailalua Pavilion, Malo'o

By mm17, as the road nears the shore, you'll see breakers that note the waning of the barrier reef. West Maui lies a few miles across the channel. Pockets of sandy beach appear past mm18, and the jagged ridges inland give way to open green slopes, with a pleasing assortment of trees. At mm20 you get to east Molokai's best beach, **Murphy Beach Park**, a.k.a. **20-Mile Beach**, an opportunity to snorkel or take a dip. The park's fishpond and swerving strip of palmy sand are a prime beach walk, with views of Maui and the tiny seabird sanctuary island offshore to the north—**Kanaha Rock** and Moku Hoʻoniki. Camping is available at the **Waialua Pavilion**, where Kamehameha V spent his formative years.

NOTE: ROAD NARROWS AFTER MM20. FOR ALL-ISLAND TOUR, TURN AROUND AND MAKE THE 40-MINUTE DRIVE BACK TO KAUNAKAKAI. TO CONTINUE ALL-ISLAND TEXT, SKIP TO "BEGIN WEST MOLOKAI TOUR" PARAGRAPH, PAGE 195.

EAST MOLOKAI TOUR CONTINUED. Sleepy Molokai becomes more so, as Highway 450 narrows after Murphy's Beach. Some areas are definite one-laners. You'll curve inland and climb to a viewpoint at **Puhakuloa Point**, below which the tiers of waves attract local surfers by the six-pack. This is known locally as **Tooth Rock**, or Rocky Point. The highway leaves the coast, at **Sandy Beach**, and climbs into the grassy hills and ironwood forests near mm22.

You'll navigate the toe of east Molokai, reaching an elevation of about 600 feet through the lands of **Puʻu o Hoku Ranch**. You want horse pics, you got 'em. You'll pass ranch headquarters and a road on the right to **Kalanikaula Sacred Kukui Grove**, named for Molokai's famous kahuna. Then, near mm26, where the road hairpins left, is a fabulous overlook of **Halawa Valley** and Bay. Inland to the left is 500-foot **Hipuapua Falls** and the top part of 250-foot cascade of **Moaula Falls**. To the north and west is Molokai's roadless north shore, where sea cliffs reach 3,000 feet.

The parklike road then makes a symphonic descent to the **Halawa Beach Park**, which features two, small sandy beaches, one on either side of the stream—straight at road's end. Snorkeling, body surfing, and board surfing are possibilities. A trail leads inland to both falls, which descend from forks of the stream. This valley was one of Hawaii's earliest settlements, dating from as early as 600 AD, and many archeological sites are yet to be discovered. Two tidal waves in the mid-1900s did damage, to both ruins and plant life. TURN AROUND AND DRIVE BACK TO KAUNAKAKAI. SEE NEXT PARAGRAPH TO CONTINUE TOUR.

BEGIN WEST MOLOKAI TOUR (AND TO CONTINUE ALL-ISLAND AND EAST MOLOKAI TOUR) GO WEST FROM KAUNAKAKAI ON HIGHWAY 460, THE MAUNALOA HIGHWAY.

Kalaupapa Peninsula

Just past mm1 is **Kioea Beach Park**, which has no beach to speak of but is notable for its **Kapuaiwa Royal Coconut Grove**, planted for Kamehameha V in the 1860s. It's the only accessible royal grove remaining in Hawaii. Heads up for falling coconuts if walking beneath the trees.

After mm4 turn right on Highway 470, the Kalae Highway. The road sweeps over the isthmus, greening up with Norfolk pines, ironwoods, and koa trees. Just before mm4, on the left by a golf course, is the **Molokai Museum &Cultural Center**, alongside the Meyer Sugar Mill site. This place gets high marks. Near mm5 you'll reach the north side of the island, where, just past the **Molokai Stables**, the **Kukuiohapu'u Trail** switchbacks down to the **Kalaupapa Peninsula**, a National Historical Park. This is the site of the leper colony overseen by Father Damien in the late 1800s. *More Stuff:* The 3-mile, 1,600-foot hike down is by permit only. Put this on your bucket list, and call Damien Tours or Molokai Stables.

After the trailhead, the road enters 34-acre **Pala'au State Park**, passing a picnic pavilion and campground, and comes to a dead end. A short trail to the right of the parking area leads through cypress and eucalyptus about .25-mile to the **Kalaupapa Lookout**. The squat peninsula far below was formed by a relatively recent wave of lava that created a 2.5-mile nub pointing due north. On the tip you'll see the lighthouse, built in 1909. The Kauhako Crater near the base of the peninsula is now a lake. After absorbing the view, head back to the parking lot and, if you have time, go left on another .25-mile trail that leads to **Phallic Rock**. Few will be able to resist the hike, although those expecting a towering monolith will be disappointed. Partially sculpted by human hands, the rock is an ancient Hawaiian fertility symbol that even today is the locale for the occasional tete-a-tete.

For East Molokai Tour, skip to "Return to Kaunakakai" paragraph, page 198, and drive there. Continue West Molokai and All-Island tours below.

Backtrack on Highway 470 and, after the golf course, turn right on Highway 480, which is Farrington Avenue.

Note: Both tours from here are similar, but All-Island Tour people need to manage time, bearing in mind it takes about 30 minutes to drive back to the harbor from west shore beaches. The West Molokai Tour people can take more time at each stop. At the Farrington junction are the coffee plantation groves, where **Coffees of Hawaii** offers complimentary pick-me-ups, as well as wagon tours. Coffee has supplanted cane as a cash crop. **The Cook House**, housed in an old sugar shack, is a plate-lunch dream.

Continue on Highway 480. Pass mm2, and turn left as Highway 480 becomes Pu'upe'elua Avenue. Then turn right, heading west at Highway 460. You'll pass the small airport and head out on a red-dirt straightaway. Just before mm13, you'll be able to see **Oahu** to the northwest, alight on the sea.

At mm15, turn right on Kaluakoi Road, toward the resort. You'll descend on a grassland road, sparsely lined with ironwoods. After 3 miles, turn right

Kepuhi Beach, Papohaku Beach and Park

toward the **Kaluakoi Villas**, and follow the resort's road to its end, near the gift shop. A path leads from the modest, but tasteful condo complex to **Kepuhi Beach**, which has grass terraces shaded by coco palms and sandy patches interrupted by black-rock reefs—places for good snorkeling. A path leads to the right, past a lava point, to the north end of the beach that is favored by surfers. To the left, a road and path skirts a golf course site, past Pu'u o Kaiaka, to Papohaku Beach Park; see next paragraph for driving instructions. Coast hikers will have room to roam both north and south.

BACKTRACK FROM THE RESORT AND TURN RIGHT ON KALUAKOI ROAD. CONTINUE FOR 1 MILE AND TURN RIGHT INTO PAPOHAKU BEACH PARK. **Papohaku Beach Park** is a beach camper's fantasy. Large native trees and coco palms decorate its sprawling lawn, which opens up to the beach—some 3 miles of open sand, the longest in Maui County. Snorkeling and bodysurfing features are included. *More Stuff:* The road continues for several more miles, passing a short trail to Po'olau Beach on the way. At road's end are several miles of road and trail, fronted by a half-dozen beaches, that end at Molokai's southwest tip.

FOR ALL-ISLAND TOUR, DRIVE BACK TO KAUNAKAKAI; SKIP TO "RETURN TO KAUNAKAKAI" PAGE 198. FOR WEST MOLOKAI TOUR, CONTINUE BELOW.

Kaunakakai

Backtrack on Kaluakoi Road—watch out for deer—and turn right at the top of the grade toward **Maunaloa**. West Molokai's only town, once a camp for pineapple workers, is less than two miles away. Its lazy asphalt track is stained red and and bordered by Norfolk pines and native Hawaiian trees. It was once the home of Molokai Ranch which allowed visitors the opportunity to experience authentic ranch life. The ranch ceased all operations in 2008.

Wind is frequent in Maunaloa, and near the **Big Wind Kite Factory & Plantation Gallery**, you'll often see colorful creations dancing in the sky. Maunaloa in ancient times is thought to be the birthplace of hula, the most Hawaiian of dances that enacts history and legend. *More Stuff:* The road continues down to the coast—you can see breakers from town—to **Hale o Lono Harbor**, which is the start of the yearly outrigger race to Maui. Other dirt roads fan out over southwest Molokai.

Return to Kaunakakai – All tours

Save time for a stroll around **Kaunakakai**. The grocery, mercantile, and gift shops along the main street, Ala Malama Avenue, are a throwback to a simpler time. These are not tourist shops. Then stroll out toward **Kaunakakai Wharf**. Before reaching the water, you'll pass the gardens at **Malama Cultural Park**. At the water is **Wharf Beach**, not a great swimming area, but in the afternoon you might see one of the local canoe clubs putting in.

At the end of the wharf, opposite the ferry docking area, is a cruising sailboat harbor. Take a look back at Molokai and get a mental imprint to take away with you. Your memory of the place will have a way of catching up to the experience a day or two (or a year or two) after your ship has returned to Lahaina.

Kaunakakai Harbor

Free Advice & Opinion

DISCLAIMER

Think of this book as you would any other piece of outdoor gear. It will help you do what you want to do, but its depends upon you to supply responsible judgment and common sense. The publisher and authors are not responsible for injury, damage, or legal violations that may occur when someone is using this guidebook. Please contact public agencies to familiarize yourself with the most current rules and regulations. Posted signs and changes in trail status determined by public agencies supersede any recommendations in this book. Be careful, have fun.

HIKING

Never walk downhill with your hands in your pockets … A cell phone is safety insurance on remote trails … You see fewer cell phones in Maui because people here see their friends in person … Stay out of stream valleys in the rain … If stranded by a flooding stream, sit and wait it out before crossing … Don't cross if water is above your crotch … Flash-flood threat is greatest on the northeast coast and Hana Highway … You often can hear a rumbling flood coming, along with the smell of fresh earth … If the stream rises a little, get to high ground … Backtrack when you get lost … Never try to walk cross-country in Hawaii … Watch your watch: Note when you leave the car, and allow time for your return before sunset, plus an hour insurance time … Ancient roads don't contour, they undulate … Always bring water … Wear bright clothes, other than green colored … Parents: never take your eyes off the kids …

Hunter's are out on weekends and holidays … All beaches are public places to the high-tide line … If you're feet are burning on the surface of hot sand, dig down a few inches … On woodland trails, don't take your eyes off the ground for more than two steps … If you hike in Maui, you will slip … Hiking poles are a third leg … Lawyers' Paradox: Paths with the least amount of danger have the most warning signs … And vice versa … In sunny conditions, try to hike before 10 a.m. and after 2 p.m. … Never climb or walk under cliffs and outcroppings; Hawaiian rocks are unstable … Going down steep hills, you want to fall on your butt, not forward … Wild pigs of 200-pounds or more have right-of-way on trails …

Do not remove or disturb rocks at a heiau or other archeological site; these places are still being discovered and preserved ... Same goes for plants; Hawaii is home to the largest reserves of endangered species ... Hike with a buddy ... Stay on trails ... If you get caught out at night, sit down and wait for morning; don't hike at night ... Always hike with a prepared knapsack; see *Calabash* ... Carry water on all hikes, and drink when you're not thirsty ... Haleakala is high; plan to be short of breath and adjust your pace for the altitude ... Bring warm clothing ... Both hypothermia and heat exhaustion are possible during the same day on Haleakala ...

Never turn your back on the ocean at tide pools and beach walks ... You need a permit to camp on beaches, or anywhere else, on Maui ... Erosion is a big problem here; don't cut switchbacks on trails ... If you must hike alone, always let someone know where you're going ... Assess how long a hike will take before you leave; see *How to Use This Book* ... Forests on Maui are too deep to walk through ... Edges of cliffs might appear solid, when they are only a mat of grasses ... In groups, don't lose sight of the person behind you ... Stay calm if lost or in trouble.

KAYAKING

Kayaking is the easiest way to snorkel the Kinau preserve ... Kayaks with no rudders or freeboards are no good in the wind ... Always call and get weather and marine reports ... Ask local outfitters for trip advice ... File this under unnecessary advice: stay at least 100 yards from a whale ... Wind shifts and sudden choppy water can mean a storm is brewing ... Keep your center of gravity low ... Lash your paddle to the boat ... Wear a life jacket ... Don't go out alone ... Maintain your balance: a canoe or kayak won't tip by itself ... Make your outbound voyage into the wind, to have the wind with you on the return ... Sunscreen your neck ... Don't trap sea turtles between boats.

SNORKELING

Rubber booties help with rocky entries ... Swim fins are not made for walking forward, except by professional clowns ... To enter the water, back in; or, put on your mask, dive in, and put on the flippers while you're bobbing around ... Most snorkeling tours take you to places you can get to from shore ... Most fish will be around the rocky points between sandy coves ... Or in coral beds ... Walking on coral reef crushes living things ... Only monk seals are allowed to be naked on Hawaiian beaches ... Lifeguards generally will place hazard signs on beaches, but don't rely on it ... Wave action means more rip currents and danger from shore breaks ... Stay away from wave action in rocky areas ... Check depth of the water first before diving ...

Don't touch a Portuguese man-of-war, a jellyfish with tentacles ... MSG helps on man-of-war stings ...To test for rip current, lie face-down in the water and observe if you are being carried away ... If caught in a rip current, don't swim against it ... Swim perpendicular to the current to break free ... Lifeguards will be at most county beaches, but not at state beaches ... Always swim with a buddy ... Good surfing conditions are poor snorkeling conditions ... Some people say snorkeling waters are clearest in the morning ... Don't feed the fish; it disturbs the ecological balance of the reef ... Presence of other swimmers does not mean conditions are safe ... Avoid a sunburn by wearing a T-shirt or rash guard ...

Calm water means safer swimming ... But watch for boat traffic ... Touching a finger to the top of your head is a diver's sign to say you're OK ... Incoming waves mean water needs to go back out to sea through a channels; channels can be observed as blue underwater canals, or choppy places where the waves aren't breaking ... Sticking your finger or hand in a hole in the reef is a bad idea ... Shark attacks are rare, but to make them even more rare, stay out of murky waters near streams, and don't swim at dusk or before dawn ... Don't touch sea turtles ... Sea urchins will sting if you touch them ... Watch the water for several minutes before entering to assess possible hazards ... Try to enter at sandy areas ... If in doubt, don't go out.

HEALTH

Haole Rot, or sun-splotched skin, is cured by Selsun Blue shampoo ... Pump or treat stream water before drinking ... Green coconuts are full of water; smash the stem end on a rock ... Coconut water helps ailing kidneys . . . Wind evaporates sweat; don't forget to drink water when hiking in breezes ... Beware of the white ooze when handling just-picked mangoes; it will burn your skin ... Accidents happen; tragedies happen when you're not prepared for accidents ...

Tropical sun is fierce; use waterproof sunscreen with SPF 15 or higher, containing zinc oxide and Parsol 1789 ... Wear a wide-brim hat ... Avoid streams and ponds when you have cuts or abrasions ... Treat even small cuts with antibiotics ... Leptospirosis, a bacteria in fresh water, causes flu-like symptoms ... Dengue fever is, in rare cases, carried by mosquitoes; use repellent in jungle environments ... Don't eat strange plants or fruits; some are poisonous ... Drinking water helps prevent heat exhaustion ... So does wearing loose-fitting clothes ... Provide shade and elevate the feet if someone collapses ... 1 to 2 liters per person per day, drink it for health and as a liquid safety precaution.

SURFING

Rules one through ten: beginners should hire an instructor ... Outfitters and instructors will happily give advice to novices ... Biggest summer surf: West shore beaches; Biggest Winter surf: east shore beaches ... Eddie would go ... Check *Best of* for beginners' beaches ... See *Resource Links* for instructors ... More waves to surf means Hawaiian surfers are less surly about wave space ... Hawaiians invented surfing; this is the place to learn ... A reasonably good athlete can stand up in one day with a long board on small waves.

DRIVING

Preventing road rage, local-style: park for a while and watch the sea ... Pull over for local traffic on the Hana Highway ... Aloha driving: go the speed limit and don't tailgate ... Broken glass at a parking spot is a sign of break ins ... Save your driving tours for weekdays ... Be in Paia by dawn to avoid the Hana Highway traffic ... Or leave later, and explore to Nahiku ... One rental car parked attracts others on scenic highways ... Driving in Maui traffic is okay, but getting across traffic is hard ... Always turn right ... See the *Driving Tour* at the start of each trailhead section for specifics of road conditions ...

Take valuables with you when leaving your car ... Check your insurance coverage (including that with your credit card) before leaving home ... Hang bead leis from your rearview mirror to make your car appear more local ... Vandals are only supposed to break into tourist cars ... Your rental car company may advise leaving your car unlocked ... Bring a package of baby wipes to freshen up after a hike or after eating a papaya while driving ... Four-wheel drive doesn't help with Maui's biggest hazard on remote roads: they are narrow ... Drive safely ... Drive Aloha.

Maui Calabash

LITERALLY, A CALABASH IS A GOURD USED AS A WATER VESSEL. IN HAWAII, THE CALABASH IS A GROUP OF FRIENDS, LIKE FAMILY, THOUGH NOT BLOOD RELATED.

TIMELINE

1,750,000 BC: West Maui volcano breaks the surface.

900,000 BC: Haleakala sees daylight.

200: First Polynesians voyage to Hawaii from the Marquesas.

800: Second wave of Polynesians, from Tahiti; round-trip migrations.

1300: Round-trip migrations cease; Hawaiians alone in the islands.

1500-EARLY 1600S: Reign of King Pi'ilanai and his heirs. Major heiaus and the road around Maui (alaloa) constructed.

1736: End of reign of King Kekaulike.

1765: Beginning of reign of King Kahekili.

1776: Kahekili defeats invaders from Big Island at Battle of the Sand Hills.

1777: Queen Ka'ahumanu is born—Kamehameha's favorite wife and enlightened leader.

1778: British Captain James Cook sights Maui's windward coast, but doesn't land.

1787: French Captain Jean Francois La Perouse becomes the first known Westerner to set foot on Maui, at Makena. Calls it "dismal coast."

1790: Most recent lava flow on Maui, at Cape Kinau (although new charcoal dating suggests the eruption was 300 to 500 years ago). Native population of Hawaii 300,000. Kamehameha the Great defeats Maui's King Kahekili at Iao Valley. American ship *Eleanor*, under Captain Simon Metcalf, slaughters 100 Hawaiians in Olowalu Massacre.

1802: Kamehameha I declares Lahaina capital of Hawaiian kingdom.

1810: Hawaiian Islands united under single rule of Kamehameha the Great, after Kauai capitulates without a battle.

1819: Kamehameha the Great dies. Queen Ka'ahumanu topples old religion of sacrifices and kapus. First whaling ship arrives in Lahaina from Massachusetts.

1823: First New England missionaries arrive, Reverend Richards.

1824: Queen Ka'ahumanu bases code of laws on Ten Commandments. Kamehameha II dies while visiting England.

1825: Conflicts between lawless whalers and missionaries, who have support of the queen, as well as Kamehameha's heirs to the throne.

1826: Mexican ship brings mosquitoes to Maui.

1828: First sugar mill.

1831: Lahainaluna High School, the first west of the Great Divide, is established.

1832: Queen Kaʻahumanu dies.
1835: Missionary Dwight Baldwin arrives.
1842: Some 40 whaling ships visit Lahaina.
1852: Prison erected in Lahaina.
1860: Visiting whaling ships number 325.
1870: Henry P. Baldwin and Samuel Alexander, sons of missionaries, buy their first 12 acres to plant sugar. Their heirs become major land owners.
1850: Capital of Hawaii moved from Lahaina to Honolulu.
1852: First Chinese immigrants arrive to work sugar plantations.
1870: Native population of Hawaii 56,000; mortality due to Western diseases.
1885: First Japanese immigrant workers arrive.
1893: United States Marines enter Pearl Harbor, annex Hawaii as a U.S. Territory. James Dole appointed first governor.
1901: Dole organizes Hawaiian Pineapple Company. Buys Lanai in 1922.
1916: Haleakala made part of national park system; becomes park in 1961.
1926: First Hana Highway, for vehicles, completed.
1934: Inter-island air mail begun.
1936: Pan American Airlines crosses the Pacific. Haleakala Visitors Center built.
1941: Japanese attack Pearl Harbor.
1946: Hotel Hana Maui becomes the island's first resort; tidal wave kills 12 at Hana.
1959: Hawaii becomes the 50th state.
1961: Kaʻanapali becomes Hawaii's first master-planned resort.
1969: Kipahulu added to Haleakala National Park.
1970: Maui population 46,000.
1980s: Haleakala designated as International Biosphere Reserve.
1993: Resolution by United States Congress apologizes to Hawaiians for the overthrow of the Hawaiian Kingdom.
1990s: Wal Mart, Home Depot, Costco.
2000: Maui population 135,000.
2002: Hawaiian Nation strive to restore status of Hawaiian Kingdom.
2005: National travel magazine's readers vote Maui's beaches the best in the U.S.
2008: State closes Ahihi-Kinau Natural Area for "two-year study."
2012: Oracle CEO Larry Ellison buys the island of Lanai

Baby Beach, Lahaina

THE WORLD'S VACATION HOT SPOT

Only Hawaii can lay claim to being the world's vacation hot spot. Just offshore the Hawaiian Islands, under water that is two-miles deep, molten lava has been roiling up from the mantle of the earth for nearly 100-million years. Volcanic magma from this unique hot spot piles up and eventually bursts the surface, where, to make a long story short, the magic of rainwater, weather, and evolution transform the lava into tropical islands.

The hot spot remains in the same place. Meanwhile, the earth's crust has been moving northwest, rotating over it like the shell of an egg rotating around its yolk. The rate of movement is about four inches per year. Once at the surface, the lava forms shield volcanoes that rise several miles high, which then move slowly northward on this geologic conveyor belt—only to have wind, waves, and rain slowly erode the peaks and submerge them once again into the sea.

Submerged volcanoes are called seamounts. The Emperor Seamounts that are now some 2,500 miles away off the western tip of Alaska's Aleutian Islands started out at the Hawaiian hot spot. Midway Island, about 1,300 miles distant in the middle of the Pacific, is actually the northwest terminus of the Hawaiian Archipelago, a chain of about 130 islands and sea-washed atolls that comprise the state.

The eight major islands normally associated with Hawaii are the highest mountain range in the world, if measured from their summits to the ocean floor. But they're getting shorter all the time, and they will inevitably be reclaimed by the tides. Kauai, the most-northwesterly among the major islands is several million years older than Maui and, since its birth, has moved about 300 miles and eroded some 5,000 feet in elevation. Maui's Haleakala, still an active volcano, towers 10,000 feet, but was once about 15,000 feet above sea level.

The good news is, new islands continue to emerge. Today, about 20 miles off the southeast coast of the Big Island, magma is boiling into seawater to form the volcano of Loihi, which will one day be the ninth among the primary islands. Time-shares are not yet available.

Volcanoes aren't the only forces of nature that has created Hawaiian real estate. Rising and falling sea levels, caused by waning and waxing ice ages, have created a riddle: What is now four islands, that used to be six islands, that used to be one island? Answer: Maui County. Today, the county consists of Maui, Kahoolawe, Lanai, and Molokai. Way back when, Maui was two islands, West Maui, which is about a million years older than East Maui, or Haleakala. Similarly, Molokai is comprised of two nearby volcanoes of different ages that used to be separated by water. In yet another geologic time, all these islands were combined as one—Maui-nui—when vastly larger polar ice caps resulted in a much lower sea level.

Today, with 728 square miles, Maui is second largest in the major Hawaiian chain—although the Big Island is five times larger. Maui has the most beaches and best swimming among the islands. Its sister islands, less than 10 miles away, provide always changing offshore views. The environs of East and West Maui are vastly different, making a visit like two islands in one. And Haleakala is almost like a third island—a lunar landscape high in the sky. Rain forests, deserts, waterfalls, wildlife ponds, tropical beaches—the list goes on and Maui has it all.

These tumultuous lands of Hawaii have moved about 300 feet north since the prehistoric migration of human beings arrived—the last place on earth to be settled—less than 2,000 years ago. The human race made its way across Asia, then island-hopped down through Indonesia to Fiji, New Zealand, and finally to Tahiti and the other Polynesian islands of the South Pacific. The first Hawaiian voyagers were the legendary Menehunes, the little people, who are thought to have sailed northward some 2,000 miles from the Marquesas. Petroglyphs, irrigation ditches, and fishponds supply archeological evidence to support the mythological origins of these first settlers.

Around 1000 AD, a second wave of Polynesians began to arrive on Hawaiian shores, this one primarily from Tahiti. The second wave is thought to have subjugated the Menehunes, whose numbers were relatively few. Navigating 100-foot long sailing canoes hand-hewn from logs, the Tahitians brought with them most of the plants commonly associated with Hawaii, such as coconut palms, breadfruit, bananas, taro and many others that were to form the cornerstones of their agrarian life.

For several centuries, back-and-forth migrations are thought to have taken place from Tahiti to the nine major Hawaiian Islands, two of which—Maui and Hawaii—were actively spitting lava. The history of these migrations has been preserved over the centuries through hula and chanting. The mythological exploits of gods and demigods, as told in the hula, have their origins is real acts by real people. For instance, the demigod Maui-tikitiki-a-Taranga—from whom the island derives its name—was probably an ancient explorer and warrior. Legends say he captured the sun at Haleakala thereby insuring a longer growing season for the people. This myth may have derived from the man's understanding of the solstice and its relation to crop production.

Around 1300 AD, the migrations from the South Pacific ceased. The Polynesians became Hawaiians, isolated from the rest of the world by several thousands of miles of blue Pacific in all directions—the most-isolated landmass on earth. Effectively, the Hawaiians were as independent as the people of earth are today, alone on a planet in the middle of an ocean of space. This isolation lasted for nearly 500 years, during which time Hawaiian civilization flourished. Learning to live in concert with the abundant land and sea became both religion and science.

Each village was located in an ahupua'a, a triangle-shaped parcel of land that included a seacoast and stream that extended over farmlands and had its origins in the interior woodlands. Expertise in farming, fishing, building, weaving—all crafts—was overseen by a kahuna, who passed knowledge to the next generation. All in nature was preserved and nurtured for future generations.

These several centuries were Hawaii's golden era, as each island prospered independently under ruling chiefs. On Maui during the 1500s, Chief Pi'ilani built huge heiaus and began a roadway system around the island that was furthered through the royal lineage of his sons. On all the islands the ruling chiefs, or ali'i, traced their genealogical heritage to common ancestors, and thus the bloodlines of the ancients, along with their knowledge, was handed from generation to generation.

By the time British Captain James Cook sighted *Mowee* in 1778, the Hawaiian population had grown to an estimated 300,000—and growth pains were evident. During the 100 years prior to Cook's sighting, the islands of Hawaii had been at war. The success of their way of life had brought about population increases that in turn created struggles over finite space and resources. On Maui, Chief Kekaulike and, later, Chief Kahekili, engaged in land and sea battles with the ruling chiefs of the Big Island. The Hana coast of Maui often changed hands between rulers of these two islands.

CALABASH | 211

These skirmishes ended in 1790, when the Big Island's Kamehameha I, defeated the forces of Maui in the Iao Valley. After negotiating a truce with the chief of Kauai, Kamehameha the Great became the first king of Hawaii, ruler of all islands. As smart as he was big and ferocious, he used cannons from a captured American trading vessel to defeat his enemies on Maui once and for all.

Beginning in 1800, new forces converged on Maui, many of them, but not all, for the betterment of the common people. Educational and societal reforms were made by Kamehameha's heirs to the throne, and more significantly by the influence of Queen Ka'ahumanu and Queen Keopuolani. The reforms were aided by the influence of missionaries who arrived during this period, helping to develop the best school system west of the Rockies and a literacy rate superior to the average among Americans at that time.

Also arriving during the 1800s were merchant ships from all points on the compass. British and American ships called in droves, replenishing fresh water and food supplies of trading vessels bound for the Orient. Sandalwood became the island's first export, and forests were denuded. Whaling was huge well into the 1800s, with several hundred lawless vessels dropping anchor in Lahaina during the heyday.

But the real boom came with sugar, as America's sweet tooth was satisfied by Hawaiian cane. Vast tracts of land were altered to become cane fields. Some of the sons of missionary families, like Baldwin and Alexander, went on to become cane growers and rulers of state government.

Since the native population decreased to some 50,000 people, due to diseases brought by Europeans, laborers flocked here from throughout the world. Maui's ethnic diversity—Filipinos, Chinese, Japanese, Portuguese, and many others—is a result of labor demands needed to satisfy the sweet tooth.

Eventually, these business interests developed to the point where the United Sates, in 1898, annexed Hawaii as an U.S. Territory. Statehood came in August of 1959. In spite of its American heritage—forever established by the events of World War II—the islands remain distinctly Polynesian.

An effort to restore Hawaiian sovereignty is alive today, and many schools and organizations foster the language, dance, and way of life that developed over the centuries when this island nation was a world apart. Similarly, efforts are underway to re-establish public access to the majority of land that is now in the hands of a half-dozen corporations—and to safeguard from development Maui's natural beauty that was preserved by the ancients, and today is the basis for the island's tourist industry.

HALEAKALA MISCELLANY

Haleakala's oldest rocks are 910,000 years old ... the oldest island in the Hawaiian Archipelago, Kure Atoll, is 28-million years old ... Historical maps and interviews suggest the last eruption was in 1790; new charcoal dating by volcanologist peg the date at 1450 to 1600; whichever, current seismic rumblings say it's still an active volcano ... The summit is 10,023 feet ... When you make the drive up, you pass through as many biological life zones (seven) as you would on a trip from Mexico to Alaska ... Haleakala used to be about 15,000 feet: erosion ... Measured from the ocean floor, Haleakala is 28,000 feet ...

Haleakala crater is technically not a crater, but an eroded valley, pocked with cinder cones ... The "crater" is 19 square miles ... The National Park is 52 square miles ... That's about one-tenth acre per visitor, if the yearly total all came on the same day ... Rainfall: Summit, 40 inches; Headquarters, 53 inches; Kipahulu, 187 inches ... Maximum wind recorded: 128 m.p.h. in 1990, but the wind indicator broke ... Temperatures: Average, 53 degrees, High, 80 degrees, Low, 11 degrees ... To walk all the trails you need to do 27 miles.

MAUI MAN

If you thought a map of Maui looks like the head and shoulders of a man lifting out of the water, you weren't being silly. Legend says (as recounted in Inez Ashdown's Ke Alaloa O Maui*) that the Goddess Pele agrees with you.*

> "As you study the map of Maui you note that it resembles the head, neck and shoulders of a man. That is how Pele formed the brave land named for the demigod, Maui, whom she loved dearly. His head is West Maui, with Lahaina, Land-of-prophecies, as his mouth and Eke Crater as his ear. Kahakuloa, the Everlasting-master, is his forehead. Ma'alaea is his throat and Kahului is the nape of his neck. His broad shoulders are all of East Maui, with the Haleakala Crater as his heart."

WHALES, SHARKS, DOLPHINS, TURTLES AND OTHER CREATURES

Whales

Dolphins, porpoises, and whales are all cetaceans—83 species of warm-blooded mammals ... Blue whales, at 100 feet, are the largest ... A whale's tongue can weigh as much as an elephant ... Humpbacks range from 40- to 60-feet in length, with females slightly larger, and can tip the scales at more than 80,000 pounds ... The oldest known humpback was 48 ... A swimming whale's tail goes up and down; fish tails go from side to side ... They can motor up to 20 mph, but cruise around 5 mph ... They can dive for about 15 minutes between breaths ... A month-long cruise gets humpbacks from summer feeding areas in Alaska to winter breeding areas in Hawaii and Mexico ... February and March are the best months to whale watch ...

Newborn calves weigh in at 3,000 pounds ... A whale birth has rarely been documented ... Neither has mating ... Gestation is 10 to 12 months ... Hawaiian population before commercial whaling, 1905: 15,000; by 1966: 1,000; Today, after endangered species status of 1970s: 7,000 ... Humpbacks do not have vocal cords, and how they produce their songs is unknown ... Songs are made up of phrases and last 6 to 18 minutes ... Feeding takes place in Alaska; they use reserves to migrate and do not feed in Hawaii ... They wean their calves here.

Sharks

Hawaii has 40 species, ranging from the 8-inch pygmy to the 50-foot whale shark ... Maui has had 3 shark attacks over 12 years, including one fatality ... Cars pose a much greater risk to people than do sharks ... About eight species are seen near shore: reef blacktip, Galapagos, reef whitetip, scalloped hammerhead, blacktip, gray reef, sandbar, and tiger ... Tiger sharks are the biggest, reaching 18 feet, and the most dangerous ... Tigers range from island to island in Hawaii ... Sharks can hear and smell over a distance of 2 miles ... They can also detect prey by sensing electromagnetic fields ... Sharks only bite humans by mistake ... oops ...

To avoid sharks: Swim with a buddy ... Stay out of the water at dawn and dusk, when sharks feed near shore ... Don't bleed in the water, or enter with open cuts ... Stay out of murky water and away from streams ... Don't splash around or wear shiny jewelry ... Stay away from spear fishermen ... And, as if you need this one, do not provoke or harass a shark.

SEA TURTLES

Three species are native to Hawaii: green, hawksbill, and leatherback ... Lifespans are unknown, but they start dating after age 25 ... Turtles are featured in petroglyphs and Hawaiian mythology ... Green turtles are the most common; vegetarians, weighing 200 pounds, they migrate hundreds of miles every several years to mate and nest in the French Frigate Shoals, which are in the northwestern part of the Hawaiian Archipelago ... Hawksbills are endangered, with perhaps only 50 adult females left in Hawaii; one of the few nesting grounds is Maʻalaea Bay ... Directed by starlight and moonlight, hawksbills nest on beaches; efforts are underway to modify coastal electrical lighting that has confused them, causing deaths ... Leatherbacks can be 8-feet long and weigh up to a ton; you'll find them in deep offshore waters feeding on jellyfish.

HAWAIIAN SPINNER DOLPHIN

Spinners swim close to shore during the day ... No one knows for sure why they corkscrew when leaping from the water ... They go out at night to deeper water to feed on squid and small fish ... Their diurnal migrations are opposite those of sharks, their main predator ... Life-span is around 20 years ... Gestation period is 10 to 12 months ... Calves stay with their mothers for 7 months after birth ... Mothers give birth every 2 or 3 years ... Marine debris and boats, along with shoreline development, pose the greatest threat to the spinners ... Other dolphins is Hawaiian waters include, bottlenose and spotted ... Some of the best places to see spinners are Lanai and Little Beach ... Let them come to you, and don't chase after them ... These are wild animals.

NENE

The Hawaiian goose, is the state bird ... It's the rarest goose in the world ... Do not feed them ... Most likely sightings are at the Halemauʻu Trail and Kolua Cabin, Haleakala ... They'll come to you, don't go after them ... Observe nene crossing signs when driving; they're for real.

Nene

Monk Seals

One of only two native Hawaiian mammals ... The other is the hoary bat; sorry people ... Only 1,300 Hawaiian monk seals remain, and they are endangered ... The Caribbean monk seal became extinct in 1952 ... Most monk seals live in the northwest Hawaiian Archipelago ... If you see a monk seal "hauled-out," it's a local; they live where they are born ... Stay at least 100 feet from a beached seal ... Old monk seals are 25 to 30 years ... Pups are about 3 feet and 30 pounds at birth ... Six weeks later, at 200 pounds, they're on their own ... Sharks are their main predators—but marine debris and habitat destruction historically has been more deadly.

Coral

Reefs may look like rocks, but coral is actually colonies of tiny animals that are related to sea anemones ... They have cylindrical bodies called polyps that secrete stony cups of limestone around themselves ... Corals have developed over 500 million years ... Tender moment: That oily shimmer sometimes in the water is coral climaxing, as part of its reproductive process... Home for coral: between the 30th latitudes, in saltwater less than 300 feet deep ... Coral comes in many shapes, like cauliflower, lobe, rice, mushroom, and finger ... Called the rain forest of the sea, some old-growth coral is 200 years old ... Thank coral for white-sand beaches ... 80 per cent of reefs in the United States are in Hawaii ... Don't touch the living coral.

Et ceteras

There are no native Hawaiian reptiles or amphibians ... Used to be 140 native Hawaiian birds; 70 are now extinct, 30 are endangered, and 12 are on the brink of extinction ... Hawaii's landmass is .2% of the United States' total; 75% of the country's plant and bird extinctions have occurred here ... One-quarter of the fish you see snorkeling are found only in Hawaii.

climate

Weather webcam: www.hawaiiweathertoday.com

Weather phone: Maui, 808-866-944-5025
Lanai, 808-565-6063
Molokai, 808-522-2477

RAINFALL (PER YEAR)

Kaupo coast 12"
Kihei 15"
Lahaina 17"
Kahului 21"
Kula 23"
Kapalua 31"
Haleakala 57"
Hana 83"
Iao Valley/West Maui Mountains 200"
Hanawi Reserve/East Rain Forests 350"

Mauka, or mountain, showers occur any time of the year, mostly on windward slopes and valleys. In ancient Maui, several dozen different types of rain were identified. Maui's latitude is 20° 50', north, which is south of the Tropic of Cancer. The climate is subtropical, with average humidity of 56 to 72 percent.

TEMPERATURES (TYPICAL, DEGREES FAHRENHEIT)

	Summer (hi/lo)	Winter (hi/lo)
Lahaina	87/77	80/70
Kahului	85/75	79/65
Kihei	89/79	82/72
Hana	84/74	78/64
Kula	82/64	66/45
Haleakala	65/45	52/29

Ocean temperature is mid- to high-70s—refreshing upon entry, but instantly comfortable.

Keanae YMCA Camp

WINDS
Trade winds blow from the northeast, from 7- to 28-days per month, with the highest frequency coming in June. Kihei and Ka'anapali are the most sheltered from trade winds, and their accompanying storms. The windiest spots are Ma'alaea and Kahului, where the winds are funneled across the isthmus. The Kaupo coast and Hana get direct winds, but are not subject to accelerated winds caused by the funneling effect. Wind speeds average 12 mph, lightest during the winter, but gusts of 25-to-30 mph are common. Winds on Haleakala can reach hurricane force. Kona winds come from the southwest, most often in the winter. *The Hawaiians have some 40 different names for the winds on the various parts of the island.*

SURF
During the winter, surf is largest on the eastern shores, reaching more than 20 feet near Paia. The pattern shifts during the summer, when western shores of Kihei and Lahaina get their seasonally high surf—the Kona surf. North shores and the southern coast have active coastal surf year round. Maui has more than 80 accessible beaches, with more miles of swimming beach than any other island, including the Big Island which is five-times bigger. *When Hawaiians speak of the eight seas, they are referring to the channels that separate all the islands, which all have different characteristics.*

THE GREEN FLASH
In Hawaii, conditions are optimal for observing the green—or emerald—flash, the illusive burst of color that occurs at times just as the sun settles into the horizon. Scientists say green wavelengths of color separate from orange and red wavelengths, as they are bent, prismlike, around the curvature of the earth. Has to be on a hazeless, flat horizon. Whatever, the green flash is rare and fortuitous.

WHAT TO DO IN 'BAD' WEATHER

TOO WINDY ... GO TO:
> Valley Isle, TH11-TH14; or to Sunny South, TH1-TH7.

TO RAINY ...GO TO:
> Sunny South, TH1-TH6; or Valley Isle, TH10-TH12; or Haleakala, TH48 through TH52. Or see *Museums and Attractions in Resource Links.*

TOO HOT ... GO TO:
> Valley Isle, TH16-TH20; Windward Coast, TH21-TH24; Hana Highway, TH37 to TH41; or Haleakala, TH45-TH47

TOO MUGGY ... GO TO:
> Valley Isle, TH16-TH20; or Haleakala, TH45-TH47

TAKE ADVANTAGE OF CLEAR WEATHER, GO TO:
> Valley Isle, TH15-TH20; or Windward Coast, TH22-TH25; or Hana Highway, TH36-TH41; or Haleakala, TH46; or Outer Islands, TH53-TH55

PACKLIST

Maui is a shopper's paradise. You may prefer to arrive with just the basics and leave dressed head-to-toe Hawaiian style. Shop Wailea, Kaanapali or Makawao for upscale resortwear or load the cart at WalMart, the Lahina Cannery Mall or Kaahumanu Center, where there's plenty of aloha wear and inexpensive T-shirts to bring home to friends.

ONE-WEEK VACATION

Shoes
- Slippers (a.k.a. zoris, go-aheads, thongs, slappers, flip-flops)
- Plane and hotel shoes (loafers, clean athletic shoes, or boat shoes)
- Hiking shoes (light weight hikers or cross-trainers, to get muddy)
- Surf shoe (optional, Teva or bootie-style)

Dress, or Khakis plus dri-fit shirt for plane, hotels
Swimming suit
Two or three pair shorts
4 or 5 short sleeve tops, synthetic dri-fit
1 or 2 long sleeve tops (Haleakala hikers bring 2 for layering)
Gore-Tex shell, or equivalent, rain jacket
Fleece vest, lightweight (optional)
Sun hat
Sunglasses
Gloves (optional, for warmth on Haleakala, and to protect hands on lava hikes.)
Retractable hiking poles
Mask, fins, snorkel
Knapsack
- Antibiotic
- Band Aids
- Energy bars, emergency food
- Flashlight
- Handkerchief
- Mosquito repellent
- Small bottle hydrogen peroxide
- Sunscreen, lip balm
- Swiss Army knife
- Water bottles
- Water purification tablets or pump
- Whistle

FARMER'S MARKETS

Ka'ahumanu Shopping Center, Kahului
    Friday, 9:30 a.m. to 5 p.m., 877-3369
Kahului Shopping Center , 877-3369
    W 7:30 a.m. to 1 p.m., 573-1934
Keanae Open Market — 2nd Sat. every month
Honokowai Market, Kahana, 669-7004
    M, W, F, 7 a.m. to 11 a.m.
South Kihei Market, 875-0949
    M, W, F, 1:30 p.m. to 5:30 p.m.
Maui Swap Meet, Kahului, Pu'uhene Avenue
    Saturday, 7 a.m. to noon, 877-3100
Hana Farmers & Crafter's Market,
    Tu, W, Th, 10 a.m. to 4 p.m.
Kumu Farms, Wailuku, 244-4800
    Tu thru Sun, 10 a.m to 5 p.m.

FREE HULA SHOWS

Whalers Village, Ka'anapali, 661-4567
    Mon., Tu, Wed., F, Sat, 7 p.m. to 8 p.m.
Lahaina Cannery Mall, 661-5304
    Sat and Sun, 1 p.m.(Keiki Hula);
    Tue and Th, 7 p.m. (Polynesian Dance)
Old Lahaina Center, 661-9913
    Tue., Fri., 11:30 a.m.
Ka'anapali Beach Hotel, 661-0011
    Nightly, 6:30 p.m. to 7:30 p.m.
Kapalua Shops, 669-3754
    Thu., 10 a.m. to 11 a.m.
Lahaina Center, 667-9216
    Wed., 2:30 p.m., Fri., 6 p.m.

LUAUS

Honuaula Luau, Marriott, 808-875-7710
Feast at Lele, 800-248-5828, 667-5353
Drums of Pacific, Hyatt, 808-667-4727
Old Lahaina Luau, 800-248-5828, 667-2998
Ka'anapali Sunset Luau at Black Rock,
    808-877-HULA

surfin' da web

INFORMATIONAL LINKS:
www.co.maui.hi.us/ (county government)
www.gohawaii.com
www.lanai.com
www.hawaii.gov
www.hawaiiweathertoday.com (live cams)
www.hookele.com (cultural)
www.infomaui.com
www.mauidirect.com
www.kpoa.com (radio)
www.makena.com (golf)
www.maui.about.com
www.maui.net
www.pulamalanai.com
www.mauiaccommodations.com
www.mauifishing.com
www.mauimapp.com
www.mauinews.com
www.molokai-hawaii.com
www.nps.gov/hale/ (Haleakala)
www.ohanapages.com
www.spotlighthawaii.com
www.tnc.org/hawaii (Nature Conservancy)
www.visitmaui.com
www.visitmolokai.com
www.hawaii-forest.com
www.windsurfari.com
www.trailblazertravelbooks.com
www.hawaiitrails.org
www.hawaiistate.hi.us/dlnr
www.hi.sierraclub.org
www.thisweek.com
www.bestplaceshawaii.com
www.hawaii-nation.org/
www.alternative-hawaii.com
www.maui-golf.com/
www.go-lanai.com/
www.surfinggoatdairy.com
www.muleride.com
www.hawaiianbeachrentals.com

LINK CALABASH
www.trailblazerhawaii.com
www.surfingmavericks.com/xx105
www.mauiwedding.net
www.mauimenusonline.com
www.madeinmaui.com
www.hawaii.gov/ogg
www.hotelmolokai.com
www.mauinokaoi.net
www.mauihi.com
www.mauioceancenter.com
www.bluehawaiian.com
www.mauifilmfestival.com
www.mauiculture.net/kuhikuhi
www.lanairesorts.com
www.hawaiianair.com
www.maui.cc.com
www.mauimagazine.net
www.lanaionline.com
www.hotellanai.com
www.aloha-hawaii.com
www.pacificwhale.org
http://wikitravel.org/en/Maui
www.extremesportsmaui.com
www.actionsportsmaui.com
www.mauiprincess.com

Trailblazer KIDS

The Hawaiian word keiki (KAY-key) means both 'child' and also the green shoot of a new banana plant. Bananas are plants, not trees, and each year a new generation must be nurtured to maturity, just like children.

In Hawaii, children are reared not only by the family, but also by the ohana—the extended family of 'aunties' and 'uncles' that make up the community. In recent years on Maui, this ohana-based rearing has been reinforced by new, 'immerging' schools, which further not only the Hawaiian language, but also traditional crafts and customs. Activities are listed in order of trailhead numbers.

ALL-STAR ATTRACTIONS

Maui Ocean Center, TH9, page 47
The best aquarium in Hawaii—a world-class attraction. Pricey.

Hawaii Nature Center-Iao Needle, TH25, page 92
The state park, county gardens, and the center's hands-on museum combine for Maui's best tropical experience.

Hana Highway, Driving Tour, page 111
A rain forest thrill ride with multiple sideshows. Paia town for picnic food.

Pi'ilanihale Heiau-Kahanu Gardens, TH39, page 128
The greatness of ancient Hawaii lives on.

Haleakala National Park, TH46, page 156
Take a trip to a desert island two miles in the sky.

Molokini Island, TH53, page 177
A former cone volcano is now a natural marine aquarium, just few miles offshore

Lanai, TH54, page 181
Ride the ferry from Lahaina and take a vacation within a vacation.

KEIKI POOLS

Ahihi Cove, TH2, page 32
Schools of snorkelers gather since it's right on the road.

Ulua Beach, TH6, page 40
Sits in the middle of other pretty Wailea Resorts beaches.

Charley Young Beach Park, TH7, page 41
Coco palm terraces make this slightly more attractive than other Kamaole beaches.

Koieie Loko Ia Fishpond, TH8, page 44
Ancient, restored fishpond is next to the humpback whale center.

Olowalu Beach, TH12, page 61
Tour boats anchor offshore; flat-sand entry is easy.

Pu'unoa (Baby) Beach, TH13, page 65
Where Lahaina's moms & dads go. Sweet.

Honolua Marine Preserve, TH16, page 72
Fabulously fishy coral. Storm runoff can muddy the waters.

Baby Baldwin Beach, TH30, page 101
A tropical swimming pool with a sand grandstand.

Pools of Oheo, TH44, page 137
This national park can be a zoo during prime conditions.

NATURE WALKS

Wetlands Boardwalk, TH9, page 45
Bet the kids run down the long ramp.
Dragon's Teeth, TH15, page 69
Waves explode on a weirdly jagged reef. (Watch out.)
Nakalele Blowhole, TH17, page 74
A short adventure walk to a saltwater geyser. (Stay back.)

Ohai Loop Trail, TH18, page 76
Mellow coastal bluff trail on a wild coast.
Tropical Gardens of Maui, TH25, page 92
The bridge over the stream adds to the green adventure (admission is charged).
Twin Falls, TH35, page 119
Easy wide path up a garden, alongside white water.
Keanae Arboretum, TH37, page 124
An inviting path into a park with massive trees.
Pipiwai Trail, TH44, page 137
Waterfalls, bridges, and a bamboo forest are just the ticket for active families.
Sliding Sands Trail, TH46, page 159
Haleakala's signature hike. Don't forget the sunscreen and water.

A DAY AT THE BEACH

All the ingredients to log some towel time: normally safe swimming and wave play, with sand and a shoreline that will look good in the family album.

Big Beach, TH3, page 34
Maluaka Beach, TH4, page 35
Po'olenalena Beach, TH5, page 36
Keawakapu Beach, TH6, page 40
Kamaole Beach Parks, TH7, page 41
Pu'unoa (Baby) Beach, TH13, page 65
Kahekili Beach Park, TH14, page 67
Kapalua Beach, TH15, page 69
Baldwin Beach Park, TH31, page 102
Hamoa Beach, TH42, page 135

LITTLE WALKS TO BIG PLACES

McGregor Point vistas, TH11, page 56
Whale watch at sunset.
Lahaina Seawall, TH13, page 64
See seagoing Lahaina from land.
Lipoa Point, TH16, page 72
Watch surfers, or go farther to a seascape.

Kahakuloa Head, TH20, page 78
A seaside perch to watch whales and birds.
Kukuipuka Heiau, TH22, page 87
Up steps to an airborne view.
Kahuna Point, TH34, page 109
Hidden down a rural road; home to Halehaku Heiau.
Fagan's Cross, TH41, page 132
A mini-workout to the best view of Hana.
White Hill, Red Hill, TH47, page 158
Get as high as possible on Haleakala.
Skyline Trail, TH47, page 162
Even the trailhead parking lot is high in the sky.
Huialoha Church, TH52, page 173
Grassy banks, wave or rock skipping along the little beach. Away from it all.

BEST PICNIC PARKS

Polo Beach, TH6, page 40
Nice shaded tables at the gateway to Wailea resort beaches.
Kamaole III Park, TH7, page 41
Get a plate lunch across the street and spend the day—plenty of locals do.
Waipuilani Park, TH8, page 44
Tucked away in north Kihei, grassy expanse with lonely beach.
Haycraft Beach Park, TH9, page 47
A little secret down the street from Maui Ocean Center.
Olowalu Landing, TH12, page 60
No facilities, but this spot has many pluses.
Launiupoko Beach Park, TH12, page 61
Pull off the road to tables under palms. Classic, but with traffic close by.
DT Fleming Beach Park, TH15, page 69
Locals and surfers gather. Don't count on swimming.
Waiheʻe Beach Park, TH24, page 90
A forested beachside beauty that is off the tourist radar.
Kaumahina Wayside, TH37, page 123
This view park on the way to Hana was spruced up in 2005.
Waianapanapa State Park, TH40, page 130
Lots to do along Hana's most-scenic coastline. Spooky cave exploring.
Kipahulu Point Park, TH44, page 140
This is where world-traveler Charles Lindbergh wanted to end his days.
Rice Park, Driving Tour, Page 150
Great view from Kula. Easy pull off.
Polipoli Springs, TH47, page 162
A pleasing high-forest getaway that won't seem like Maui.

FAMILY FREEBIES

Hawaiian Islands Humpback Whale Sanctuary, TH8, page 44
Also snorkel in the saltwater pond and visit little Vancouver Monument.

Lahaina Town, TH13, page 62
A seagoing tourist town with both glitz and history. Let 'em run under the big banyan tree. See the hula show daily at Lahaina Cannery Mall.

For the Birds, Ka'anapali, TH14, page 66, 808-661-1234

The luscious grounds of the Hyatt Regency are home to penguins, flamingos, swans, parrots, and a pair of Indonesian cranes. Stop by and say Aloha.

Maui Swap Meet, TH28, page 97
Everybody can find a personal souvenir and a tempting snack.

Kanaha Beach Park, TH29, page 98
Take a ringside seat for the windsurfing and kiteboarding spectacle.

Waianapanapa State Park, TH40, page 130
Picnic, hike, swim—either in the ocean or a fresh pond.

HAWAIIAN HISTORY ADVENTURES

King's Trail, TH1, page 29
Prepare for an adventure; best example of an ancient Hawaiian highway.

Koieie Loko Ia Fishpond, TH8, page 44
Swim around in a pool made centuries ago.

Olowalu Petroglyphs, TH12, page 58
Maui's best ancient rock pictures, and among Hawaii's best.

Kepaniwai Heritage Gardens, TH25, page 92
See the different countries that combine to make Hawaii at this garden park.

Historical Buildings Tour, TH27, page 95
The Baldwin House Museum still reflects its former residents. Picnic under the trees.

Keanae Village-Wailua, TH37, page 122
Agrarian Old Hawaii is on display. Not tourist towns. Fresh buttery banana bread for sale.

Pi'ilanihale Heiau, TH39, page 129
A temple rising from the jungle.

Nu'uanu Landing-petroglyphs, TH51, page 170
Some of Maui's first arrivals left their mark.

Tedeschi Winery, TH47, page 164
King Kalakua loved the parklike grounds, high in cowboy country. Cool off those sunburns.

A BAG OF TRICKS

Atlantis Submarine Ride, Lahaina, 800-381-0237
Yes, a real under water journey in the fish-filled coral waters.

Ulalena show at the Maui Theater, Lahaina, 856-7900
Hula and chanting—the old song and dance— tell the history of Hawaii.

Lahaina-Ka'anapali Railroad (Sugar Cane Train), 667-6951
A 12-mile, narrated ride on vintage open-air cars may be the fastest thing over the land during heavy traffic periods. One 400-foot long trestle crosses high over a stream valley. Pricey; sugar cane is gone.

Rooftop Golf, Ka'anapali, 661-2000
Atop the Embassy Suites resort is a putt-putt course with a birdie view.

Maui Tropical Plantation, 244-7643
Tram rides, outrigger canoe on a quiet lagoon, and a tame zipline. All family members will enjoy the spacious scenic grounds.

Old Lahaina Luau, 667-1998
A moonlit spectacle of traditional Polynesian song and dance. Here's your chance to eat poi, and many other more tasty traditonal dishes of a big Hawaiian feast. Need to put this one in the vacation budget.

Resource Links

PUBLIC AGENCIES
County of Maui
Department of Parks & Recreation, 270-7230
Aquatics Division, 270-6137
Beach Parks, camping, 270-7389
Recreation Program, 270-7383

State of Hawaii
Department of Land and Natural Resources, 984-8109
Aquatic Resources Division, 243-5294
Kanaha Pond, Forestry and Wildlife Division, 984-8100
Historic Preservation Division, 243-5169
Iao Valley State Park, 882-6206
Natural Area Reserves, 873-3506
Polipoli Springs Recreation Area, 984-8109
Parks, Camping, 984-8109
Pala'au State Park (Molokai) 567-69-23
Na Ala Hele Trails, 873-3508 or 3509
Waianapanapa State Park, 984-8109
Volunteer Services, 586-7200

Federal
Haleakala National Park, 572-4400,
Kipahulu District, 248-7375
Weather, 877-5111
Road Closures 986-1200
Kealia Pond Wildlife Refuge, 875-1582

TRANSPORTATION
See Getting Around Maui *in the front of this book for more travel information.*

Air from the Mainland
American, 800-433-7300, 244-5522, www.aa.com
Hawaiian, 871-6132, 800-367-5320, www.hawaiianairlines.com
Your vacation starts at the airport with these guys.
Delta, 800-325-1999, www.delta.com
Alaska, 800-252-7522, www.alaskaair.com
United, 800-241-6522, www.united.com

Area code is 808 for all numbers, unless otherwise listed.

MOLOKAI AND LANAI
  Mokulele Airlines, 866-260-7070, www.mokuleleairlines.com
  Hawaiian Air, 567-6510, www.hawaiianairlines.com

CAR RENTALS
  Alamo, 800-327-9633, 871-6235
  Avis, 800-321-3712, 871-7575
  Budget, 800-527-7000, 871-8811
  Dollar, 800-800-4000, 877-2731
  Hertz, 800-654-3011, 877-5167
  Aloha Cars-R-Us, 800-655-7989
  Aloha Rent a Car, 877-452-5642
  BioBeetle, 877-873-6121
  Maui Cruisers, 249-2319

  LANAI
  Dollar, 565-7227
  Lanai Cheap Jeeps, 649-9517

  MOLOKAI
  Mobetta Car Rental, 308-9566
  Molokai Rental Car, 344-7612
  Alamo, 567-6381

PUBLIC BUSES, Maui Bus, 270-7511, or Robert's Hawaii, 871-6226

FERRIES
Also ask for car rentals and tours.
  Expeditions (Lanai), 800-695-2624, 661-3756
  Lahaina Cruise Company (Molokai), 667-6165
    Hawaii Ocean Project tours

WEST MAUI EXPRESS (SHOPPER SHUTTLE)
  Connects all of West Maui, 877-7308

AIRPORT SHUTTLE, 875-8070, 661-6667, 800-977-2605
TAXIS, 244-7278, 874-8294, 665-0003

VISITOR INFORMATION
Also contact Public Organizations.

    Maui Visitors Bureau, 800-525-6284, 244-3530
    Maui Chamber of Commerce, 871-7711
    Activity Owners Association of Hawaii, 800-398-9698
    Destination Lanai, 800-947-4774, 565-7600
    Molokai Visitors Association, 800-800-6367, 553-3876
    Weather forecast, 877-5111, 877-3477
        Lanai, 565-6033; Molokai, 552-2477

SUPPLEMENTAL MAPS
Free maps are available in shopping centers, on the plane, and from the visitors bureau. Trailblazer's maps and directions are enough for you to get around the island, but a street map and detailed, all-purpose map is a good idea. (A GPS and USGS topo maps, while informational, are not useful for hiking. The hardest part here is finding the trailhead. After that, rough, dense topography requires that you stay on trail and turn back if you lose the trail. On coastal walks, you just need to know where the ocean is.)

Map of Maui, the Valley Isle, University of Hawaii Press. Full Color Topographic,
    2840 Kolowalu Street, Honolulu, HI, 96822. *Best all-purpose map. Indexes place names and shows unpaved roads.*
Maui Recreation Map, Department of Land and Natural Resources, 984-8100.
    Available free. Shows hunter's forest reserves, state hiking trails.
The Ready Mapbook of Maui County, Odyssey Publishing, 888-729-1074,
    935-0092. *Best street map. In book form.*
Maui County Bicycle Map, Maui Visitors Bureau, 244-3530
Maui County Shoreline Access Guide, County Parks Department, 270-7389

NEWSPAPERS, MAGAZINES & NEWSLETTERS
    Maui News (daily), 244-3981
    Haleakala Times, 579-8020
    Ka Waiola (Maui Tomorrow), 244-2570
    Keepers of the Coast (Surfrider Foundation), 243-0858
    Lahaina News (weekly), 667-7866
    Maui No Ka Oi Magazine, 242-8331
    Maui Time Weekly, 242-9393
    Maui Weekly, 875-1700
    Lanai Times, (monthly), 565-3816
    The Dispatch (Molokai), 552-2781
    Molokai Advertiser-News, 558-8253

Area code is 808 for all numbers, unless otherwise listed.

MUSEUMS & ATTRACTIONS

Alexander & Baldwin Sugar Museum, 871-8058
Bailey House Museum, 244-3326
Baldwin Museum and Courthouse, 661-3262
Hale Pa'ahao prison, 667-1985
Hana Cultural Center & Museum, 248-8622
Hawaii Nature Center, Iao Valley, 244-6500
Hui Noeau Visual Arts Center (Baldwin Estate), 572-6560
Humpback Whale National Marine Sanctuary, 800-831-4888
Kealia Pond National Wildlife Refuge, 875-1582
Keawala'i Congregational Church, 879-5557
Old Lahaina Luau, 667-1998
Maui Ocean Center, 270-7000
Maui Swap Meet, 244-3100
Maui Tropical Plantation 244-7643
Molokai Museum & Cultural Center, 567-6436
Pi'ilanihale Heiau, 248-8912
Lahaina Ka'anapali Railroad (Sugar Cane Train), 667-6951
Tedeschi Winery, 878-1266, 878-6058
Ulalena Show at Maui Theater, 856-7900
Whale Museum, 661-5992
Wo Hing Museum, 661-3262

GARDENS

Ali'i Kula Lavender, 878-3004, 878-8090
Garden of Eden, 572-9899
Kahanu National Tropical Botanical Garden, 248-8912
Kula Botanical Garden, 878-1715
Maui Nui Botanical Garden, 249-2798
Maui Tropical Plantation, 364-6622
Kumu Farms, 244-4800
Tropical Gardens of Maui 244-3085

PRESERVATION AND CULTURAL GROUPS
Call ahead of your visit to arrange to volunteer.
Coastal Lands Conservation, 538-6616
Fishpond Ohana Restoration, 879-7926
Friends of Kukuipuka, 242-4931
Friends of Moku'ula, 661-3659
Hana Cultural Center, 248-8522
Hawaiian Islands Humpback Whale
    National Marine Sanctuary, 800-831-4888, 879-2818
Hawaiian Nation, 242-6840
Hawaiian Natural History Association, 985-6051
Huialoha Church Resortation Fund, 791-5638
Hui Noeau Visual Arts Center, 572-6560
Malama Honokowai, 249-8811
Malama Kahakai (coastal preservation), 579-9802
Maui Arts & Cultural Center, 242-2787
Maui Cultural Lands (Malama Honokowai), 572-8085
Maui Historical Society, 244-3326
Maui Museums Association, 871-8058
Olowalu Cultural Preserve, 683-0378
Pacific Whale Foundation, 800-942-5311, 249-8811
Protect Kaho'olawe Ohana, 573-7819
Sierra Club, 579-9802, 573-3454; hikes, 573-4147
Surfrider Foundation, 800-743-7873, 243-0858
Lanai, The Nature Conservancy 565-7430
Waihe'e Coastal Dunes & Wetlands, 244-5263

RECREATIONAL OUTFITTERS, TOURS
Bicycle
Cruiser Phil's, 893-2332
Maui Mountain Cruisers, 871-6014
Haleakala Bike Company, 575-9575
Maui Downhill, 518-2233
Mountain Riders Bike Tours, 877-4944
South Maui Bicycles, 874-0068; West Maui Cycles, 661-9005

Ziplines
Maui Zipline Company, 633-2464
Pi'iholo Ranch Zipline, 800-374-7050
Skyline Eco-Adventures, 878-8400
Twin Falls Zipline, 573-1529

HELICOPTERS

A number of reliable companies fly Maui's skies, but you won't find a safer, more luxurious, or more adventurous ride than on Blue Hawaiian Helicopters. Aboard the quiet Eco-Star, you can cruise from Molokai to the Big Island, from Haleakala to the lush valleys Hana Highway in between. 1-800-745-2583, 871-8844

HIKES

Sierra Club, 419-5143, 538-6616 *Contact for schedule of hikes.*
D. T. Fleming Arboretum, 572-1097 *Free tours Ulupalakua.*
East Maui Irrigation (EMI) waiver, 579-9516
   Waivers for Hana Highway area for Sierra Club and Mauna Ala hikes
Hawaii Nature Center, Iao Valley, 244-6500
Hike Maui, 879-5270, 866-324-6284 *These guys are pros.*
Kapalua Resort Center, 665-9110
   Free coastal & mountain trials on resort land. Free shuttle.
Kipahulu Ohana, 248-8558 *Cultural, botanical walks near Pools of Oheo*
Mauna Ala Hiking Club, Box 329, Pu'uene, HI 96784, 875-8171
   Join for $5 ($7 with card) and get EMI waiver to hike Hana Highway
The Nature Conservancy, 572-7849 *Waikomo Ridge*
Olowalu Culural Preserve, 633-0378 *Volunteer in historic valley.*
PATH (Public Access Trails Maui) 244-9233
Waihe'e Valley Plantation, 244-2120; Wailuku Water Co., 244-7051
   Looks like the Swinging Bridges hikes are closed for now.

HORSES

Molokai Mule Ride, 8567-6088
Ironwood Ranch, Kapalua, 669-4991
Pi'iholo Ranch, 800-374-7050
Makena Stables, 879-0244
Mendes Ranch, Kahakuloa, 244-7320
Pony Express Tours, Kula, 667-2200

KAYAKS, CANOES

Makena Kayak, 879-8426
Maui Kayaks Eco-Adventures, 874-4000
Maui Ultra Dive (also surf), Kihei, 875-4004
South Pacific Kayaks, Kihei, 800-776-2326, 875-4848

SURFING

You get a bang for your buck hiring a surfing guide.
Girls Gone Surfing, 280-0103
Goofy Foot, Lahaina, 244-9283, 229-6737
Surf Dog Maui, 250-7873

surfing, cont'd—
    Outrageous Adventures, Lahaina, 1-877-339-1400, 669-1400
    Second Wind, 877-7467
    Soul Surfing Maui, 870-7873

Snorkel and Scuba
Ask about boat size and cancellation policy.
    Maui Dive Shop, 879-1775; Kihei, 879-3388, 879-1533;
        Kahana, 661-6166, 669-3800; Ka'anapali, 661-5117;
        Lahaina, 661-5388; Ma'alaea, 244-5514
    B&B Scuba, 875-2861
    Boss Frogs, Kihei (ask for other locations) 875-4477
    Ed Robinson's Diving (scuba), 800-635-1273, 879-3584
    Extended Horizons (scuba), 667-0611
    Four Winds, Wailuku, 879-8188
    Hawaiian Rafting Adventures, 661-7333
    Lahaina Divers (scuba), 800-998-3483, 667-7496
    Maui Undersea Adventures, 2801477
    Mike Severns Diving (scuba), 879-6596
    Trilogy Excursions, 888-225-6284

Windsurfing/Kiteboarding/Stand Up Paddle
    Action Sports Maui, 871-5857
    Hawaiian Sailboarding Techniques (HST), 871-5423
    Hi-Tech Surf Sports, 888-717-0683
    Proflight Paragliding (Haleakala), 874-5433
    Second Wind, 877-7467

Whale Watching, Cruises
Also see Best Of section for places to view whales from land.
The ferries to Molokai and Lanai double as whale-watching excursions.
    Expeditions, Lahaina (Lanai ferry), 661-3756
    Lahaina Cruise Company (Molokai ferry),
        Hawaii Ocean Project, 667-6165
    Pacific Whale Foundation, 800-942-5311, 249-8811
    Blue Water Rafting, 879-7238
    Maui Adventure Cruises Lahaina, 661-5550
    Gemini, Lahaina, 669-0508
    Pride of Maui (also snorkel), 242-0955
    Teralani, Ka'anapali, 661-7245
    Ultimate Whale Watch, 667-5678

Area code is 808 for all numbers, unless otherwise listed.

Golf
Makena Golf Course, 891-4000
Kapalua Golf, 888-227-6054
Dunes at Maui Lani, 873-7911, ext. 2
Waiehu Municipal Golf Course, 244-5934

Molokai
Damien Tours, Kalaupapa, 567-6171
Halawa Falls Cultural Hike, 553-4355
Historical Hike West Molokai, 800-274-9303
Kalaupapa National Historical Park, 567-6802
Molokai Mule Ride, Kalaupapa, 800-567-7550, 567-6088
The Nature Conservancy 553-5236
Molokai Ranch Hawaii, 877-726-4656, 552-2741
Pu'u O Hoku Ranch, 558-8109
Molokai Bicycle, 553-3931
Snorkeling with Bill Kapuni, 553-9867

Lanai
The Nature Conservancy, 565-7430
Adventure Lanai Ecocentre, 565-7373
Luaiwa Petroglyphs, 565-7600

Where to stay

Calling is a good way to find out which places have aloha. Inquire about amenities and location specifics, and be sure to ask if you are getting the lowest rate. Almost all listings are oceanfront or ocean view. Prices vary by region, as noted below. Some luxury resort hotels are more than $400 per night; economy-minded travelers should be able to find a place for about $75 per night. Some condominiums have monthly rates. Camping and rustic cabins are available for much less. For island-wide bed & breakfast referrals, try Hawaii Bed & Breakfast, 800-262-9912.

All area codes are 808 unless toll-free numbers are noted.
(H) = Hotel, resort, (C) = Condos (B) = Bed & Breakfast, cottages, (A) = Rental agency

SUNNY SOUTH (Makena, Wailea, Kihei, North Kihei)

Best swimming beaches and sunny weather. Arid surroundings. Wailea is a high-end resort strip. Kihei has mid-range condos and resorts, most across the road from beach parks. North Kihei's beaches aren't as popular, and the area is quieter and often more economically priced.

Makena
Makena Surf Resort (C) 800-528-8348

Wailea
Anduz Maui at Wailua (H) 879-1234
Four Seasons (H) 874-8000
Grand Wailea Resort (H) 875-1234
Outrigger Palms at Wailea (H) 879-5800
Polo Beach Club, Wailea Eluua Village (C) 879-1595, 866-1368

Kihei
Condominium Rentals Hawaii (A) 800-367-5242
Hale Pau Hana (C) 879-2715
Kihei Beach Resort (C) 800-367-6034
Kihei Maui Vacations (A) 879-4000
Kihei Surfside (C) 874-3194
Mana Kai Maui (C) 879-1561
Maui Kamaole (C) 8799-2778
Maui Parkshore (C) 879-1600
Maui Vista (H) 874-5252
Royal Mauian Resort (H) 879-9257
What a Wonderful World (B) 879-9103

North Kihei
Aston Maui Lu (H) 877-977-6667
Kauhale Makai, (C) 879-8888
Kealia Resort (H) 800-265-0686
Kihei Holiday Resort (C) 206-661-1316
Koa Resort (C) 800-541-3060,
Luana Kai Resort (H) 879-1268
Maui Schooner Resort(H) 879-5247
Waipuilani (C) 879-1458

VALLEY ISLE (Lahaina, Ka'anapali, Kahana, Kapalua)

Excellent swimming beaches. Tropical greenery inland. Lahaina is a quaint but active tourist town, with moderate to high room rates. Ka'anapali is a high-end resort strip. Kahana has mid- to high-end condos and resorts, packed together but with back-door ocean settings. Kapalua has higher-end resorts and nice cove beaches. Weather is sunniest in Lahaina-Ka'anapali.

Lahaina

Aloha Lani Inn (B) 661-8040
Lahaina Inn (H) 661-0577
Lahaina Roads, Pu'upana (C) 800-669-6284
Lahaina Shores Resort (H) 866-934-9176
Makai Inn (B) 662-3200
Aina Nalu Resort (C) 800-462-6262,
Pioneer Inn (H) 800-457-5457, 661-3636
Plantation Inn (H) 667-9225

Ka'anapali

Aston-Maui Ka'anapali Villas (C) 677-7791
Hyatt Regency (H) 800-233-1234, 661-1234
Ka'anapali Beach Hotel (H) 800-262-8450
Sheraton Maui (H) 661-0031
Westin Maui (H) 888-625-4949, 667-2525

Kahana-Kapalua

Hale Kai (C) 800-446-7307, 669-6333
Hale Napili (C) 669-6184
Honokeana Cove (C) 669-6441
Kahana Sunset (C) 800-669-1488, 669-8700
Kahana Village (C) 800-824-3065, 669-5111
Mauian Hotel on Napili (H)
    800-367-5034, 669-6205
Napili Bay (C) 888-661-7200
Napili Sunset (C) 800-447-9229, 669-8083
Napili Surf Beach Resort (C)
    800-541-0638, 669-8002
Polynesian Shores (C)
    800-433-6284, 669-6065
Ritz-Carlton (H) 800-262-8440, 669-6200

WINDWARD COAST (Maʻalaea, Wailuku, Kahului, Paia)

Yes, it can be windy. Kahului and Wailuku are working towns, with some resorts on the bay; rates are low to moderate. Maʻalaea is a long beach; rates are moderate. All windward coast listings are centrally located, most convenient for trailblazers who plan to spend days exploring. Paia has mostly B&Bs in quiet settings, with moderate rates. Weather is not the sunniest, but beaches are good. Also there's quick access to the Hana Highway and Haleakala.

Maʻalaea
Kanai A Nalu (C) 244-3911
Maʻalaea Bay Rentals (A) 800-367-6084
Maʻalaea Surf (C) 879-1267
Noni Lani Cottages (C) 879-2497

Kahului-Wailuku
Banana Bungalow Hostel (B) 244-5090
Maui Seaside Hotel (H) 877-3311
Northshore Inn (H) 986-8095
Old Wailuku Inn (H) 244-5897

Paia
Hoʻokipa Bayview Cottage (B) 800-258-6770
Inn at Mama's Fish House (H) 870-9764
Maui Vacation Properties (A) 800-782-6105
Paia Inn Hotel (H) 579-6000
Spyglass House, Beach House (B) 269-0093

KULA

Cool country settings are away from beaches and resorts.

Country Garden Cottage (B) 878-2858
Haiku Plantation Inn (B) 575-7500
Hawaiian Islands B&B (B) 800-258-7895
Kula Lodge (H) 878-2517, 878-1535
Kula Lynn Farm (B) 878-6320
Malu Manu (B) 888-878-6161
Peace of Maui (B) 572-5045

HANA

A beautiful non-resort area, away from the rest of Maui. For quiet, outdoor adventures. Not as sunny. Rates range from economy to pricey.

AlaʼAina (B) 248-7824
Ekena Bed & Breakfast (B) 248-7047
Hamoa Bay Bungalows (B) 248-7884
Hana Aliʻi Holidays (A) 248-7742
Hana Kai Maui Resrot (H) 800-346-2772
Hana Paradise Cottages 248-7746
Hana Oceanfront Cottages (C) 248-7558
Luana Spa Retreat, 248-8855
Tradewinds Cottage (B) 248-8980
Traavasa Hana (H) 855-868-7282, 248-8211

LANAI

Hotel Lanai, 800-795-7211, 565-7211
Jasmine House, Dreams Come True (B) 566-6961
Lanai City House (B) 565-6071
Four Seasons at Manele Bay (H), 565-2000
Lodge at Koele (H), 565-4000

MOLOKAI

Hotel Molokai (H) 954-7415
Kahale Mala (B) 553-9009
Kaluakoi Villas (C) 800-367-5004, 552-2721
Molokai Friendly Isle Realty (A) 553-3666
Molokai Shores (C) 553-5954
Molokai Lodge (camp and lodge) 877-726-4656, 660-2710
Dunbar Beachfront Cottages (B) 800-673-0520

CAMPING & RUSTIC CABINS

County of Maui Beach Parks, 270-7389
Beach camping won't be a wilderness experience. Kanaha is good. The county parks on Lanai and Molokai are excellent.

Molokai
County of Maui, 553-3204
Hawaiian Homelands, 567-6104
Molokai Ranch (private), 877-726-4656

Lanai
Hulopoe Beach Park, 565-3978

State Parks and Cabins, 984-8109; Molokai, 558-8150
Waianapanapa, Polipoli, Pala'au, Waialua
Waianapanapa has excellent beach cabins, although rustic, near Hana. Polipoli is a high-elevation cabin, forest location. Pala'au and Waialua are great places on Molokai.

Haleakala National Park, cabins, tents, and backpacking, 572-4400
Hosmer Grove and Oheo campgrounds;
Holua, Kapalaoa, Paliku cabins
Hosmer is high-elevation tent camping. Oheo is excellent beachside camping. The cabins are rustic and set in dramatic locations. Prepare for cold weather.

YMCA Camp Keanae, 248-8355
Rustic cabins, dorms and tent sites available. Memorably beautiful ocean bluff location.

Where to eat

Cuisine may range from burgers to gourmet, and prices from cheap to swank, but these eateries are all island-style winners. Give them a call before you go to see if they meet your tastes. Not all serve dinner.

(C) Cheap or take-out (M) Moderate, family (P) Pricey, special occasion
(under $10) ($10-$20) (over $20)

All area codes are 808.

WAILEA-KIHEI
Annie's Deli & Catering, Kihei (C) 875-8647
Da Kitchen, Kihei (C) 875-7782
Gannon's Wailea (P) 875-8080
Gogi Korean Taco Truck, Kihei (C) 276-4711
Hawaiian Moons Natural Foods (C) 875-4356
Kihei Kitchen (C) 879-2230
Momma's Ribs & Rotisserie, Kihei (C) 875-7755
Monkeypod Kitchen by Merriman (P) 891-2322
Tommy Bahama Café, Wailea (P) 875-9983

MA'ALAEA-LAHAINA-KAPALUA
Aloha Mixed Plate, Lahaina (C) 661-3322
Bamboo Fresh, Lahaina (M) 661-8999
Beach Bums Bar & Grill, Ma'alaea (M) 243-2286
Cool Cat Cafe, Lahaina, (C) 667-0908
Gerard's, Lahaina (P) 661-8939
Honolua Store, Kapalua (C) 665-9105
Kimo's, Lahaina (P) 661-4811
Lahaina Coolers (M) 661-7082
Leodas Kitchen and Pie Shop, Olowalu (M) 662-3600
Local Food, Lahaina (C) 667-2882
Mama'a Ribs & Rotisserie, Kahana (C) 665-6262
Merriman's Kapalua (P) 669-6400
Plantation House, Kapalua (P) 669-6299
Roy's Kahana Bar & Grill (P) 669-6999
Sansei Seafood Restaurant, Kapalua (P) 669-6286
Shark Pit Maui, Lahanina (M) 298-7776

WAILUKU-KAHALUI

Ichiban Restaurant (C) 871-6977
King's BBQ, Wailuku (C)244-8848
Maui Coffee Roasters (M) 877-2877
A Saigon Café, Wailuku (M) 243-9560
Sam Sato's, Wailuku (C) 244-7124
Slightly Salty Food Truck (C) 310-913-1845
Tasty Crust Restaurant, (C) 244-0845
Waikapu on 30, Wailuku (C) 242-1130
Zippy's Kahului (M) 856-7599

PAIA-KULA

Cafe Des Amis, Paia (M) 579-6323
Cafe Mambo & Picnics, Paia (C-M) 579-8021
Hali'imaile General Store (P) 572-2666
Komoda Store & Bakery, Makawao (C) 572-7261
Kula Lodge (P) 878-1535
Makawao Steak House (P) 572-8711
Mama's Fish House, Kuau (P) 579-8488
Mana Foods, Paia (C-M) 579-8078
Paia Fish Market (M) 579-8030
Pukalani Superette (C) 572-7616

ROAD TO HANA

Aunty Sandy's Banana Bread, Keanae, 248-8031
Nutcharee's Authentic Thai Food Hana, 248-8855
Travaasa Hana (P) 248-8211
Laulima Farms, Kipahulu (C) 248-8669

LANAI

Blue Ginger Café (M) 565-6363
Canoe's (M) 565-6573
Lanai City Grille (P) 565-7211
Pele's Other Garden (M) 565-9628

MOLOKAI

Big Daddy's (M) 553-5841
Hotel Molokai (P) 553-5347
Kualapu'u's Cookhouse (M) 567-9655
Manae Goods & Grinds (C) 558-8498

STORES, GIFTS, ART, CRAFTS
Joe's Kula Auto at Historic Calasa Garage, Kula, 878-1818
Ed Lane, Kihei, 875-0828
Fabric Mart (Hawaiian galore), Kahului, 871-5770
Gecko Trading Co. Boutique, Makawao, 572-0249
Hasegawa General Store, Hana, 248-8231, 248-7079
Hot Island Glass, Makawao, 572-4527
Kaupo Store, 248-8054
Kula Marketplace, 878-2135
Lahaina Arts Society, 661-0111
Lahaina Cannery Mall, 661-5304
Made in Maui Association, 871-7711
Lavaka and Sons (wood carving), Lahaina 757-0202
Maui Crafts Guild, Paia, 579-9697
Maui Creations, Kahului, 873-7955
Maui Hands, Paia, 579-9245; Makawao, 572-2008
Ululani's By the Bay, Kahakuloa, 244-7151
Upcountry Harvest, Kula, 800-575-6470, 878-2824
Whalers Village, Ka'anapali, 661-4567

Hawaiianologists
Hawaiian quilts: Wailani Johanson, 661-0325
Steel guitar: Henry Allen, 669-6189
Hula: Kumu, 553-8348, Tommy and Noa Akima, 242-2927,
    Nina Maxwell, 572-8038
Leis: Gordan Bailey, 878-3828
Carving: Sam Kaai, 572-0076
Hawaiian language: Kiope Raymond, 878-3564
Lauhala weaving: Pohaku Kaho'ohanohano, 572-5626

Lanai
Heart of Lanai Gallery, 565-6678
International Food & Clothing, 565-6433
Petroglyphs on the Square, 565-6587
Richard's Market, 565-6047

Molokai
Big Wind Kite Factory, 552-2364
Kamakana Fine Arts, 553-8520

HAWAIIAN GLOSSARY

The Hawaiian language was first written by missionaries in the 1820s, who transcribed phonetically. *Hawaiian Grammar*, which is now out of print, was published by Lorrin Andrews in 1854. Only 12 letters were needed—A, E, I, O, U, plus the consonants, H, K, L, M, N, P, and W. Note that there is no B. and S. in Hawaiian.

Hawaiian can be thought of as a dialect of the Polynesian language; others include Samoan, Tahitian, Marquesan, and Maori. The original home of the Polynesians was India, and after a long period of migrations they reached the South Pacific, as their language transformed with their travels. Today, an increasing number of schools in Hawaii are centered around teaching the language, as well as the crafts, dance, and legends. Vowels may follow each other, but consonants stand alone. A "W" is sometimes pronounced as a "V," when in the middle of a word. Words always end in a vowel. The funny apostrophe (') between some vowels is called an okina. It creates a glottal stop in the word; for instance, in "ahupua'a," the ending is pronounced "ah-ah." Among all words, stress is usually placed on the second to the last syllable, unless the word only has two syllables, in which case the last is stressed.

Selected Words

a'a – sharp, broken lava
ahupua'a – a division of land around which a village lived; watershed
aina – land, country
ahi - fire
akaaka – to laugh
akua – God, deity
ale – an ocean wave
ali'i – chief or chiefess descended from original chiefs or nobles
aloha – hello or goodbye, welcome or farewell, love and best wishes
aumakua – a class of ancient gods;
hale – house
haleakala – house of the sun
hana – work
haole – foreigner, sometimes Caucasian
hau – breeze, dew; a king of tree
heiau – temple, church, worship ground
hoaloha – a friend
hoku – a star
holua – a sled, or sliding place
honi – to touch, taste, kiss
honu – a turtle
ho'okipa – to entertain, to lodge
huhu – angry, offended
hui – group, meeting
hukilau – group net fishing
hula – dance that enacts the stories that become myths
Iao needle – Jupiter appearing as the moving star
ike – to see, know
iki – small, little
imu – pit or oven used for roasting
ipo – sweetheart, darling
ka'a – cart or car
ka'anapali – rolling precipice
kahului – gathering together
kahuna – teacher, expert, priest
kai – the sea
kama'aina – native born, or longtime resident
kamaole - childless
kanaka – the people
Na Ala Hele — trails for walking

selected words, cont'd—

kane – man
kapalua – two borders
kapu – forbidden, no trespassing
kaupo – night landing
keanae – the mullet
keawakapu – the sacred harbor
keiki – child, or young banana plant
kihei – a man's garment, cloak
kipahulu – sojourn at forest fringe
kokua – help
kopaʻa – sugar
kukui – a type of tree; lamp or torch
kula – country, field
lahaina – cruel sun
lanai – deck, porch, patio
laulau – fish, pork, sweet potatoes and taro leaves in steamed pouch
lei – garland of flowers, vines, or beads worn around the neck
lolo – dumb
lomi lomi – a traditional massage
lono – report or news; one of the great gods
luau – feast
mahalo – thank you
mahina – lunar month
makai – toward the sea
makahiki – fall celebration of return of peace and fertility; a year
makena - abundance
malama – solar month; light
mana – spiritual power
mauka – toward the mountain, inland
mauna – mountain
Mele Kalikimaka – Merry Christmas
menehune – dwarf person; legendary first settlers
moana – ocean
molokini – many ties
moku – island
Na Ala Hele -- "trails for walking"
nalu – surf breaking on the beach
nani – pretty, beautiful

nene – Hawaiian goose
niu - coconut
ohana – family
ohia – mountain apple
oluolu – please
olowalu – many hills
oʻne – sand
opala - rubbish
pahoehoe – smooth, undulating lava
paia - noisy
pali – cliff
paniolo – Hawaiian cowboy
pele – the goddess of volcanoes
peleleu – a large, double canoe
poi – pasty food made from taro
pono – good, blessed; in balance with nature
puka – a hole
puʻu – hill or cinder cone
pupu – snack or hors d'oeuvres
tutu – grandmother
ula - red
ulu – the breadfruit tree
ulupalakua – ripe breadfruit ridge
wahine – woman
waianapanapa – glistening water
wai – fresh water
waiheʻe – slippery water
wailea – water of lea, goddess of canoe makers
wailuku – water of breaking waves
wiki – fast, quickly

Index

20-Mile Beach 194
accommodations 238-241
Ahihi Bay 31
Ahihi Cove 25
Ahihi-Kinau Natural Area 29, 31-33
airlines 12, 230
Alau Island Seabird Sanctuary 136
Alelele Falls 140-141
Alexander, Samuel T. 122
Ali'i Beach Parks 192
Ali'i Kula Lavender Garden 162
Andaz Maui Resort 41
Aquarium 31, 33
Association of Fishponds 44
attractions 224-228, 233
Awalua Beach 61
Baby Baldwin Beach 102, 103
Baby Beach (Lahaina) 65
Baby Beach (Spreckelsville) 102
Bailey House Museum 95-96
Bailey, Edward 96
Baldwin Beach Park 83, 102-104
Baldwin House Museum 62
Baldwin, Dwight D. 62, 102, 122
Baldwin, Harry A. 102
Baldwin, Harry and Ethel 154
Baldwin, Henry P. 43, 103, 122
Bamboo Forest Falls 122
Banyan Tree Square 62
Battle of the Sand Hills 45
beach parks 230
Beau Chien Beach 30, 31
Bellstone Pools 50, 77, 78
bicycles 234
Big Beach 27, 34, 35
Big Spring 128
Big Wind Kite Factory 198
Black Rock 66, 67
Black Sand Beach (Makena) 27
Black Sand Beach (Hana) 132, 133
Blue Angel Falls 130
Blue Ginger 183
Blue Hawaiian Helicopters 190
Blue Pool 130
botanical gardens 233
Bottomless Pit 160
Boundary Trail 161
Bradbury, Alan 123
Breakwater 47

buses 231
Calasa Service 150
camping 230, 241
Cape Hanamanioa 30-31
Cape Kinau 29
car rental 12, 231
Chang, Ali'i 162
Chang's Cove 38
Chang's Point 27, 36, 37, 38
Charley Young Beach Park 41, 43
children 224-228
Church of the Holy Ghost 150
climate 217-219
Coffees of Hawaii 196
Cook, Captain James 85, 210
Cook House, The 196
Coral Gardens 57
Cove Park 44
cruises 236
cultural groups 234
D. T. Fleming Arboretum 164
D. T. Fleming Beach Park 51, 70, 72
Damien, Father de Veuster 193, 196
De la Perouse, Admiral Compte 29
Dickey, C. W 154
Dole, Sanford (Park) 183
dolphins 215
Dragon's Teeth 70-71
driving times 12
Dumps 31, 33
Eddie Pu Trail 41, 42
Edison, Thomas 64
Eke Crater 87
Eke Crater Trail 75, 76
Ellison, Larry 181
Emma, Queen 59
Emperor Seamounts 208
Fagan, Paul 133
Fagan's Cross 133
Fairmont Kea Lani Resort 40
Falls at Makahiku 140
farmer's markets 221
ferries 231
Five Caves 36
Five Graves 36
Four Seasons 40
Four Seasons Manele 181
Francis Xavier Mission 79
Garden of Eden 123
Garden of the Gods 185

INDEX | 249

gardens 233
Gecko Trading Company 153
glossary 247-248
Gold Coast 9, 25
golf courses 237
Golf Links 73
Grand Wailea Resort 40
Great Tahiti 164
green flash, the 219
Halawa Beach, Valley 194
Hale Hoʻokipa 130
Hale Kane Heiau 173
Hale Paʻahao 64
Hale Pai 64
Hale Piula 62
Haleakala National Park (Kipahulu) 115-116, 138-141
Haleakala National Park (Nuʻu) 169
Haleakala National Park 146, 156-160, 173
Haleakala Park Headquarters 156
Haleakala Ranch Trail 154
Haleakala Visitors Center 158
Haleakala Volcano 211
Halehaku Heiau 109
Halekiʻi Bay 173
Halekiʻi-Pihana Heiau State Park 82, 90
Halemauʻu Trail 156, 157
Haloa Point 38
Halua Pond 32-33
Hamilton, Laird 107
Hamoa Beach 115, 136-137
Hana 133-136
Hana Airport 132
Hana Bay 134
Hana Beach Park 134
Hana Cultural Center 114, 134
Hana Highway 111, 119-131
Hana Maui Trail 133-134
Hana Ranch 133
Hana Wharf 134, 136
Hanakoʻo Beach Park 66, 67
Harrison, George 123, 127
Hasegawa General Store 135
Hawaii Nature Center 81, 92
Hawaiian Archipelago 208
Hawaiian Canoe Club 98
Hawaiian goose 215
Hawaiian Humpback Whale Sanctuary 44
Hawea Point Conservation Area 68-70
hawksbill turtles 45, 213

Haycraft Beach Park 47
health tips 203
Helio's Grave 141
Henry Fong Store 163
hiking tips and safety 200-201
Hill of Earthquakes 34
historical dates 206-207
Hoʻokipa 104-107
Hoʻokipa Lookout 83
Hoʻomanu Church 140
Hoaloha Beach Park 98
Hoapili Trail 30
Hoapili, Chief (Governor) 62, 64
Hokukano 165
Holua Cabin 158
Honokahua Burial Site 70
Honokohau Falls 76
Honokowai Beach Park 71, 72
Honokowai Village 71
Honoliʻi Park 95
Honolua Bay 51, 68, 74
Honolua Marine Preserve 72-74
Honolua Ridge Trail 71
Honolua Store 52
Honolulunui Bay 128
Honomanu Bay 124-125, 127
horseback rides 235
Hosmer Grove Nature Trail 146, 156
Hosmer, Ralph 156
Hotel Hana Maui 133
Hotel Lanai 183
hotels 238-231
House of the Sun 156
Huakini Bay 167, 169
Huelo 121
Hui Noeau Arts Center 154
Huialoha Church (Fund) 173
hula shows 221
Hulopoe Beach (Bay) 181, 182
Hulu Island 85
Humpback Whale Sanctuary 27, 44
humpback whales 212
Hyatt Regency 66
Iao Needle 92
Iao Stream 94
Iao Theater 96
Iao Valley 58
Iao Valley Botanical Garden 92
Iao Valley State Park 81, 91, 92-94
Iao Valley, Battle of 92

information 232
Ironwoods 70, 72
Island Marine Ferry 190
Jaws 107-109
Jodo Mission 64, 65
Ka'ahumanu Church 95
Ka'ahumanu, Queen 62, 134
Ka'anapali 66-68
Ka'anapali Historical Trail 66
Ka'ahumanu, Queen 210
Kaeleku Plantation 130
Kahakuloa Head 77, 79
Kahakuloa Protestant Church 78
Kahakuloa Village 50, 78
Kahanu Tropical Botanical Garden 113, 128-130
Kahekili Beach Park 66-67
Kahikihui 164
Kahili Golf Course 56
Kahili'ili Beach 60
Kahului 81
Kahului Harbor 96
Kahuna Point 109
Kakaele Blowhole 51
Kakahaia Beach Park-Refuge 192
Kalaeloa Cove 31, 33
Kalakaua, King David 138, 147, 164
Kalama Park 27, 44
Kalanikaula Sacred Grove 194
Kalanikupule, Chief 58
Kalaniopu'u, King 45
Kalaupapa Lookout 196
Kalepolepo Beach Park 44
Kalokoeli Pond 192
Kamalo Harbor 193
Kamanamana Village 30
Kamaole Beach Parks 41-43
Kamehameha I, The Great 58, 59, 61, 62, 90, 92, 95, 109, 134, 192
Kamehameha II 61
Kamehameha III 62
Kamehameha V 194, 195
Kamehameha, IV 59
Kamakaou Preserve 193
Kanaha Beach Park 83, 97-100
Kanaha Pond Wildlife Sanctuary 83, 99-100
Kanahena Cove 34
Kanepu'u Nature Preserve 185
Kapahakapao Loop Trail 154
Kapalaoa Cabin 159

Kapalua 52, 68-72
Kapalua Beach 68, 71
Kapalua Coastal Trail 68
Kapalua Resort Cener 71
Kapilau Ridge Trail 94
Kapoli Beach Park 47
Kapuaiwa Royal Coconut Grove 195
Kapukaulua Burial Site 132
Kauiki Head 134
Kauakini Gallery 79
Kaulanapueo Church 121
Kaumahina State Wayside 112, 124
Kaunahuna Beach 29
Kaunakakai 191
Kaupo 171, 173
Kaupo Gap 159
Kaupo Ranch Wildlife Marsh 170
Kaupo Store 171
Kaupo Trail 171
kayaking 201-202, 235
Kealia Coastal Boardwalk 45
Kealia Pond 27
Kealia Pond Wildlife Refuge 47
Keanae 124-126
Keanae Arboretum 125
Keanae Peninsula 112-113
Keanae Stream (Pool) 126
Keanae Village 125-126
Keawakapu Beach 27, 40, 41
Keawalai Church 27, 36
Keka'a Beach Park 66, 67
Kekaulike, Chief 173
Keomuku Village 186
Keomuku Highway 184
Keoneoio Village 29
Keopuolani, Queen 64
Kepaniwai Heritage Gardens 81, 91-92
Kepuhi Beach 197
Kianaio Beach 29-30
Kiea Beach Park 195
Kihei 41, 43-44
Kihei Boat Ramp 42, 177
Kihei Canoe Club 27, 43
Kilea cinder cone 58
King Kamehameha Golf Club 56
King's Trail 25, 29-30132, 166
Kings Highway 56
Kipahulu 138-141
Kipahulu Ohana 140
Kipahulu Point Park 140

Kipapa O Kihapiʻilani Trail 132
Koʻolau Forest Reserve 121-124
Koʻolau Gap 156
Koieie Loko Ia Fishpond 44
Koki Beach Park 136
Kokulau Islands 173
Kolea Road 123
Kuau Beach 107
Kuhiwa Bamboo Forest 128
Kukuipuka Heiau 87
Kula 36
Kula Botanical Garden 162
Kula Forest Reserve 160-161
Kula Lodge 149
Kula Marketplace 149
Kulanaokalai Beach 61
Kuloa Point Trail 139
Kumu Farms 95
La Perouse Bay 25, 29-31
La Perouse Monument 31
Lahaina 52'
Banyan Tree Square 53
Lahaina 61-66
Lahaina Beach 65
Lahaina Cannery Mall 64
Lahaina Harbor 62
Lahaina Pali Trail (East) 55-56
Lahaina Pali Trail (West) 56-57
Lahaina Seawall 62, 66
Lahainaluna High School 64
Lanai 181-187
Lanai City 183-184
Lanai Expeditions 182
Lanai Expeditions 47
Laulima Farms 140
Launiupoko Beach Park 61
Launiupoko Ahupuaʻa site 60
Launiupoko Valley 60
Lehoula Beach 137
Leleiwi Pali, Overlook 158
Lelekea Bay 141
Liholiho 61, 62
Lindbergh, Charles (gravesite) 140
Lipoa Point 51
Lipoa Point 73, 74
Little Beach 27, 34, 35
Loaloa Heiau 173
Lodge at Koele, Four Seasons 184-185
London, Jack 146
Lower Paia Beach Park 106, 107

Lualailua Hills 165, 166
luaus 221
Lupi Road 121
Maʻalaea Bay 27, 43, 44-47
Maʻalaea Harbor 47
Mahan Ridge Trail 71
Mai Poina Oe Iau Beach 43, 44
Makamakaole Falls 87
Makapipi Road 128
Makawao 153-154
Makawao Forest Reserve 154
Makena Landing 35-37
Makena Resort Maui 33, 36
Makena State Park 27, 33-35
Mala Wharf 65, 66
Malama Cultural Park 198
Malama Honokowai 71
Maliko Bay (Landing) 107, 109
Malo, David 64
Maluaka Beach 36
Mamaʻs Cove 107
Mamaʻs Fish House 107
Mamane Trail 161
Mana Foods 106
Manawainui Gulch 166
maps 232
Maui Aquarium 31
Maui Art Center 98
Maui Country Club 100
Maui County 8
Maui Dive Shop 177
Maui Historical Society 96
Maui Land & Pineapple Co 71
Maui Man 211
Maui Nui Botanical Garden 98
Maui Ocean Center 47
Maui Ocean Club 66
Maui Swap Meet 81, 96
Maui Tropical Plantation 95
Mauna Olu Seminary 55
Maunalei Arboretum 71
Maunaoloa 198
McGregor Point (Lighthouse) 27, 55, 56, 57
Mendes Ranch 86
Menehune Footprints 164-165
Metcalf, Captain Simon 59
Mokapu Beach 40, 41
Mokeʻehia Island 85
Mokuʻula Island 62
Mokuleia Marine Preserve 72, 74

Molokai 188-198
Molokai Museum & Cultural Center 196
Molokai Ranch 198
Molokai Stables 196
Molokini 177-178
monk seals 216
Montana Beach 104
Mount Eke 77
Mount Lanilili 87
Mud Flats 47
Munro Trail 187
Murdock, David H. 181
Murphy Beach Park 194
museums 233
Nahiku 113, 127-128
Nakalele Blowhole 74-75
Napili Beach 68, 71
Natural Arch 167
Nelson, Willie 153
nene 215
newspapers 232
Nonou Bay 170
nonprofit groups 234
North Kihei 43-44
Nuʻu Bay 169-170
Nuʻu Landing 170
Nuʻu petroglyphs 170
Oasis Beach 29-30
Ohai Loop Trail 51, 76
Ohala Heiau 132
Old Airport Beach 67
Olinda Road 153, 154
Olivine Pools 77
Olowalu Beach 60
Olowalu Cultural Preserve 58
Olowalu Landing 53, 59, 60-61
Olowalu Valley 58
Oneloa Beach 68-70, 72
Our Lady Seven Sorrows Church 193
Pacific Whale Foundation 44, 47
Pahihi Gulch 169
Paia 104-107
Pailolo Channel 191
Pailoa Bay 132
Palauea Beach 27, 38
Paliku Cabin 173
Papaʻea Road 122
Papalaua Beach Wayside 57
Papawai Point 57
Papohaku Beach Park 197

PATH Maui 154
Paukukalo 98
Pauwela Point 108
Peahi Point 107
Petroglyph Hill 58
Phallic Rock 196
Piʻilani, King 30, 68
Piʻilanihale Heiau 128-130
Pine Isle Market 183
Pipiwai Trail 140
planning 220
Poʻolau Beach 197
Poʻolenalena Beach 37-38
Poelua Road 76
Pohaku Park 71
Polipoli State Park 160, 161
Polihua Beach 185
Polo Beach Park 27, 40, 41
Polynesian migrations 209
Pools of Oheo 114, 139-140
Popoalaea, Princess 131
Popoiwi Heiau 173
preservation group 234
Puʻu Kaeo 71
Puʻu Maneoneo 170
Puʻu Olai 27, 34
Puʻuʻulaula 160
Puʻunoa Beach 65
Puʻupehe Cove 182
Puʻupiha Cemetery 65
Puaʻaka State Wayside 128
Puamana Beach Park 66
public agencies 230
Queen Kaʻahumanu Birthplace 134
rainfall 218
Red Hill (Makena) 34
Red Hill Summit 160
Red Sand Beach 135, 136
Redwood Trail 162
resorts 238-241
restaurants 244-245
Rice Park 150
Richards, William 64
Ritz Carlton 52, 70
Royal Lahaina Resort 67
safety tips 200-204
sailing 236
Sandy Beach 194
Sapphire Pools 127
Science City 160

scuba 236
sea turtles 213
seals 216
Shark Cove 182
sharks 212
Sheraton 66
Shipwreck Beach 186
Shops at Wailea 40
shuttles 231
Sierra Club 38
Skyline Trail 160, 161, 162
Slaughterhouse Beach 72, 74
Sliding Sands Trail 160
snorkel tours 236
snorkeling tips and safety 202-203
Spartan Reef 100
spinner dolphin 215
Spreckels, Claus 100
Spreckelsville (Beach) 99, 100, 102
St. Augustine Shrine 127
St. Gabriels Church 127
St. Joseph Church 173
State of Mind Beach 104
Stevenson, Robert Louis 147, 164
Stuck-in-Irons House 64
S-Turns 71
Sugar Beach 43
Sugar Cove 102
Sun Yat Sen Park 150
Supply Trail 156
surf 219
surfing instruction 235
surfing safety and tips 204
Sweetheart Rock 182
Swinging Bridges 89
Tall Lord 50
taxis 231
Tedeschi Winery 164
Thompson Road 163
Tie Trail 162
trade winds 219
transportation 230-231
Travaasa Hana 133
Tropical Gardens of Maui 91
Turtle Town 36
turtles 213
Twin Falls (Botanical Preserve) 119-121
Twin Falls Farm Stand 119
Ukuhame Wind Farm 55
Ulua Beach 40, 41

Ululani's Shave Ice 78
Uluplakua Ranch 147, 164
Vancouver Monument 43
Vancouver, Captain George 29, 43
Venus Pool 137-138 Muolea Point 138
visitor information 232
Wahikuli Beach Park 65
Wahikuli Interpretive Trail 67
Wahinepe'e (Road) Falls 124
Waianapanapa Caves 131
Waianapanapa State Park 131-133
Waiehu Beach Park 90
Waihe'e Beach Park 89-90
Waihe'e Coastal Dunes & Wetlands 90
Waihe'e Ridge Trail 86
Waihe'e Valley (Stream) Plantation 89
Waihou Springs Forest Reserve 153-154
Waikalai Plateau 76-77
Waikamoi Ridge Nature Trail 112, 123
Waikomo Ridge Trail 154, 156
Wailea 38-41
Wailea Beach 40
Wailua 127
Wailua Falls 141
Wailuaiki Road 128
Wailuku 82, 95-96
Wailuku Cross 94
Wailuku Female Seminary 96
Waimoku Falls 140
Waine'e Graveyard 64
Waiohuli Trail 161
Waiola Church 64
Waipoli Road 160, 161
Waipuilani Park 44
Wall of Tears 93
Wash Rock 57-58
Wawau Point 102
weather 217-219
Whale Day 44
whale watching cruises 236
Whaler's Village 66, 67
whales 212
White Hill 159
Wianapanapa State Park 113
Winfrey, Oprah 163
Windmill Beach 73, 74
windsurfing 236
Wo Hing Museum, 64
Wright, Frank Lloyd 56
Young, John 59

Happy trails!

For publisher-direct savings to individuals and groups, and for book-trade orders, please contact:

DIAMOND VALLEY COMPANY
89 Lower Manzanita Drive, Markleeville, CA 96120

Phone-fax 530-694-2740
www.trailblazertravelbooks.com
wwwtrailblazerhawaii.com
e-mail: trailblazertravelbooks@gmail.com

All titles are also available at bookstores and websites, as well as in e-Book form
Please contact the publisher with comments, corrections, and suggestions.

Diamond Valley Company's
TRAILBLAZER TRAVEL BOOK SERIES

ALPINE SIERRA TRAILBLAZER
Where to Hike, Ski, Bike, Fish, Drive
From Tahoe to Yosemite

"A must-have guide. With you every step of the way."—Tahoe Action

GOLDEN GATE TRAILBLAZER
Where to Hike, Walk, Bike
In San Francisco and Marin

"Makes you want to strap on your boots and go!"—Sunset Magazine

KAUAI TRAILBLAZER
Where to Hike, Snorkel, Bike, Paddle, Surf

"Number one, world-wide among adventure guides."—Barnesandnoble.com

"Accurate, informative, probably the best."
Koke'e Museum

MAUI TRAILBLAZER
Where to Hike, Snorkel, Surf, Drive
Maui, Molokai, Lanai

"The best of them all."—Maui Weekly
"For off the beaten track." New York Times

HAWAII THE BIG ISLAND TRAILBLAZER
Where to Hike, Snorkel, Surf, Bike, Drive

"Top three world-wide among adventure guides."—Barnesandnoble.com

OAHU TRAILBLAZER
Where to Hike, Snorkel, Surf
From Honolulu to the North Shore

"Marvelously flexible. A well-marked trail of tropical adventures."
—San Francisco Chronicle

NO WORRIES HAWAII
A Vacation Planning Guide for
Kauai, Oahu, Maui, and the Big Island

"Really a travel planning guide without peer."
—Guide to Travel Guides

NO WORRIES PARIS
A Photographic Walking Guide

"A beautiful way to discover Paris on foot."
Chicago Tribune

"Trailblazers are deserving of ongoing praise. You are guaranteed a unique experience that is high quality and perfect for independent travelers."—Midwest Book Review

"Trailblazers are the essential books to pack when planning a trip to Hawaii."—About.com

"Long story told short—there are no guidebooks for Hawaii that begin to compare to the Trailblazer books."—Maui Weekly

Made in the USA
Columbia, SC
02 April 2019